T0339159

MENASSEH BEN ISRAEL

Menasseh ben Israel

Rabbi of Amsterdam

STEVEN NADLER

Yale

UNIVERSITY

PRESS

New Haven and London

Frontispiece: Exterior of the Portuguese-Jewish Synagogue (1639–1675), Amsterdam, by Romeyn de Hooghe, circa 1686. (Courtesy of the Bibliotheca Rosenthaliana, Special Collections of the University of Amsterdam)

Copyright © 2018 by Steven Nadler. All rights reserved. This book may not be reproduced, in whole or in part, including illustrations, in any form (beyond that copying permitted by Sections 107 and 108 of the U.S. Copyright Law and except by reviewers for the public press), without written permission from the publishers.

Yale University Press books may be purchased in quantity for educational, business, or promotional use. For information, please e-mail sales.press@yale.edu (U.S. office) or sales@yaleup.co.uk (U.K. office).

Set in Janson type by Integrated Publishing Solutions. Printed in the United States of America.

ISBN 978-0-300-22410-8 (hardcover : alk. paper) Library of Congress Control Number: 2018931347 A catalogue record for this book is available from the British Library.

This paper meets the requirements of ANSI/NISO Z39.48-1992 (Permanence of Paper).

10 9 8 7 6 5 4 3 2 1

For Richard H. Popkin, z"l

CONTENTS

MENASSEH BEN ISRAEL

1

Prologue: On the Houtgracht

ON A COLD, raw Monday in late November 1657, the members of the Talmud Torah congregation of Amsterdam gathered in their ornate synagogue beside the canal known as the Houtgracht to hear their chief rabbi deliver a eulogy for his recently deceased colleague. Rabbi Saul Levi Mortera began with a homily on a verse from Psalms—"Bless, O my soul, the Lord and everything that is within me bless his holy name" (Ps. 103.1)—in which he explained that outer appearances may mislead one as to the true state of a person's soul. "These people may be quite beautiful to behold—fashionable, bedecked in jewels, lacking none of the accoutrements of glory and prestige . . . while inside they are nothing but intrigue and deceit, and every vile blemish."[1] A truly righteous person, he said, requires no bodily embellishments or external honors whatsoever. "It is not the position that honors the man, but it is the man who honors the position." Nor do the virtuous, upon their passing, need some fancy tomb or gravestone. Citing the words of the Talmud, Rabbi Mortera reminded the mourners that "we do not build a monument for the righteous; their words are their memorial."[2] He then applied this lesson to the rabbi whose life he was honoring.

> This *tzadik* [righteous person] does not need an imposing monument or sarcophagus to honor him for the sake of his position. "His words are his memorial": the words in the books he wrote will preserve his memory. Indeed, the truth is that he did have an honored position; his position honored him and he it . . . He was a teacher and a mentor from his youth in this distinguished place, in the greatest congregations of the region. And he honored his position through his distinguished achievements, which earned him constant praise and glory and honor.

Rabbi Menasseh ben Israel had died the week before, in Middelburg, while on his way back to Amsterdam from London. After his body was brought to the city and prepared for burial by the congregation's Bikur Holim society, it was loaded onto a barge and drawn along the Amstel River to Ouderkerk aan de Amstel, the small village five miles from Amsterdam where this community of Sephardic Jews had their Beth Haim cemetery. Menasseh was only fifty-three years old. He served these descendants of Portuguese and Spanish exiles his entire life and was utterly devoted both to his congregants and to the country that had given them refuge. But his final years had been difficult, filled with disappointment and sorrow.

He lost both of his sons. His business affairs were a mess and his family was in financial straits. His long campaign for the readmission of the Jews to England, as far as he could tell, had come to naught. He never was able to secure the royal patronage that would have given him the kind of stature he felt he deserved, not to mention financial security. He died probably thinking his life had been a failure.

Still, in his lifetime Menasseh enjoyed tremendous respect well beyond the confines of the Amsterdam Jewish community, beyond even the borders of Holland. In fact, he was much more highly regarded among European gentiles than among his own people. He was seen by non-Jews as a learned and accessible authority on matters of Judaica, and they did not hesitate to make use of his expertise. They especially valued him as *the* Jewish expositor of a common Messianic vision, wherein the worldly empires will be swept away by a "Fifth Kingdom" ruled by a savior sent by God. While Menasseh certainly did not share his Christian friends' conviction that the Messiah's arrival will be accompanied by the conversion of the Jews, he was broad-minded enough to proclaim that God's providential care is universal: there will be a place in paradise for all of the virtuous, regardless of religious persuasion. Even the vicious, should they voluntarily repent of their sins, would eventually enjoy everlasting salvation. In Menasseh's view—defending as he did a robust doctrine of free will and the immortality of the soul—each individual is responsible for his own fate, in both the short term (including the length of his lifetime) and, more important, the very long term.

All of this theological and philosophical activity—pursued through numerous books, pamphlets, and lectures, as well as a wide-ranging correspondence—was carried out with great displays of erudition. Menasseh's works overflow with citations from Hebrew Scripture, Talmud and rabbinic commentaries; the writings of early Church fathers; medieval Jewish and Christian philosophical treatises; Jewish mystical texts, including Kabbalah; and ancient pagan thinkers, all marshaled to support his ideas and refute those of his opponents.

However, Menasseh's broad intellectual engagements also made him suspect in the eyes of many of his fellow Amsterdam Jews. The other rabbis were unhappy with his ecumenical efforts and conciliatory attitude toward Christian doctrines. The community's lay leadership regarded him as a bit of an insubordinate maverick and was troubled by his personal relationships with non-Jews. With his generally defiant nature, he was considered by many to be a nuisance.

There was certainly no love lost between Menasseh and his senior colleague Mortera. Menasseh chafed under the chief rabbi's authority and felt he was underappreciated (and underpaid) for his sermons and his teaching. Mortera, for his part, did not have a lot of respect for Menasseh as a scholar and as a role model for his congregants. Nevertheless, in his eulogy for Menasseh he put aside their differences. He spoke of his "great sorrow" upon the rabbi's passing, and saved his final praises for Menasseh's skill as a speaker and accomplishments as a writer. "His beautiful eloquence, his delightful words, were not in his mouth alone, but also by his hand, in his books which he wrote in such an elegant style . . . his radiance has shone throughout the world."

With these remarks, the Portuguese Jews of Amsterdam said farewell to a man who, through good times and bad, came to represent not only their community but, to so many of his contemporaries, Judaism itself. Menasseh ben Israel was, for much of the seventeenth century, the most famous Jew in the world.

2

Manoel/Menasseh

As GASPAR RODRIGUES NUNES SAT in his cell waiting for his fourth session with the Lisbon Inquisition, he was in excruciating pain. His three previous stints on the rack and the hoist had seriously damaged his thirty-nine-year-old body. During the first round of torture, on August 28, 1596, Gaspar was stripped naked and bound with cords attached to his arms and his legs. He was then given several twists on the rack across his body. According to his Inquisitor's report, "the defendant continually screamed for help."[1] When he was commanded to confess his sins, Gaspar defended his innocence. The torturer was directed to apply more pressure, and was rather focused in his method. "In view of his saying that he had nothing to say, a twist was added to the first one in the flesh of both his arms; and since he said nothing he was given another twist, in addition to the first, in the muscle of the right arm near the hand."[2]

After a month to reflect on his offenses—and to heal somewhat—Gaspar was once again subjected to this cruel examination, despite the fact that the first torture "had not been properly carried out because of the mishap which [Gaspar] seemed to have suffered"; apparently he had fainted and his limbs swelled up, so the session ended prematurely. Still, he confessed nothing. On the third occasion, the Inquisitors decided that hanging him by his arms tied behind his back might be a more effective technique. This time, Gaspar did indeed confess. He said that while he had been baptized as a child and lived outwardly as a Catholic for decades, he was "a Jew and had believed in the Law of Moses for the last sixteen or seventeen years." He admitted, that is, to being a "Judaizing" converso, one of many so-called New Christians who, raised in a family that several generations earlier had been forcibly converted from the Jewish to the Catholic faith, continued to practice their ancestral religion in secret. The Inquisitions of Spain and Portugal did not care if you were a Jew; indeed, since the expulsions and forced conversions at the end of the fifteenth century, there were, at least officially, no more Jews in the Iberian peninsula. However, they did care, very much, if you were an insincere Christian.

The Lisbon authorities were not satisfied with Gaspar's confession—it seems he had not named enough names—and so yet another torture session was scheduled for early February 1597. It was now almost four years since Gaspar's arrest, and he was a broken man, both mentally and physically. Gaspar told his examiners that "his arms were in a bad way and that he would not be able to withstand further torture." According to the physician who examined him before the next round, "[Gaspar] was not fit for having his hands brought behind his back for tying, because during the *polé* [hoisting] torture some time ago his right shoulder was dislocated and was reset in a plaster which is still on him."[3]

In light of this, the members of the Holy Tribunal decided that this was enough. Gaspar Rodrigues Nunes, "maimed in his right arm and hand" and his body covered with lesions, was released from prison on February 27. He was ordered to appear at an *auto-da-fé* in Lisbon, where he would be "reconciled" with the Church. He was forced to give up all of his property, accept a form of house arrest, attend mass regularly, and wear the *sanbenito* outside the home.

What may have made Gaspar's experience yet more painful was the identity of the person who had denounced him. It was his wife, Felipa Rodrigues, who had been in custody for suspicion of Judaizing since October 1591. She, in turn, had been denounced by her cousin, and confessed that she and Gaspar had been observing Jewish fasts for some time. Her statements impugned not only her husband but his father, Àlvaro Rodrigues, who was arrested with his son. Felipa's denunciation of her father in-law was backed up by none other than his own daughter, Gaspar's sister, Branca Marques, who claimed that Àlvaro had, when she was a young girl, instructed her "to believe in one sole God who created heaven and earth, land, sea and sands, and to commend herself to Him and to believe only in Him and to keep the Sabbath . . . and to believe only in the Law of Moses."[4]

We will never know how many of the New Christians accused of insincerity in the faith in the late fifteenth and sixteenth centuries really were secretly practicing Judaism.[5] Many denunciations were undoubtedly false and based on suspect motives: personal malice, professional envy, greed. However, Judaizing was certainly not some figment of the Inquisition's imagination. Many families did, under cover, observe Jewish customs in some attenuated form or another—by refusing to eat pork, observing fasts, or saying prayers and lighting candles. In the case of Gaspar Rodrigues Nunes and his relatives, we certainly do seem to be in the presence of a clan of Judaizing conversos. The family's subsequent history testifies to this.

And then there is the proud acknowledgment, many years later, by Gaspar's own son.

He was born and baptized Manoel Dias Soeiro in 1604. His city of birth, if we take his word for it—and we should—was Lisbon. In a letter he wrote in 1648, Manoel (now going by his Jewish name, Menasseh) told his correspondent, "I am a Lisbonian by birth [*yo soy por patria Lisbonense*]," while in one of his treatises, *The Hope of Israel*, he refers to "my native city Lisbon [*mi patria Lixboa*]."⁶

The only complication lies in Menasseh's marriage banns, which were recorded by a Dutch civil magistrate in 1623 when he was living in Amsterdam. The parties to a marriage were required to state their place of birth, and in his banns "Manasse ben Ysrahel" is noted as being *van Rochelle*—that is, from La Rochelle, France—while his older sister, whose banns were registered at the same time, is listed as *van Lisbonne*.⁷ This raises the possibility that the family left Lisbon before Manoel was born. If this was the case, then when he proclaimed Lisbon to be his "native city," he must have meant only the city of his father and forefathers. A more likely explanation, though, is that he was indeed born in Lisbon but, less than two decades removed from that city dominated by the Inquisition, he had some reason for dissembling in an official public document. For one thing, a lie about his birthplace would protect relatives still in Portugal, who would immediately come under Inquisitorial suspicion if they could be connected with people of Spanish or Portuguese descent now living as Jews.⁸

Manoel's paternal grandfather Àlvaro Rodrigues (born in 1526) was a nail seller with a shop in Lisbon, on a street colloquially known as the "Arco dos Pregos," or Nail Arcade. Àlvaro's son, Gaspar—Manoel's father—followed him into the nail busi-

ness. Both men had been born in Beja, in a south-central region
of Portugal known as Lower Alentejo; the family moved to Lisbon and set up business there sometime after Gaspar's birth in
1558.

Felipa was Gaspar's first wife. It was not a good marriage,
and her denunciation of her husband may have stemmed from
his treatment of her—at least that is what Gaspar alleged when
given the chance by his Inquisitors to impeach her testimony
by showing that it was based on prejudice rather than truth. He
claimed that she was his "capital enemy because from the day
they started their household he has been treating her continu-
ously very badly, giving her many beatings and smacks for the
reason that she demands an accounting from him as to whence
he came home late at night." She would often flee to their
neighbors for protection. At one point, he admitted to having
threatened her with a sword, and said that he "threw a chair at
her head or hit her with it, by which he inflicted a great wound
on her that required seven or eight stitches."[9] Gaspar's narrative was more than just a sly way of undermining her credibility
as a witness to his Judaizing, however, since one of their neighbors called Gaspar "a nasty old man" and confirmed the inci-
dent with the sword.[10]

Despite their domestic problems, Gaspar and Felipa had
three children before their incarceration: Violante, Caterina,
and Àlvaro, who were put in the care of their uncle, Felipa's
brother, while their parents were in the Inquisition's dungeons.
A fourth child was born after their release, in 1598, but the
marriage seems, for all intents and purposes, to have been over.
The torture took just as serious a toll on Felipa's mental health
as it did on Gaspar's physical well-being. In a petition to the
Inquisition to be excused from her own house arrest, she claimed
that she was "very ill with great melancholies and inflamma-
tions of the heart, with privation of her senses." Felipa had apparently lost her mind, a claim backed up by a doctor's testi-

mony that, although she was lucid on occasion, "at the slightest provocation the former insanity will return."[11]

In the end, we do not know for certain what became of Felipa Rodrigues, but she must have died from her illness. Sometime after 1598, Gaspar Rodrigues Nunes was remarried, to Antónia Soeiro. Their daughter was born in 1602, followed by two sons.

Writing in Amsterdam several decades later, their first son Manoel (Menasseh) related that his late father Gaspar "was deprived of all of his properties by the Spanish Inquisition because he was a Jew. Three times he was subjected to cruel tortures, and as a result lost the good health of his body."[12] Menasseh never forgot his father's ordeal—Gaspar's physical infirmities must have served as a constant reminder—or the sufferings of others still in Spain and Portugal. In one of his books he called the Spanish Inquisition (which, after the union of Spain and Portugal in 1580, oversaw the hunt for heresy in Lisbon) "that horrible monster." He spoke of the "cruelties . . . that it daily uses against poor innocents, old men and children, of every age and sex."[13]

After his release from prison, Gaspar remained under surveillance by the Inquisition, so life in Lisbon must have felt rather insecure. The threat of rearrest on the slightest pretext—rumor started by an unscrupulous business rival or even a relative seeking to save his or her own skin—hung over him and his family. Thus, sometime just after 1604—if Manoel was indeed born in Lisbon—they decided to flee Portugal.[14]

Their first stop was the island of Madeira, a Portuguese colony in the Atlantic Ocean southwest of the Iberian mainland. Although this put some distance between them and the Lisbon authorities, Madeira was still rather dangerous territory for New Christians suspected of Judaizing. Spies were everywhere, and the Inquisition's scrutiny of lands within its dominions, no matter how remote, never flagged. Hoping to find some peace well beyond the reach of his once and possibly future interrogators, Gaspar moved the family to La Rochelle, in western France. In this port city there was a sizable population of Spanish and Portuguese merchants, many of whom were undoubtedly New Christians also practicing Judaism in secret. Because La Rochelle at this time was dominated by Huguenots who themselves had experienced Catholic oppression but who now enjoyed some independence from the French crown, it was a more tolerant environment for Iberian conversos.[15]

La Rochelle was only a temporary haven. After the death in 1610 of King Henri IV, who had been raised as a Protestant, the city was under constant threat by the Catholic forces of Louis XIII. It would not have been wise to count on it being a long-term sanctuary. (La Rochelle would, in fact, fall to the king's army in 1628.) Even though there was no French Inquisition, France was not a welcoming place for Protestants, for Jews—their 1394 banishment from the kingdom was renewed by Louis in 1615—and especially for ostensible Christians practicing Judaism in secret.

Meanwhile, the long struggle by the Dutch for independence from Spain, begun in the 1570s, had allowed the province of Holland, and especially its largest city, Amsterdam, to flourish. By the early seventeenth century, this cosmopolitan northern port, now dominated by Calvinists, had become an attractive destination for Iberian New Christian merchants. Amsterdam was especially alluring to those conversos who wished to return to their ancestral religion.

Therefore, sometime between early 1613 and the spring of 1614, Gaspar, Antónia, and their three children decamped for the Dutch Republic (more formally known as the United Provinces of the Netherlands) and the safer and, hopefully, more prosperous environs along the Amstel River. As Menasseh would put it many years later, "[they] secretly fled to these provinces for asylum of liberty and conscience."[16]

Jewish families had begun settling in Amsterdam right at the turn of the century, as soon as it seemed both safe to dwell in provinces that had so recently been a part of the Spanish domains and, just as important, economically desirable to do so. The earliest Jews of Amsterdam were almost all Sephardim, arriving either directly from Spain and Portugal or from other cities in the post-expulsion Sephardic diaspora, including Venice, Hamburg, Fez, and Salonika. Many also came from the Dutch-speaking provinces still under Spanish control. Antwerp in particular, *the* Flemish center of trade and originally part of the Dutch rebellion, saw a significant drop in its New Christian (not to mention Protestant) population once it was reconquered by a now vindictive Spain. With the ascendance of the Dutch Republic as both an economic power and a more tolerant place, Amsterdam was a natural new home for these international entrepreneurs and their families, whose religious sincerity the Catholic governors of the Spanish Netherlands continued to regard with suspicion.

They came first as professed Christians. In Dutch notary documents of the period, they are always referred to as "Portuguese merchants" and are present in Amsterdam as early as 1591. In the first formal text pertaining to these immigrants as a group, from September 1598, the Amsterdam burgemeesters (mayors) decreed that the foreigners would be allowed to take the oath of citizenship, but warned them that public worship outside of the Dutch Reformed Church was forbidden. At this point, there was, at least officially, no question of allowing Jews (crypto or otherwise) to settle in the city. The burgemeesters might have regarded this as so remote a possibility that it was not even up for consideration. They noted in their decree that the Portuguese "are Christians and will live an honest life as good burghers."[17]

And yet, it is unlikely that the city's leaders were totally unaware of who these Portuguese "Christians" really were. Indeed, just a few years later, it was a fairly open secret in Amsterdam that the refugees, initially there for the sake of business, were taking advantage of Dutch toleration to return to their religious roots. The Amsterdam regents seem to have had no problem with this. They were not yet ready in the first decade of the seventeenth century to welcome Jews with open arms or explicitly allow them to worship, but they saw that there was little harm, and potentially great economic advantage, in tacitly granting them the asylum they sought. Spain's loss would be Holland's gain.

The precise historical beginnings of an organized Jewish community in Amsterdam are obscured by several romantic myths.

There is the story of Maria Nuñes and other Portuguese New Christians fleeing the Inquisition sometime in the 1590s. When their ship was intercepted by the English—who were then at war with Spain and Portugal—and brought to London, the aristocratic captives were paraded around town. The elegant Maria charmed the city's high society. Even Queen Elizabeth was taken by the young woman's grace and beauty. However, Maria politely resisted the queen's entreaties to stay and join her court—as well as a marriage proposal by the commander of the fleet that had captured her—and pleaded for them all to be allowed to continue their journey to the United Provinces, where they intended to convert (back) to Judaism. The queen, impressed by Maria's steadfast virtue, relented and the group was given safe passage across the North Sea to settle in Amsterdam.[18]

Then there is the tale of Moses Uri Halevi, an Ashkenazic Jew living in Emden, in the German territory of East Friesland near the Dutch border.[19] One day in 1602, we are told, there arrived in his town two ships bearing Portuguese merchants and their families. After seeing a house with a Hebrew motto above the door (*Emet ve-shalom yesod ha'olam*, "Truth and peace are the foundation of the world"), the visitors sought out its owner and asked him to circumcise their men, "because they were children of Israel." Halevi cautioned them that it was too risky to undertake this in a Lutheran city like Emden, and directed them to go to a particular house on the Jonkerstraat in Amsterdam. He later met them there and, with his son Aaron, performed the circumcisions and led them in prayer.

These narratives place the origins of the Amsterdam Jewish community in individual acts of faith and courage. This is what founding myths do. But they are not without a kernel of truth. The archival records show that in 1597, four Portuguese merchants and a Maria Nuñes landed in Amsterdam.[20] And Moses and Aaron Halevi were real individuals—their narrative comes down to us from Aaron's son Uri—who daringly took on a leadership role when it was clear that the Dutch were unsure what do to with these exotic newcomers who had long been accustomed to hiding their identity.[21] In the early years of Jewish residency in Amsterdam, there were a number of awkward and difficult incidents that eventually forced the city's leaders to formulate a deliberate policy.

On one occasion, a Friday evening service was interrupted by the Amsterdam sheriff and his men. They had been tipped off by neighbors hearing a strange language emanating from the house in which the Jews were welcoming the Sabbath. Convinced that the unfamiliar sounds must be Latin, the constables, good Calvinists that they were, burst into the house expecting to find a Catholic mass surreptitiously (and illegally) being celebrated. The gathering was broken up and Moses and Aaron Halevi were arrested. However, when it was explained to the sheriff that the language he heard was Hebrew, not Latin, and that the people in the house were Jews, not Catholics, the Halevis were released without charges.

The first true Jewish congregation in Amsterdam was organized by a man named Jacob Tirado. In 1603, Tirado, with the assistance of Moses Halevi, began holding occasional Jewish services in his home.[22] Once it became a regular gathering for worship, the group took the name Beth Jacob ("House of Jacob"), in honor of its founder. Tirado would soon leave Amsterdam for Jerusalem, where he died in 1620. When the Beth Jacob congregation learned of his passing, its rabbi, in his eulogy, addressed the following words not just to his congregants, but to the city's entire Jewish population:

> He was called "our father," for he was the father of this Jewish community and this synagogue. May God remember to his credit how he nurtured it as a father does a son, at considerable risk to life and fortune, and how he sustained it with his financial resources, sending abroad for scholars, purchasing a Torah scroll out of his own pocket. Indeed, he paid all the expenses of the synagogue from his own resources, without help from any others. Thus it is appropriate to call him "our father Jacob."[23]

Beth Jacob enjoyed its status as Amsterdam's sole Jewish congregation for only a few years. By 1608, with more than two hundred Portuguese Jews in the city (out of a total municipal population of 700,000), a second congregation, Neve Shalom ("Dwelling of Peace"), was formed.[24]

It was not long before the two Amsterdam congregations realized that they needed experienced rabbis to help these former conversos and their descendants learn about and conform to the norms of rabbinic Judaism and forge a proper Jewish community. Jewish liturgical rituals, life-cycle events, and everyday practices—including circumcision, kosher butchering, prayer and Torah study, observance of the festivals, and funerary customs—had been lost during generations of living as Catholics in Spain and Portugal. So in 1609 the members of Beth Jacob brought Joseph Pardo, originally from Salonika but then residing in the older Jewish community of Venice, to Amsterdam to lead them. Neve Shalom, meeting in the home of Samuel Palache, Morocco's Jewish ambassador to the Netherlands, followed suit and hired Judah Vega, from Constantinople. A third congregation was founded in 1619, after a dispute within Beth Jacob over liturgy, orthodoxy, politics, and (perhaps the most intractable issue of all) synagogue property split the congregation into two factions. Rabbi Pardo and his followers left Beth Jacob to set up their own congregation, which they eventually called Beth Israel.[25]

These earliest rabbis in Amsterdam had a difficult job.[26] Besides educating the community in the basics of Judaism, much of their effort was devoted to correcting longstanding heterodox practices and deeply embedded misconceptions. They sought especially to eradicate traces of Catholicism that had, over generations, corrupted both the crypto-Judaism that the New Christians once practiced in Iberia and the Judaism that they now openly observed in Holland. Amsterdam's Sephardim would call the Passover matzah "holy bread"; on Yom Kippur they said prayers for "grace and salvation"; and Purim was known as the "Feast of Saint Esther"—a particularly popular holiday since it honored a heroine who, like the conversos themselves, had to hide her Jewish identity.

While relations between the congregations—each with its own governing board, or *ma'amad*, whose members were called *parnassim*—were not always easy, they managed to cooperate on essential communal matters. In 1614, Beth Jacob and Neve Shalom banded together to buy the land in Ouderkerk for a cemetery. And in 1616, they set up a single Talmud Torah association for educational matters, a joint Bikur Holim society to look after the sick and transport the dead for burial, and the

Santa Companhia de Dotar for supplying dowries to orphan girls and poor brides.

There was no getting around the fact that Amsterdam was now home to a thriving, and growing, Portuguese-speaking Jewish population. The question for the municipal authorities, though, was what to do about it.

When Gaspar, Antónia, and their three children arrived in Amsterdam, the city had just begun seriously to address the issue of its resident Jews. Although the States General—the central political organ of the Dutch Republic, composed of representatives of the seven provinces—was, at this time, not opposed to allowing Jews openly to practice their religion, Amsterdam itself was still officially forbidding public worship. This was probably for the sake of plausible deniability on the part of the relatively liberal city regents in the face of anti-Jewish pressure from the more intolerant elements of the Dutch Reformed Church. After all, who can tell what goes on behind closed doors? However, the municipal leaders knew that such an implicit arrangement could not last as a viable long-term policy.

In 1616, the Amsterdam city council, in an ordinance that was basically an acknowledgment that the Jews were there to stay, laid down several directives meant to regulate the Jewish community, and especially relationships between its members and non-Jews. Among other things, Jews were told not to criticize the Christian religion; they were forbidden to try to convert anyone to Judaism; and they were not to have "fleshly conversation" (that is, sexual relations) with gentiles.

The conservative faction of the Dutch Reformed Church was not happy about seeing yet another "sect" allowed to establish itself in this newly independent Calvinist land. The Dutch Republic still struggled with the problem of confessional identity, and not only Catholics but also Lutherans and members of dissident Reformed movements (such as Mennonites and Anabaptists) felt the heat as the more orthodox ecclesiastics and their political allies pressed the municipal authorities to safeguard the mainstream denomination's dominant status. The Dutch Reformed Church may not have been an "established" church, like the Church of England, but in Holland, Utrecht, and other provinces it was *the* public church.[27] The city of Amsterdam's warnings to the Jews were, in part, intended to appease the local Reformed consistory. Still, religious toleration was enshrined in the founding document of the Dutch Revolt. The Union of Utrecht of 1579—which served as a kind of national constitution during the Dutch Golden Age—proclaimed, in its thirteenth article, that "every individual should remain free in his religion, and no man should be molested or questioned on the subject of divine worship."

In 1619, the States General concluded that each province should decide for itself whether and under what conditions (if any) to accept Jews. It stipulated, as well, that while it was permissible for a town to assign Jews to a particular residential quarter, it could not compel them to wear any special marks or clothing. That same year, the Amsterdam city council finally granted the Jews living there the right to practice their religion openly, although it also imposed some restrictions on their political, social, and economic rights and liberties. While a Jewish individual could purchase citizenship, it would not be inherited by his children. Nor could Jews become members of certain guilds and professions. And intermarriage with Christians was absolutely forbidden. Jews were also told to maintain a strict observance of Jewish law. This was probably a warning to keep to themselves, at least in matters of faith, and not blur confessional lines. At the same time, the Jewish community was given a great deal of autonomy and allowed to manage its own religious, social, political, and economic affairs (although the Dutch claimed jurisdiction when it came to criminal matters). Jews were also free to engage in business with the Dutch—in fact, their livelihoods depended on their doing so—and to mix socially with them. All in all, it was quite an open environment, especially by seventeenth-century standards.

Like many of the recent Portuguese arrivals in Amsterdam, Gaspar and his family settled right away in the Vlooienburg/Breestraat neighborhood, a new part of the city built on reclaimed marshland to house the growing population. The Vlooienburg island was bordered on one side by a section of the Amstel River—the "Binnen Amstel" (Inner Amstel), since it flowed within the confines of the city center—and, on another side, by the Houtgracht, or "Wood Canal," so-called because the streets around it were home to the city's wood (*hout*) trade. (In the late nineteenth century, the Houtgracht was filled in; the area is now the Waterlooplein and home to City Hall, an opera house, and an open-air flea market.)

The island's inner lanes were crowded with residences, while the avenues on its periphery were lined with wharves, warehouses, and markets. The wooden houses in the island's center were smaller and less sumptuous than the stately brick homes on the Sint Antoniesbreestraat (Saint Anthony's Broadstreet), the wide thoroughfare just across the Houtgracht, where wealthier Sephardic Jews tended to live. While many non-Jews lived in the Vlooienburg/Breestraat quarter—especially artists and art dealers—it soon became known as the Jewish neighborhood. (The lower part of the Sint Antoniesbreestraat would, by the end of the seventeenth century, be called the Jodenbreestraat, or Jews Broad Street.) It was not a ghetto, however. Jews could live anywhere they wanted in Amsterdam. But given the premium on space in a dense city constricted by rivers and canals, this new neighborhood is where the affordable housing was. (In the 1630s and 1640s, when indigent Ashkenazic Jews fleeing pogroms in eastern Europe began arriving in Amsterdam, the interior of Vlooienburg island would become even more crowded, perhaps resembling the tenements of New York's Lower East Side in the early twentieth century.)

With their wealth and goods having been confiscated by the Inquisition, and after many years of wandering (Lisbon to Madeira to La Rochelle to Amsterdam)—during which Gaspar would not have had many opportunities to establish himself in a profession and earn a decent income—the Rodrigues Nunes family must have arrived in Amsterdam quite poor. They may even have had to rely on charity from the young Portuguese-Jewish community there to pay the rent—they certainly could not have afforded to buy a house, even on the Vlooienburg island—and provide food for their first couple of months in this strange northern city.

The first ten years of Manoel's life were ones of transience and evasion. The family stayed long enough in Madeira and La Rochelle for each of these places to feel like home—or long enough, at least, for Manoel later (as Menasseh) to tell people that he was "from" one or the other. But they were no doubt aware all along that these cities afforded only temporary refuge. There may have been several other, quite brief layovers at less agreeable locales as well.

This must have been an extremely difficult period. Gaspar was still healing from his ordeal with the Inquisition—he would never be physically well again—and the family had no property to speak of. Moreover, safety was always a concern. Although La Rochelle held out the possibility of dropping the Catholic facade, there was always a need for caution. This Protestant city may have been well outside the Inquisition's bailiwick, but there were Spanish spies even here. Equally worrisome was the fact that France was still technically off-limits to Jews.

It was only when Gaspar, Antónia, and the children reached Amsterdam, around the time that Beth Jacob and Neve Shalom finally secured land for a Jewish cemetery, that there was any real hope for stability and an end to the secrecy. The relief must have been tremendous. Menasseh often expressed much gratitude toward the Dutch, and to the city of Amsterdam in particular. This was home. While his brother would travel far and wide over the course of his career as a merchant, Menasseh left the United Provinces only twice, briefly, before he turned fifty. Writing in later years, in English and in response to "the reproaches cast on the Nation of the Jewes," he called the Dutch Republic "the country wherein I have lived all my life time under the benign protection, and favor of the Lords, the States Generall, and Magistrates of Amsterdam."[28] He elsewhere called himself "Portuguese by birth, but Batavian in spirit."[29]

Once settled in Vlooienburg, all the members of the family went through a formal conversion to Judaism. Father and sons were circumcised, and everyone assumed Jewish names. Gaspar Rodrigues Nunes was now Joseph ben Israel, and he gave his sons the names of the sons of the biblical Joseph: Manoel became Menasseh, and the younger son (whose Portuguese name is unknown) became Ephraim. Antónia, whom Menasseh says was "born into a not insignificant family," took the name Rachel, and her daughter was now Hester (or Esther).[30] Like many of the Portuguese Jews of Amsterdam, they did not entirely dispense with their Portuguese names. These Iberian identities were often used when doing business with the Dutch. Jacob Tirado, for example, was known by the gentiles with whom he did business as Jaimes Lopes da Costa. For dealings with firms in Spain and Portugal and their colonies, however, the Portuguese Jews took on Dutch aliases, so as to conceal their Iberian origins from the agents of the Inquisition and thereby protect any relatives still in Catholic lands.

Concerned to put his family once again on a solid financial footing, Joseph did not wait long to set himself up in business— one that no longer involved nails. Already in October 1614, possibly just a few months after landing in Amsterdam, "Gaspar Rodrigues Nunes" appears on a notary document concerning commerce on a Dutch ship that was stranded off the coast of France. He was listed among a large number of Amsterdam merchants, with both Portuguese and Dutch names, "who are interested in the goods and money coming from the ship of skipper Pieter Fransz that ran aground at Boulogne" and who, through the notary, are granting power of attorney to a Dutch agent based in Rouen "to recover these goods and money in France and put an attachment on them."[31]

Joseph was also eager for the family to become respectable members of Amsterdam's Portuguese-Jewish community. The family joined the Beth Jacob congregation upon their arrival, and the same year that Joseph was dealing with a stranded freighter he made his first payment of Beth Jacob's *finta* tax. This general assessment, essentially dues required of every member of the congregation, was based on an individual's personal wealth. In May of 1614, Joseph paid a *finta* of six guilders. This was not as low as what some other congregants owed—the minimum was supposed to be two guilders—but not nearly as high as that paid by more wealthy members like Rohiel Jesurun and Baruch Ossorio, who each paid thirty guilders that month.[32] For a family just trying to recover financially after losing everything in Portugal and then wandering for several years, this had to have been somewhat of a hardship. The family must have been living in relative poverty. Still, contribute they did.

Above all, Joseph was determined that his family members should become good and knowledgeable Jews. In 1616, he and the twelve-year old Menasseh joined a recently established study group, the Santa Irmandade de Talmud Tora (Holy Brotherhood for the Study of the Law).

The rabbi, or *hakham*, of Beth Jacob at the time was still Joseph Pardo. When Pardo and a number of congregants left

in 1618 to form Beth Israel, he was replaced by Saul Levi
Mortera, the only rabbi in the Amsterdam Portuguese-Jewish
community in this period who was not of Sephardic background.[33] Mortera was born in 1594 to an Ashkenazic family in
Venice, and probably studied with that city's famous but flawed
rabbi, Leon de Modena (he suffered from a serious gambling
addiction).[34] Mortera left Venice for Paris in 1612 when his
employer and mentor, Elias Rodrigues Montalto—a physician
and former converso whom Modena had converted back to
Judaism—was appointed the official doctor at the court of
Marie de' Medici, Henri IV's widow. (A special dispensation
was needed to allow these Jews to reside in France.) Mortera
served as Montalto's secretary, Hebrew teacher, and spiritual
adviser until the good doctor's death in Tours in 1616. The closest Jewish cemetery was the one serving Amsterdam's Portuguese congregations, and so Mortera brought Montalto's body
to Ouderkerk for a proper burial. When the members of Beth
Jacob asked Mortera to join their congregation, he accepted,
swayed perhaps by the fact that in this northern city, unlike
Venice, Jews did not have to live in a ghetto. That same year,
he married into the community; his bride, Ester Soares, was a
recent arrival from Lisbon.

When Mortera took over from Pardo as rabbi of Beth
Jacob, he was only twenty-four years old. Despite his youth, he
was already a learned scholar well prepared for the task of guid-
ing these new Jews in living according to *halakha*, or Jewish
law. Unlike so many members of his congregation—and much
of the Amsterdam Portuguese-Jewish community at large—he
was fluent in rabbinic texts and Jewish theological and philosophical literature. His sermons—which early in his tenure
had to be translated into Portuguese for his audience—were
intellectually rich, erudite exegeses on biblical texts informed
by citations not only of Talmud and various *midrashim*, but also
of patristic authors, medieval Jewish and non-Jewish thinkers,

and Italian humanists.[35] Mortera was well read and well traveled, a European intellectual who now also happened to be a rabbi charged with helping to reeducate a community of former New Christians.

Not having gone through the converso experience in Spain or Portugal, Mortera had little understanding of the difficulties that Amsterdam's Sephardim faced in adjusting to the demands of a proper Jewish life. He also had no sympathy for the relatives of Amsterdam Jews still forced to live as Christians in Spain and Portugal, and even contempt for those who stayed there willingly. He was not shy about expressing his views in the synagogue, and often had quite severe things to say about conversos who refused to leave their comfortable lives in the "lands of idolatry." In one of his sermons, he accused them all of "hypocrisy" and claimed that "God detests them for concealing their true faith in Him."[36] Responding to a query from a Spanish priest in Rouen, he warned that "Jews who are not circumcised and who do not observe the law in lands where they are not permitted to do so" risk eternal punishment. If they continue to confess the Catholic faith (even "against their wishes"), engage in the worship of images, attend mass, and deny that they are Jews "when, in their hearts, they really are," then they are "guilty before God." In Mortera's view, despite the Mishnah's claim that "all Israelites have a portion in the world-to-come [*olam ha-ba*]," there were certain sins for which even a Jew could permanently forfeit his or her place in the world-to-come, and apostasy was one of them.[37]

Joseph Pardo and—after Pardo's departure from Beth Jacob to Beth Israel—Mortera were the young Menasseh's rabbis, with Pardo presumably presiding when Menasseh became a *bar mitzvah* in 1617. But Menasseh's earliest education, in Hebrew language and Scripture, was overseen by the Neve Shalom rabbi who taught in the elementary school jointly directed by the two congregations. As Menasseh succinctly put it, in some autobiographical remarks at the end of one of his treatises, "I was tutored in Hebrew letters by Rabbi Isaac Uziel."[38]

Uziel, originally from Fez, Morocco, came to Amsterdam from the North African city of Oran, arriving shortly after Menasseh's family. By all accounts, Uziel was a stern and somber man. And while he was, unlike Mortera, a Sephardic Jew, according to one contemporary he, like Mortera, had a hard time empathizing with the travails of the converso experience. Daniel Levi de Barrios, the seventeenth-century poet-historian of the Portuguese-Jewish community of Amsterdam, reports that "some members [of Uziel's congregation] disapproved of his sermons, either because of their harsh and offensive parts or because, as powerful people, they did not think that they deserved to be reproached in any way." Uziel, De Barrios says, "would in his sermons scold . . . with the burning zeal of the prophet Elias." On De Barrios's telling of the origins of the Beth Israel congregation, Uziel's demeanor caused some congregants to leave Neve Shalom, "so they might no longer suffer being corrected by the righteous Uziel." He says that "they united with others to build a new synagogue, which they called Beth Israel," and appointed a more amiable rabbi, David Pardo, the son of Joseph.[39]

Menasseh, however, greatly admired Uziel, who apparently was a close friend of the family.[40] Some years after Uziel's death, when Menasseh was supplementing his rabbinic salary with a publishing business, he honored his late rabbi by bringing out a printed edition of his Hebrew grammar.[41] *Ma'aneh lashon* (The Gift of Speech), by Isaac ben Abraham Uziel, was probably the grammar from which Menasseh himself learned Hebrew, and it would be among the first things to come off his brand new printing press.

One of Menasseh's fellow pupils in Uziel's elementary classes was a boy named Isaac Aboab da Fonseca. Like Menasseh, Aboab was born in Portugal, in 1605; and his family, having escaped the lands of the Inquisition, also made a temporary stay in France, in St. Jean-de-Luz. They arrived in Amsterdam in 1612 and joined the Neve Shalom congregation. We do not know how Menasseh and Aboab, who were only one year apart in age, got along as children in Uziel's class—probably no better and no worse than is typical for schoolmates. Uziel likely treated his students with no more leniency or mercy than he showed his congregants, and the boys may have bonded in their shared suffering under a harsh regime. Nonetheless, later in life relations between the two men would be rather tense. Aboab turned out to be one of Menasseh's nemeses, someone whose status (and salary) in the Amsterdam Jewish community Menasseh greatly resented.

Menasseh was a precocious student. Already in 1619, he gave his first sermon to the Beth Jacob congregation. He was quite proud of his oratory skills. "In my youth, I was so devoted to rhetoric and so eloquent in the Lusitanian language [Portuguese] that when I was fifteen years old my discourses [*conciones*] were very pleasing, applauded and well received."[42]

He was also a quick study in his Hebrew lessons under Uziel, for in 1621, when he was seventeen, he began composing his own Hebrew grammar book, in Portuguese and Hebrew. With a boldness bordering on chutzpah, he gave it the same title as a famous grammar by the great twelfth-century theologian, philosopher, and exegete Abraham ibn Ezra: *Safah Berurah* (The Pure Language). Menasseh's grammar probably stems from the Hebrew lessons that he himself was now giving as a *rubi* in the lowest levels of the Talmud Torah school.[43] Like the manuscript of Uziel's Hebrew grammar before Menasseh published it, as well as those of other Amsterdam rabbis, Menasseh's handwritten text was copied several times and circulated in the community, both in its schools and in its *yeshivot*, or adult learning academies.[44]

As useful as Menasseh's grammar may have been in the

classroom and even within the broader community of former conversos trying to gain at least a rudimentary knowledge of Hebrew, it was a rather mundane beginning to his writing career. This set of introductory lessons in the rules, syntax, and vocabulary of Hebrew, arising as it did out of pedagogical necessity (and revealing that Menasseh already had some knowledge of Latin), gives very little indication of the rich and influential body of exegetical, theological, and philosophical writings that he would produce in the coming decades. Little could his elementary school students suspect that their young teacher, fresh out of school himself and restless to make a name for himself, would become an international celebrity: a famous author of bestselling Judaica and the center of a pan-European network of Jews and gentiles anticipating—sooner or later—the coming of the Messiah.

In the spring of 1622, Isaac Uziel died. The Neve Shalom congregation, only two decades old, was in need of a new rabbi. They could once again import someone from abroad—Salonika, perhaps, or Venice, or Hamburg. Or, now that there was a well-established Jewish community in Amsterdam educating its own, they could look among the homegrown talent. In the end, the Neve Shalom *parnassim* went local and chose the teenager who was regarded as the late rabbi's most gifted pupil. This, at least, is suggested by what Menasseh himself had to say, ever so tersely, about the impressive change in his status. He remarked only that "after [Rabbi Isaac Uziel's] death, I succeeded in his place."[45]

If this quick and simple transition "from the cradle to the pulpit" is indeed what happened, Menasseh ben Israel, at the age of eighteen, was functioning as a rabbi (although not yet officially a *hakham*) and, like his mentor Uziel, serving as a teacher in the community's elementary school.[46] Menasseh's official ordination, whenever it occurred, probably a few years later, would have been carried out by one of the community's more senior rabbis—almost certainly Mortera, who still led the congregation to which Menasseh's family belonged.

It is extraordinary that the son of a refugee family of former conversos who, not landing in Amsterdam and beginning a real Jewish life until the age of ten, and starting with only the barest (and probably a distorted) understanding of Judaism and no knowledge of Hebrew whatsoever, could, in so short a time and at such a relatively young age, become learned and respected enough to lead the city's second-oldest Jewish congregation, educate the Amsterdam Portuguese community's youth, and help reintegrate other new arrivals.

Menasseh was, in fact, part of a remarkable coterie of young men in the second generation of Amsterdam's Sephardim. These students of Halevi, Vega, Uziel, Pardo, and Mortera, either born in the Vlooienburg neighborhood or arriving there as children, would assume leadership positions in the community and elsewhere by the early 1620s. Besides Menasseh and Aboab—who would also be named a *hakham* for Neve Shalom—there was Isaac Athias, who would go on to become a rabbi in Hamburg; and Joseph Pardo's son David, who, some years older than Menasseh, would serve as the chief rabbi of Beth Israel.[47] At the end of the sixteenth century, there were no Jews in Amsterdam. Just two decades later, the city was—like Venice, like Hamburg—a feeder of rabbis to Jewish communities elsewhere.

Not in his wildest dreams, and certainly not while suffering on the rack, could Gaspar Rodrigues Nunes have foreseen such a brilliant turn of events. Unfortunately, he did not get to enjoy the family's elevated standing in the community for long.

3

On the Nieuwe Houtmarkt

WHEN THE FRENCH PHILOSOPHER René Descartes moved
to the Netherlands as a young man, he sought only peace and
quiet. The distractions and steady stream of interruptions in
Paris had made it too difficult to carry out his work there. "As
many people know, I lived in relative comfort in my native
country. My only reason for choosing to live elsewhere was
that I had so many friends and relatives whom I could not fail
to entertain, and that I would have had little time and leisure
available to pursue the studies that I enjoy and that, according
to many people, will contribute to the common good of the
human race."[1] And then there were the censorious eyes of
the French ecclesiastic and academic authorities, who frowned
on philosophical novelty. The crowded bustle of Amsterdam—
where everyone is "so busy that they are more concerned with
their own affairs than curious about those of others"—and the
isolation of the Dutch countryside suited his purposes well,

and he ended up spending most of his adult life in the United Provinces. He had settled, he believed, in a land of milk and honey—especially milk.[2]

Descartes's idyllic report notwithstanding, the Dutch Golden Age was far from being a period of uninterrupted peace, prosperity, toleration, and great art. During the 1620s, in particular, the young Republic faced some hard times. There was international menace and domestic strife, both of which threatened its unity as a federation of self-governing provinces. One historian has called this decade "the most somber period in the history of the United Provinces. . . . Under siege and squeezed hard," Dutch society was in the grip of a *"malaise"* that was economic, political, and religious.[3]

In 1622, as Menasseh was assuming his rabbinical duties with the Neve Shalom congregation, the Dutch Republic was once again at war. The truce that had been signed with Spain in 1609, halting hostilities in the long battle for independence, had unraveled. A series of provocations by the Habsburg crown—including an embargo against Dutch trade with Spain, Portugal, and their New World colonies; interference with Dutch shipping in the Levant and the Baltic region, an important source of wood for Holland's lumber industry; and attacks on Dutch herring fishing in the North Sea—led to a serious economic slump in the United Provinces. Moreover, the Republic found itself increasingly isolated diplomatically, as relations with France, England, and the German states—all of whom had, over the previous decade, made peace with Spain and engaged in commercial disputes with the Dutch—deteriorated. The Republic had, through the "Twelve Years' Truce," gained some international recognition as a de facto sovereign nation. But its security, even its continued existence, remained precarious as Spain maintained a large occupying army in the southern Low Countries. By early 1622, the Spaniards, under the brilliant but ruthless generalship of Ambrosio Spinola, had decided to take advantage of the military situation. The battle was back on.

At the same time as the renewal of war with Spain, there were serious religious and political tensions within the Dutch Republic itself. Public life in the United Provinces was still reeling from one of its periodic major upheavals, many of which ended only with a barbaric act of violence.

Just a few years before Menasseh's family arrived in Holland, there appeared a breach in the unity of the Dutch Reformed Church. In 1610, a number of liberal Reformed ministers had issued a remonstrance or petition in which they set forth their unorthodox views on a variety of sensitive theological questions. These "Remonstrants" or Arminians (so called because they were followers of Jacob Arminius, a theology professor at the University of Leiden) explicitly rejected the strict Calvinist doctrines of grace and predestination. Both sides of the debate agreed that divine grace was essential for salvation. No one living after the Fall could possibly do good or achieve eternal blessedness through their own natural efforts and without God's free and unearned grace, which was distributed to the elect without regard to merit. But where more orthodox theologians insisted that such grace was irresistible—a person to whom grace was granted could not reject or even resist it—the Remonstrants believed that a person had the capacity, through his free will, to choose whether or not to cooperate with this divine gift. The Remonstrants also favored a separation between matters of conscience (which should be left to individuals) and matters of public policy (to be managed by civil authorities), and they distrusted the political ambitions of their conservative Calvinist opponents. Like many reformers, the Arminian partisans saw their crusade in moral terms. In their eyes, the true liberating spirit of the Reformation had been lost by the increasingly dogmatic, hierarchical, and intolerant leaders of the Dutch Reformed Church.[4]

The Remonstrants had on their side Johan van Olden-barnevelt, the advocate or general secretary (the position was later called "grand pensionary") of the States of Holland, the province's governing body, composed of representatives from the cities and towns. Because of the size and importance of Holland relative to the other provinces—a first among equals—whoever was the leader of that province's government essentially held one of the two most powerful political offices in the Dutch Republic. Depending upon the circumstances, his influence often surpassed even that of the stadholder, a national figure whose own domain extended across several provinces. (The stadholder was also the commander-in-chief of all Dutch military forces, and by tradition—especially for the weaker provinces—a symbol of Dutch unity; the position was ordinarily given by most of the provinces to members of the House of Orange-Nassau.)

With Oldenbarnevelt's support for the Remonstrant cause, what was initially a doctrinal dispute among the Calvinist clergy and university theology faculties quickly assumed political dimensions. The States of Holland, urged on by Oldenbarnevelt, upheld the right of the Remonstrants to continue preaching and to bring forward their opinions within the public church, and this in turn further antagonized the Remonstrants' opponents. The Counter-Remonstrant theologians accused the Arminians of being covert Catholics who took their lead from Rome, while Oldenbarnevelt's political enemies saw in his support for the religious liberals an opportunity to label him a traitor working on behalf of Spain, the Catholic enemy.

Within a few years, the Remonstrant/Counter-Remonstrant battle over theology became intertwined with conflicting views on domestic affairs and even foreign policy. The opposing camps disagreed on whether civil authorities had the right to legislate over the church and to control what it taught. They also fought over how to conduct the struggle with Spain. The Remonstrants sought peace, while the Counter-Remonstrants were in favor of pursuing the war against the Catholic foe without compromise. There was frequent, and sometimes quite violent, persecution of Remonstrants in a number of Dutch cities, and many Arminian sympathizers were removed from office. By 1617, the Holland stadholder himself, Prince Maurits of Nassau, entered the fray on the Counter-Remonstrant side. This was a calculated political move by Maurits. He hoped to oppose Oldenbarnevelt's policies, especially any peaceful overtures to Spain, as well as to gain support from orthodox religious leaders for his own domestic agenda (which involved increasing the stadholder's authority across provinces and thereby centralizing power in the Republic).

The orthodox Church leaders, concerned about Arminian influence, convened the Synod of Dort (Dordrecht) in late 1618. The delegates to the Synod reiterated their general commitment to freedom of conscience in the Dutch Republic, as enshrined in the Union of Utrecht. The Counter-Remonstrants controlled the gathering, however, and they made heavy-handed use of their advantage. They codified the severe Reformed dogmas concerning grace and atonement, and they succeeded in passing a resolution that restricted public worship and office holding to orthodox Calvinists. There was a purge of Remonstrants in the church and municipalities at all levels. Meanwhile, Oldenbarnevelt's enemies mercilessly prosecuted him. In the spring of 1619, he was convicted of treason. Despite the legal irregularities of the trial, he was handed a death sentence and beheaded shortly thereafter. By 1622, the Counter-Remonstrants were in clear command of the Republic's religious sphere, while their political allies, led by Maurits, had full charge of domestic and military policy.

What these developments—war, economic turmoil, the rise of religious intolerance, and a general deterioration of national unity and morale—might mean for Holland's Jews, who were now substantially invested in the province's economic well-being and reliant upon its continued political and religious good will, is apparent from a brief episode at the end of 1619, shortly after the Counter-Remonstrants gained the upper hand. The Amsterdam city council, at the urging of the local consistory of the Dutch Reformed Church, which now felt empowered to insist on the restriction of public worship to orthodox Reformed services, forced the three synagogues on the Houtgracht to close their doors. The prohibition did not last long, though—the regents of Amsterdam did not appreciate taking orders from conservative preachers, and they certainly did not want to alienate the Sephardim who now played a significant role in the city's economy—and by March of 1620, the Portuguese Jews were back in their synagogues. The consistory was not happy about this, and lodged a formal complaint with the burgemeesters. The church council was concerned that the city leaders were giving the Jews too much liberty, and longed for the good old days when Amsterdam would regularly prohibit the Portuguese settlers from doing things like using a house they had built as a synagogue (this happened in 1612) and purchasing land within the city limits for a cemetery (a request that was denied twice, in 1606 and 1608).[5]

The early 1620s brought emotional highs and lows for Menasseh. Though still in his teens, he was now among the spiritual leaders of his community. This must have been a source of great joy and not a little pride to him and his family, only recently removed from the clutches of the Inquisition, years of wandering, and destitution. Still, Menasseh had to show due deference to his own former rabbi at Beth Jacob, Saul Levi Mortera, who was ten years his senior. He also served at the pleasure of the *ma'amad* of his congregation, the governing body of *parnassim* that, like the regents of the city of Amsterdam itself, was composed of wealthy professionals and merchants selected from prominent families. The interests of these lay leaders of the community and the religious concerns of the congregations' rabbis did not always coincide, often leading to serious clashes over power and prerogative. While Menasseh would later chafe under the *ma'amad*'s authority, his gratification in such a quick and unexpected rise from student to rabbi tempered any frustrations with his congregation that he might have faced this early in his career.

In October of 1622, just a few months after Menasseh's promotion, Joseph ben Israel died. He was sixty-four years old. His late adult life must have been an experience of constant pain and infirmity as a result of the torture he had suffered twenty-five years earlier. No sooner had the family buried Joseph in the Ouderkerk cemetery—in a place of honor at the feet of Rabbi Uziel—than Menasseh's mother, Rachel, passed away as well.[6] In one of his late writings, Menasseh tells of her suffering, and relates a dream that he had shortly before her death in which he foresaw her end:

> The lady who is the crown on my head, my mother Rachel Soeira, her soul in Eden, fell on a bed of suffering and her illness was very grave, and the doctors began to despair for her, there is no judge who can decide on her cure, there are not treatments for her. And I, low and in pain, tired and exhausted from the troubles of the time and from the anguish of my soul, on the eve of her departure, I rose up high on my bed, my cauldron, a sleep which is no sleep and a wakefulness that is not wakefulness, and God showed me that she will die as I saw her burial; and close to her was buried the distinguished man of our people, and then I woke up, but that man [I thought to be] alive and well. And the next day the lady my mother z"l passed away and the next week among those coming to comfort me I saw two nephews of that man and they are dressed in black clothes of mourners, long as is the custom, so I asked one person near me the reason for the

mourning clothes and they told me that bad tidings came to them about their father's death in the land of Spain, and as I heard his words I said to myself: who knows if that is the interpretation of the dream that I had. Not four days passed and the distinguished man died and was buried near my mother, their souls shall be bound in the bundle of life with our Lord God.[7]

In the final months of 1622, the house on the Nieuwe Houtmarkt where Menasseh lived with his older sister and younger brother was a dark and sad place. It was also a relatively impoverished home, as Menasseh's low income from Neve Shalom—sixty guilders per year—was not sufficient to support all three of them with any great comfort.

Menasseh's sorrow over losing both parents within a short span of time was softened somewhat by his marriage the following year to twenty-one-year-old Rachel Abrabanel. Menasseh took great pride in marrying into a family that, he said, had an extremely venerable history. "I married my wife, Rachel, from the Abrabanel family, who asserted that they were Hebrews descended from David."[8] In light of the tradition that the Messiah is to come from the House of David, this alleged genealogical fact about his wife was, in Menasseh's mind, not without significance for the destiny of his sons.

Rachel was the daughter of the late Joseph Abrabanel, a converso who had only recently brought his family from Guimãres, Portugal, to Amsterdam, where he established himself as a respected physician.[9] The family, it has been claimed, had its roots in Portuguese-Jewish nobility. Her ancestors are supposed to have included the great fifteenth-century scholar and diplomat Isaac Abrabanel—who, after moving from Portugal to Spain, served as treasurer to the monarchs Ferdinand and Isabella just on the eve of the Expulsion—and Isaac's son Judah Abrabanel, a philosopher and author of a famous treatise, *Dialoghi d'amore* (Dialogues on Love). In 1492, after pleading, in vain, with his royal employers to reconsider their order expelling the Jews, Isaac and his family fled Iberia for Italy, settling eventually in Venice. Perhaps Rachel's father was indeed a grandson of Don Isaac and the son of Judah (although possibly the son of Judah's brother Samuel). But that raises the fraught question as to why some members of a well-known Jewish family would have ended up back in the hostile territory of Portugal in the early seventeenth century, where Joseph raised his children. The connection with the illustrious Abrabanel line—like the descent from David—may be nothing more than an ennobling family myth.[10]

On the same day in August 1623 that Menasseh (identified as being *van Rochelle*) and "Ragel Barbanel" (*van Guymerens*, that is, Guimãres) registered their marriage banns with the city, Menasseh's sister Hester (who is described as *van Lisbonne*) and Rachel's brother Jonah, a poet, did the same. Rachel and Jonah were there to serve as witnesses for their siblings' banns, and chose to take advantage of the opportunity to deepen the ties between the two families. The civil ceremony in which the Dutch magistrate granted them all permission to marry required the couples to swear that "they were free persons, and that as regards blood relationship there were no circumstances whereby a Christian marriage would be prevented."[11]

After their wedding, Menasseh and Rachel settled in a rented house on Nieuwe Houtmarkt. It may have been the same house in which Menasseh had been living with his siblings, or it may simply have been another house among the less expensive real estate on the Vlooienburg island. The term "New Wood Market" in seventeenth-century records is an imprecise designation for Vlooienburg, as the city's district for processors and purveyors of lumber.

Contemporary prints show the streets on both sides of the Houtgracht bustling with a variety of commercial and recreational activities. Well-to-do Sephardic Jews who lived in the neighborhood and poorer Ashkenazim from the inner lanes of the island, along with their gentile neighbors (many of whom were artists and art dealers) and Amsterdamers from other parts of the city who enjoyed visiting the "Jews quarter," could, while strolling along the "wood canal," stop at any of the produce or flower markets there. They might also wander into some of the art galleries a block away on the Breestraat, including the home of the dealer Hendrik van Uylenburgh, where a young painter from Leiden named Rembrandt Harmenszoon van Rijn would soon be living and working in his studio.

Within the space of a few years, Menasseh and Rachel had three children. Their first-born, in 1625, was a daughter, who was given both a Hebrew name, Hannah, and a Portuguese name, Gracia. She was followed by two boys, Joseph and Samuel.[12] Their birthdates are all unrecorded.

Menasseh, ever proud of his sons, would often boast, to both Jewish and gentile friends, that Joseph and Samuel were in the Davidic line. One of Menasseh's Jesuit admirers wrote that "Menasseh did not hesitate sometimes to proclaim to me . . . that he had attained a relationship to King David, and that his sons had achieved the same relationship, and that he had given birth to nephews of David."[13]

With a wife and three children to support, the meager salary that Menasseh was earning as rabbi for Neve Shalom and teacher in the community's elementary school was rather inadequate. In fact, Menasseh would worry—and complain—about money for the rest of his life. He would never feel that he was properly compensated by the Amsterdam congregations he served; and compared with what the other rabbis were earning, he was absolutely right.

By 1624, Menasseh was able to supplement his income for preaching and primary-level teaching by giving lessons in Talmud.[14] This would hardly have been enough to allow the family to live in the kind of comfort to which Abrabanels, at least, would have been accustomed. It was certainly not enough to buy a house or even rent something in the more upscale part of the neighborhood, on or just off the Breestraat. In October 1624, Menasseh was able to make a nominal *promessa* or charitable offering on the occasion of the funeral of David Farrar, a member of Beth Jacob and a scion of one of the leading families of the Amsterdam Sephardic community. On an important communal occasion like this, a "voluntary" donation was pretty much mandatory. His contribution of six stuivers (there were twenty stuivers to the guilder or florin) was only a third of what Abraham Farrar, a physician and the deceased's cousin, had given, but for a man of Menasseh's means it was a generous gesture—and it was twice as much as what Rabbi Mortera offered.[15] These kinds of communal gifts, fairly regular over the course of the year on the occasion of celebrations and life-cycle events, and coming on top of the *finta* and other taxes, must have taken a toll on the family budget.

It was time to start looking for other ways to bring in some money.

On March 18, 1626, Menasseh paid a visit to the office of the Dutch notary Sybrant Cornelisz. He was accompanied by an artisan named Nicolas Briot. The two men were there to sign a contract whereby Briot, a skilled type-cutter originally from Liège in the Spanish-ruled southern Netherlands, would prepare and deliver to the rabbi a full set of Hebrew type. The agreement drawn up by the notary states that "Manoel Diaz Soeiro, Portuguese merchant dwelling in this city of Amsterdam, and Nicolas Briot, type-founder also living in Amsterdam, have arranged and made an agreement as follows: Manoel Diaz Soeiro has placed an order with Nicolas Briot to make for him and deliver the kinds of Hebrew letters as mentioned further, as much of each kind as he will need." The typeface that Briot was to make should contain both unpointed (or unvocalized) characters and letters "all with their vowels and points well formed and cut."[16]

By early 1626, then, Menasseh had decided on a business plan for supplementing his annual rabbinic salary. He was going to open a printing and publishing house.

This was a smart and remarkably prescient move. There was a great need in Amsterdam for a publisher of Jewish texts, primarily works in Hebrew but also—in light of the local, Iberian-born clientele—in Spanish, a need that would only increase in the coming years.

When Menasseh began operating out of his home on the Nieuwe Houtmarkt—officially, Jews were not permitted to have open retail shops in the Netherlands—there was nobody publishing Hebrew books in the city, and only a handful of publishers doing so elsewhere in Holland.[17] The Amsterdam printer Jan Theunisz, active in the first decade of the century, did have a set of Hebrew type that he used in copies of works by the English Puritan theologian Hugh Broughton. While these books contained some Hebrew passages, Theunisz did not publish Hebrew books per se.[18]

In Leiden and Franeker, meanwhile, academic publishers were producing Hebrew texts for local scholars and their students. Both of these university towns had a history of Hebrew printing going back to the late sixteenth century. It was in Leiden, in 1585, that Christopher Plantin turned out the first Hebrew book in the northern Netherlands, a Hebrew grammar. Over the next three decades, Plantin's firm, overseen by his son-in-law Franciscus van Ravelingen (better known by his Latin moniker, Franciscus Raphelengius), published high-quality Hebrew Bibles, dictionaries, grammars, and linguistic studies. The press was barely able to keep up with the demand by academic theologians, and Plantin's finely cut type, superior to that used by Theunisz, circulated among other publishers.[19] In Franeker (in the province of Friesland), Gillis van de Rade (or, to use his business name, Aegidius Radaeus) was publishing individual books of the Hebrew Bible, accompanied by Latin commentaries, treatises on the Hebrew language, and even a work of Hebrew poetry.

Plantin had moved his business to Leiden from its original home in Antwerp, in the southern Netherlands, where there were a number of printers producing Hebrew texts. These were all Christians, of course, since this was still Spain's territory. However, there were Jewish printer/publishers of Hebrew books elsewhere in northern Europe. Moses ben Jacob Halevi was running a press in Emden, and there were Jewish firms in Basel, Frankfurt, and Prague.[20] For the Amsterdam Portuguese-Jewish community, though, the most important sources for congregational books in the first two and a half decades of the seventeenth century were Krakow and Lublin in Poland, and Venice and Ferrara in Italy. Beth Jacob, Neve Shalom, and Beth Israel were all in need of liturgical and other works in Hebrew and especially—since a good number of the Amsterdam Sephardim were, at this stage in the community's history, unable to read Hebrew—in Spanish and bilingual editions. (Portuguese was the language of the home and in the street, but Spanish was the preferred language for religious texts and high literature.) To meet this demand, the congregations turned to foreign Sephardic and Ashkenazic publishers. Many of the books imported to Amsterdam from Poland and Italy were bought in bulk on the retail market, but quite a few were printed on commission from local Portuguese-Jewish clients who were willing and able to pay for nice editions.

This imbalance in the trade of Hebrew texts, as well as Jewish literature in general in a variety of languages, would soon see a radical inversion. Slowly but surely, a skilled cohort of Hebrew printer/publishers arose in Amsterdam, and over the next several decades the city came to dominate the world of Jewish books.[21] By midcentury, Amsterdam surpassed all other

European cities in the number, variety, and quality of printed Judaica. This was, in fact, part of a larger phenomenon as publishers in Amsterdam and other Dutch cities began flooding the international market with a quantity and diversity of literary works that dwarfed what was being produced elsewhere. As one scholar puts it, the Republic came to enjoy the reputation of being "Europe's publishing house."[22]

In the sixteenth century, no book or pamphlet could be published in the province of Holland without permission of the States of Holland; this *imprimatur*, granted after the contents of the work had been examined and approved, had to be printed in the book itself.[23] In the first two decades of the seventeenth century, the States General became increasingly concerned about books that were likely to cause problems "in both ecclesiastical and political affairs," culminating in a 1615 edict intended to encourage provincial and municipal bodies to engage in the preventive censorship of offensive works. However, with the marked increase in the number of books and pamphlets being prepared for publication—and, in many cases, simply being published without being submitted for official approval—neither the province of Holland nor the States General was able to keep up, so they no longer required publishers to submit manuscripts for approval prior to publication. Printers henceforth had only to register their businesses with the local magistrates, as well as swear an oath that they would hand over any suspicious writings that had been submitted to them and that in their opinion might be a danger to the state or to piety. The control of the presses in the Dutch Republic was subsequently a decentralized affair, with the States General ceding authority to the individual provinces to manage things, and the provincial States in turn leaving it up to the cities and towns to keep an eye on their resident publishers. Consequently, there was a great deal of inconsistency throughout the Republic in the enforcement of censorship, whether before or after publication. What might be severely repressed in Groningen could well find easy distribution in Amsterdam or Leiden.

This relatively lax policy—or, at least, lax enforcement—allowed a rich and eclectic body of literature to emanate from Dutch presses. Strident political treatises, including radical democratic broadsides; controversial religious tracts by dissident Reformed sects (such as the Quakers) and anti-trinitarian factions (most alarmingly, the Socinians); "scandalous" and "soul-destroying" books by atheists, libertines, and freethinkers; even erotic literature—these and other writings in theology, philosophy, science, poetry, drama, and fiction that could not possibly be published anywhere else flourished in the tolerant literary environment of Amsterdam and other Dutch cities. The books coming out of the provinces of Holland and Utrecht reached a wide international audience and catered to readers of Dutch, German, English, Latin, Spanish, Portuguese, and especially French, which was quickly becoming the lingua franca of the Republic of Letters.

All this was, of course, of great concern to political and religious authorities elsewhere in Europe, who—like the leaders of the Dutch Reformed Church itself—saw Holland as a source of all things subversive. The Spanish and French kings were particularly frustrated with the Dutch for allowing their recently liberated territory to serve as a fount of anti-monarchical literature. However, there was little these foreign authorities could do about it, and little that Holland's regents cared to do about it. In the absence of prior restraint, the Dutch presses just rolled on.

A number of factors contributed to Amsterdam's rise as *the* major European hub for the publication of Jewish books. There was the inability of university publishers in Leiden, Franeker, and Utrecht—important centers of Hebraic scholarship in their arts and theology faculties—to keep up with the increasing local and international demand for grammars, dictionaries, and scholarly editions of Hebrew texts. At the same time, printers of Judaica in Venice and cities within the Holy Roman Empire faced greater restrictions as both the Catholic Church and Protestant authorities were ever on the lookout for Jewish literature containing anti-Christian polemics; the printing of the Talmud, especially, regarded by the Church as rife with offenses against Christianity, was strictly forbidden. Perhaps most important of all, there was the growth of a prosperous community of Jews in Amsterdam itself—Sephardic and Ashkenazic immigration increased rapidly as the century went on—that had its own liturgical and literary needs. Importing books from abroad in quantities large enough to meet those needs was simply becoming too expensive—and, eventually, unnecessary.

By the early 1640s, Amsterdam printer/publishers were producing all the essential kinds of Jewish literature: Pentateuchs (*humashim*) with *haftarah* portions from the Prophets and other writings for the weekly Torah readings; Hebrew Bibles (with and without rabbinic commentary); *siddurim*, or everyday prayer books; *makhzorim*, or prayer books for the holidays; halakhic or legal treatises; rabbinic exegeses; copies of the Passover *haggadah*; books of *selichot*, or penitential prayers for Rosh Hashanah and Yom Kippur; editions of the Mishnah; homiletical collections; kabbalistic works; even a complete set of the Babylonian Talmud, including the tractate *Avodah Zara* ("Worship of Idols"), usually singled out by Christian censors as the most offensive to Christians. The quality of Jewish books coming out of Amsterdam was high. It included both well-bound volumes set in fine type on good quality paper, as well as cheaper editions in large volume. Moreover, the in-house "correctors" or proofreaders knew what they were doing. Hebraic publishing in Amsterdam was widely admired for its exacting standards. "Printed in Amsterdam" became a valuable trademark for Jewish books, one that was often pirated by publishers elsewhere in order to enhance the marketability of their wares.

Because of guild restrictions in many cities, much of the printing of Hebrew throughout the province of Holland was done by gentiles. In Leiden, besides the Plantin-Raphelengius firm, there was Johannes Le Maire—whose output included studies of Hebrew vocalization and a Hebrew philosophical treatise with Latin translation—and the members of the Elzevir family, whose house published in 1630, in the midst of the war with Spain, a "Prayer of Holland's Jews [*Tefillat Kahal Yisrael be-Medinat Hollandim*]" for the success of the siege of 's-Hertogenbosch by the stadholder Frederik Hendrik.

In Amsterdam, the printer/publishers Johannes Janssonius and Nicolaes van Ravesteyn were competing with the business run by Joan and Cornelis Blaeu. Compared with what was coming out of Leiden, however, none of these early Amsterdam publishers had a particularly large Hebrew catalogue—just a few grammars and lexicographical works, although the Blaeu brothers did publish several volumes of Maimonides's *Mishneh Torah* with Latin translations.[24] Moreover, the scholarly academic editions that Dutch Christian publishers were producing were hardly of much use to the Jews of Vlooienburg, especially for ritual purposes.

This left the field wide open for enterprising Jewish printers.

As with most matters regarding the rights and responsibilities of Jews in the Dutch Republic, restrictions on business activities, as well as enforcement of those regulations, varied from province to province and from town to town. Exceptions (explicit or tacit) were allowed and loopholes taken advantage of, with local authorities sometimes looking the other way. Thus, as gentile printers and booksellers were discovering the value of dealing in Judaica, there also developed a notable Jewish presence in the Dutch publishing world, one that catered to the domestic and foreign demand for Jewish literature in Hebrew, Spanish, Portuguese, and Yiddish.

This relative freedom of the Jewish press did not come easy. When, in 1615, the States of Holland was first considering the conditions under which to allow the open settlement and public worship of Jews, there was debate as to whether or not there should be censorship of Jewish literature. The toleration shown by the regents of Haarlem, which in 1605 was perfectly willing to allow Jews "to print and have and use in their homes all kinds of books, in Hebrew or any other language," was not the obvious policy for most Dutch cities.[25] When the delegates Hugo Grotius (Hugo de Groot) and Adriaen Pauw submitted to the States their drafts of regulations to govern Jewish residence in the province, they suggested that Jews should be able to own and print all kinds of books—especially "the Holy Writing of the Old Testament, both in the original language and in translation"—but that they should be prevented from publishing works "containing words of blasphemy or defamation" toward the Christian religion.[26] For Grotius, who favored allowing Jews to settle in Holland, prior censorship was the only reasonable policy. He singled out the Talmud, "which contains many blasphemies against Christians," and insisted its publication or use should be strictly forbidden. Any Jewish publisher caught violating this regulation, he wrote, ought to be punished by expulsion from the Republic and have all his property confiscated; any Jew caught reading or owning proscribed books should have to pay a heavy fine. Pauw, the pensionary of Amsterdam, seconded Grotius's recommendations. He, too, welcomed Jewish settlement, just as long as they live "modest and obedient lives" and refrain "from speaking, writing, or publishing, publicly or in private, any reasons or words of blasphemy or scorn against our Lord and Savior Jesus Christ or the

Christian religion ... on pain of banishment for life and the confiscation of goods."[27]

In the end, the States of Holland was reluctant to re-create in the province just the kind of inquisitional environment from which both the Republic and its Sephardic Jews were liberated when they left behind their Iberian overlords. In its 1619 proclamation, the States ignored the recommendations of Grotius and Pauw and declined to enshrine in province-wide law any prior restraint of the press or harsh reprisals for "offensive" literature. There is no mention whatsoever of restrictions to be imposed on Jewish publishing. In Holland, at least, the Jews ended up with the same freedom of the press as ordinary burghers.

The Dutch Reformed Church, naturally, took a radically different view of things. Its ministers were not at all happy with this tolerant arrangement. The theology faculties in Leiden and Utrecht would spend most of the century protesting both the general leeway given Jewish publishing and the printing of particular works—Talmuds, of course, but also exegetical and philosophical treatises. They had a special animus against Jewish messianic writings likely to give Christians the wrong idea about God's Anointed One. A young conservative theologian named Gisbertus Voetius (Gijsbert Voet) led the charge, holding public disputations in which he inveighed against the presence of Jews in the Netherlands and the liberties they enjoyed, despite the fact that there were no Jews in his city, at least officially. He complained vehemently about the lack of censorship being exercised over what was coming off Jewish presses. (This was not the last time that Voetius fulminated against the Jews, and in a few years his vitriol would be directed at Menasseh himself.)

At the municipal level, city councils—either out of principle or economic self-interest—were generally unmoved by these ecclesiastic complaints. There is no record of prior restraint directed at Jewish publishing by any town in the provinces of Holland and Utrecht in the seventeenth century. In Amsterdam, even the local Reformed consistory was willing to let things be, just as long as Jewish books did not appear in Dutch, which would have made them a little too accessible to the general public.[28]

The Jewish printer/publishers in the Republic during the first half of the century were all based in Amsterdam—mainly because that is where the Jews were. These publishers at first came from the Sephardic community, which, in this early period, made up the vast majority of the city's Jewish population.

There was Daniel de Fonseca, a member of the Neve Shalom congregation originally from Portugal who briefly ran a printing press in 1627 and 1628 and ended up publishing only two books: a treatise on ethics by Meir ibn Aldabi and an index of commentaries on the Hebrew Bible compiled by Abraham de Fonseca (who may or may not have been related to him). Somewhat later, Imanoel Benveniste, who arrived in Vlooienburg as a young man—most likely from Italy, although he had family still in Spain or Portugal—enjoyed much more success than De Fonseca. Benveniste would become a major publisher of a wide variety of Judaica, sacred and secular, in Hebrew and Spanish, more than sixty works in all over a twenty-four-year career until his death in 1664. His output included a Babylonian Talmud and a book of prayers and lamentations on the pogroms of 1648 in the Ukraine, Volhynia, Podolia, and Lithuania.[29]

Those anti-Jewish riots and massacres in the east led to significant changes in the makeup of Amsterdam Jewry. German, Polish, Ukrainian, and Lithuanian Jews began arriving in the city in significant numbers. As they settled in the Vlooienburg district and re-created a congregational life, they had to replace the communal and private libraries they left behind. Printers thus began producing liturgical books in line with

Ashkenazic ritual and other literature in Hebrew and Yiddish (including bilingual editions).[30] Some of these publishers were themselves Ashkenazim. Around the same time as Benveniste was putting the final touches on his Talmud and printing some commentaries on the Kabbalah, Judah ben Mordecai (also known as Judah Leib ben Mordecai Gimpel), who came to Amsterdam from Posen around 1632 and served for a time as a compositor for Benveniste, and Samuel bar Moses Halevi, who arrived in the city from either Germany or Poland, were catering to the literary needs of this community by 1648. Their business partnership did not last long—it disbanded in 1651— but they were prolific and ended up producing twenty books in Hebrew and Yiddish. Their merchandise included *A Book of Prayers for the Whole Year Made According to the German and Polish Customs*, in Yiddish; a bilingual edition of a poem commemorating the riots and expulsion of Jews in Frankfurt in 1614; and a rhymed paraphrase, in Yiddish, of the Book of Esther.[31]

Amsterdam by this time, midcentury, was the European capital of Jewish publishing. Most of the printing of Hebrew books and other Judaica was taking place close by the synagogues on the Houtgracht. Between 1627 and 1660, Sephardic and Ashkenazic printer/publishers in Amsterdam put out more Hebrew books, and more Judaica generally, than the other publishers in all Dutch cities combined since Plantin cut his first Hebrew type in 1585.

And it all began with Menasseh ben Israel's visit to the notary's office on that early spring day in 1626. He was the first printer of Hebrew books in Amsterdam—Jewish or gentile. Menasseh also published more Jewish books—in Hebrew, Spanish, Portuguese, Latin, English, Dutch, and Yiddish—than anybody else. We do not know from whom he learned his craft, or even if he trained with anyone. The city of Amsterdam did allow Jews to join guilds that governed occupations deemed essential to their communal life and in which their participation did not present too much competition for Christians, and printing and bookselling qualified. There is no reason, though, to think that Menasseh entered a formal apprenticeship in a master's shop. (Neither is there evidence that, once in business, he ever joined the guild. Perhaps he did not want to take on the costs of membership.) Yet somehow he managed to acquire the knowledge and technical skills needed. Before long he became the most important and certainly the most famous Jewish printer/publisher in the world, setting a very high bar by the quality of his workmanship. What especially distinguished Menasseh when he first started out from other early publishers of Hebrew and Jewish texts in the northern Netherlands was that much of his activity was to meet the needs of Jews, not gentile scholars.

There were a number of Hebrew types circulating in Amsterdam by the time Menasseh set up shop—including that used by the Plantin/Raphelengius firm in Leiden, as well as type available from Antwerp and Paris—but none of them were up to Menasseh's exacting standards. Among the typefaces that he ordered from Briot was Descendiana, which cost him ten stuivers (half a guilder) per pound. Menasseh wanted three hundred pounds of it, delivered within six weeks. That comes to one hundred and fifty guilders. If he wanted even just one hundred pounds of the other seven typefaces, some of which were quite a bit more expensive than the Descendiana, the whole order was going to cost him more than three thousand guilders. This was a substantial sum, and just for the type. When the cost of a printing press, tools, and ongoing expenses for paper and ink are included, the capital investment for a publishing house could run close to ten thousand guilders. How could Menasseh possibly afford all this?

Most printer/publishers in the Dutch Republic relied on outside investors, both for starting and sustaining the business itself and for specific projects, and Menasseh's operation was no different. He published his first book in January 1627—*Sefer Tefillat k'minhag kahal kadosh sefarad* (A Book of Prayers According to Sephardic Rite)—and it was financed by Ephraim Bueno and Abraham Sarphati. Bueno was a wealthy physician in the Amsterdam Portuguese-Jewish community, and Sarphati was the scion of one of the oldest Sephardic families in the city. All three men had studied together in one of the community's yeshivas.

Other early supporters of Menasseh's publishing house included his brother-in-law Jonah Abrabanel, who, along with Bueno, financed the publication in 1628 of Menasseh's own *Sefer Pene Rabah*—a concordance between the Bible and the *Midrash Rabbah* in which he shows where each biblical verse receives its rabbinic commentary—and a Spanish prayer book for the five major fast days. David Pardo, rabbi of Beth Israel, and Shalom ben Joseph Shalom Gallego, whose father Joseph was an important *hazzan* (prayer leader) in the Beth Jacob congregation, together subsidized three prayer books—two in Hebrew and one Spanish—in 1631, including a Hebrew *makhzor* for the High Holy Days and a *siddur* for four fast-days of the Jewish year: the tenth of Tevet, the Fast of Esther, the seventeenth of Tammuz, and Tisha b'Av.[32]

Not all of Menasseh's financial backers came from the Amsterdam Jewish community. Hendrick Laurensz was a publisher and bookseller in his own right, one of the most important in the city. He even published some Hebrew works, which for a time he had printed in Franeker. But by the late 1620s, this Dutch literary entrepreneur was turning to Menasseh for his printing. Over the next several years, he commissioned the Neve Shalom rabbi to print no fewer than five Hebrew books, including three Bibles; a volume containing the Pentateuch with *haftarot*, the five *megillot* or scrolls (Song of Songs, Ecclesiastes, Ruth, Esther, and Lamentations), and the *Targum*, the

Aramaic translation of the Hebrew Bible by Onkelos; and a book of Psalms. Nor was he the only local competitor who took advantage of Menasseh's Hebrew type and printing skills. Johannes Janssonius also financed Menasseh's printing of a Hebrew Bible and a book of Psalms.

While some of Menasseh's backers may have been acting out of a philanthropic commitment to Jewish learning and to the liturgical and educational needs of the Sephardic community, and while some might have been just plain bibliophiles, many had a more pecuniary motive. They were investors. There was good money to be made in the publication and selling of Jewish books, particularly in the vast eastern European market. Partners and stakeholders who helped with the everyday expenses of running a printing house or with the cost of a particular undertaking might receive their return in cash (principal and interest), especially if they were not themselves booksellers. Others, however, opted for their dividend in books, which they could go on to sell at a profit. A publisher/dealer would commission and subsidize a set of books from Menasseh or Benveniste, sometimes a print run of several thousand volumes, and then list the title in his catalogue for clients or offer copies for sale in his shop. In 1640, Benveniste printed thirty-seven hundred copies of an edition of *Midrash Rabot*, a thousand of which went to his investor Jacques Pietersz.[33] Hendrick Laurensz must have been pleased with the returns on his arrangement with Menasseh, since he renewed it several times over the years.

Menasseh also relied upon non-financial support from within the Sephardic community, although in some cases he had to pay for it. In the early years of his business, we find several of the congregations' rabbis lending a hand in reviewing page proofs. Isaac Aboab da Fonseca served as corrector for the prayer book financed by Bueno and Sarphati and provided some Hebrew poems for Menasseh's *Sefer Pene Rabah*; and Saul

Levi Mortera is listed as the corrector for a collection of Hebrew prayers and songs edited by the *hazzan* Joseph Shalom
Gallego. We do not know if they charged Menasseh for their
services or if it was regarded as just another part of their duty
to the community.

When it came to hiring typesetters, however, Menasseh
seems to have had a preference for Ashkenazic Jews, at least for
books in Hebrew. This manual work would have been beneath
the dignity of the Portuguese community's rabbis, and the
knowledge of Hebrew required for the task would have surpassed the competency of most of Amsterdam's Sephardim. The
Polish-born Judah Leib ben Mordecai Gimpel was the compositor for quite a few of Menasseh's books from 1631 on. Six
years later, Gimpel was joined by two brothers from Krakow,
Jacob and Abraham bar Zvi Setzer, in typesetting a Pentateuch
with Rashi commentary. (Menasseh was not averse to also hiring gentiles for typesetting work. The same year that he hired
Gimpel, he also signed a contract with Bartholomeus Laurensz.
The Dutch compositor worked for Menasseh for nine years—
but, the contract stipulated, not on Saturdays—and then went
over to Benveniste's printing house.)[34]

Already in these early years of his business Menasseh's list
was an eclectic one. In addition to Rabbi Uziel's grammar, Joseph Shalom Gallego's book of prayers (titled *Sefer Imrey No'am*),
the Hebrew Bibles and Pentateuch financed by Laurensz, the
prayer books subsidized by Bueno, Sarphati, Abrabanel, Pardo,
and Gallego, and his own *Sefer Pene Rabbah*, Menasseh published a *humash* in Spanish; the *Sefer Hayirah*, an ethical treatise
by the thirteenth-century philosopher Jonah Gerondi; a two-
volume edition of the Mishnah with commentary; and a Spanish *makhzor* for Rosh Hashanah and Yom Kippur.

Although the secular authorities were content to allow the
Jews to publish whatever they wanted, things seem to have
been a little different within the Amsterdam Portuguese-Jewish

community. Several of Menasseh's publications have a seal of approval from the *parnassim*. In at least one case—Menasseh's own *Thesouro dos dinim*, a handy layperson's reference guide to Jewish law and ritual—the members of the governing board asked Saul Levi Mortera and David Pardo to review the work before granting their approval. The two rabbis reported back that "we find it wholly conforming to the law"; their statement, along with an *Aprovaçao e Licença* from the *parnassim* (they call it a "license to be able to print and sell") are part of the book's front matter.[35] Earning such an endorsement from within the community might not have been absolutely necessary for publishing something—it is unclear how strictly this requirement was enforced—but it probably was not a bad idea.[36]

Menasseh may, however, have been a bit too indiscriminate in his choice of printing jobs. In 1628, a little more than a year after starting his press, he began printing a first edition of the *Sefer Elim* by the physician and philosopher Joseph Solomon Delmedigo.[37] The imminent publication of this provocative work brought some trouble for Menasseh from the community's *deputados*, the joint board of governors set up by Amsterdam's three congregations to deal with matters affecting the community as a whole.

The peripatetic Delmedigo was originally from Crete, but during a visit to Amsterdam in 1626 he was persuaded by the leaders of the Beth Israel congregation to stay and serve as one of their rabbis. In a letter to Samuel ben Judah Leib Ashkenazi, the editor of one of his earlier works, Delmedigo called Menasseh "a very good friend of mine" and said it was Menasseh who asked to be allowed to publish his treatise, of which "he has already printed a few pages on beautiful paper and with marvelous types."[38] Delmedigo praised Menasseh as "old in wisdom though young in years," and offered a fine testimonial to his erudition and character. "He is a jewel of the learned world and glory for our people in the eyes of the gentiles. He also writes learned works as no other can be found in the world."³⁹

The first part of the *Sefer Elim* is a series of mathematical, scientific, and religious questions sent to Delmedigo by a Karaite Jew in Troki, Lithuania, named Zerakh ben Natan, whom he had met while traveling in the east. The second part contains Delmedigo's lengthy responses in which he deals with a wide range of topics in algebra, trigonometry, metaphysics, kabbalah, astrology, cosmology, physics, and astronomy. The most striking and controversial aspect of the *Sefer Elim* is the critical comparison of the Ptolemaic and Copernican systems of the cosmos. Delmedigo had been a student of Galileo's when he was at the university in Padua—he called the Italian mathematician and astronomer his "teacher [*rabbi*]"—and even though he played it very cautiously and did not explicitly claim that the old geocentric system was false, he had high praise for the heliocentric model.⁴⁰ In fact, he found the arguments for the Copernican theory thoroughly convincing; it is, he says, both a simpler hypothesis and better supported by the observed phenomena. He goes on to suggest that "anyone who does not accept [these arguments] can only be regarded as a perfect idiot."⁴¹ In his critique of the Ptolemaic model he mocks the idea that the heavens are constituted by crystalline spheres, an Aristotelian notion that, through Maimonides, had become deeply embedded in Jewish thought. Delmedigo also suggests that the distant stars are each a kind of sun, perhaps with planets orbiting them just as the six known planets orbit our sun.

The *deputados* learned that Menasseh "is printing in his house a book in Hebrew by Josef del Meduigo," a book that they also somehow heard contained highly unorthodox opinions. On May 13, 1629, they summoned Menasseh to their meeting room. It was decided at that gathering that Joseph Shalom Gallego would come and orally translate Delmedigo's Hebrew text into Portuguese for them and that Menasseh would clarify some "doubtful" passages of the translation. This was to be done in the presence of a committee composed of Rabbi Abraham Cohen de Herrera and three other "persons of quality," one from each congregation. This committee would then report back and, together with the *deputados*, decide on the appropriate course of action. In the meantime, they warned Menasseh, the work was not to be published.[42]

Menasseh was not pleased at being treated in this way. Among other things, he worried about the financial loss he would suffer for the work he had already done on this project (including commissioning an elaborate engraved portrait of Delmedigo as a frontispiece and numerous mathematical figures). He thus turned to the rabbis of Venice, who functioned as mentors to the Amsterdam Sephardim, for their approval to publish the work. The Venetians—led by Rabbi Modena, who was not only Rabbi Mortera's former teacher but had also tutored Delmedigo himself when the young man was in Venice during his student years in Padua—gave Menasseh the permission he sought in the summer of 1629, although they apparently had not read the entire treatise.[43] Menasseh resumed the printing of Delmedigo's treatise and by the end of August had completed two volumes in densely packed, very small type: one containing Zerakh's queries, and one containing many but not all of Delmedigo's responses.

The Amsterdam *deputados* did not appreciate Menasseh going behind their backs in this way. Knowing that he had continued with the printing of the *Sefer Elim*, they called him in for a second interview on September 2. He was told to bring the parts that he had already printed, along with those yet to be done. According to the extant minutes of the meeting, at which Cohen de Herrera and three other rabbis from the community were present, it was resolved that the investigating committee should undertake a full examination of Delmedigo's texts to see if they contained anything "contrary to the honor of God and his holy law and good morality [*contra a honra del dio e sua sta. Ley e bons costumez*]." The committee would then submit a preliminary report in writing to Menasseh, and he would be allowed to respond, also in writing, either to state his agreement with them or to provide reasons why the allegedly heterodox passages should not be prohibited.[44] A final decision would then be made about what Menasseh could and could not publish. Unfortunately, that report is no longer extant, so we do not know exactly what the committee concluded or what, if anything, it considered objectionable in Delmedigo's book. There must have been something that the committee found worthy of censure, however, since the volumes printed that August did not contain the entire work.

The whole episode left bad feelings all around, especially between Menasseh and his colleague Isaac Aboab, who was one of the rabbis selected to serve on the investigating committee. The two men got along just fine before, with Aboab not only acting as a corrector on texts being printed by Menasseh but also contributing some poems of praise to be included in the publication of Menasseh's own *Sefer Pene Rabah*. Future collaboration, however, was now very unlikely. That second meeting in September probably represents the beginning of the deterioration in their personal relations.

The decision to publish Delmedigo's treatise might have been a bit of poor judgment by Menasseh. Even if the *parnassim* had been sympathetic to the new Copernican cosmology— and some of them probably were—they had to bear in mind what their Dutch hosts would think. Menasseh only compounded the difficulty of his situation by looking to Venice for a ruling. This would not be the last time that Menasseh got in trouble with the leaders of the Amsterdam Jewish community.

4

The Conciliator

THE *Livro de Bet Haim do Kahal Kados de Bet Yahacob* was the
record book for that Amsterdam Portuguese-Jewish congregation for its first three decades. It is an important source of information on the community's membership up to 1630. Its pages
list charitable contributions, taxes (both paid and pledged), sal-
aries, and marriages. They tell us that Jacob Israel Dias paid his
finta assessment of twenty guilders in 1627, and that on April 9
of that same year Abraham Espinoza, the uncle of the future
philosopher Bento (Baruch) Spinoza, made a communal contribution in memory of his recently deceased brother, the philosopher's grandfather, Isaac.

The book's primary function, however, was to register the
burials at the Beth Haim cemetery in Ouderkerk. On page 135
of the parchment-bound manuscript, recording interments for
November 1628 (Heshvan 5389 of the Jewish calendar), there is
the following entry: "On the 26 of this month, a female child of

Menase ben Israel, in the seventh row between no. 28 and 29 in the empty space by the feet of Clara de Palacios daughter of Jacob de Palacios."[1]

The girl buried that day was not Menasseh's first-born, Hannah, who married some years later, but a second daughter. She is not named, so she must have died as an infant. This is the only mention in the historical record of this girl. Menasseh himself nowhere discusses it. It was not the last time he had to bury one of his own children; in fact, he eventually outlived three of his four offspring. The accumulating sadness over the years must have been unbearable. Eventually, it would break him. (His colleague Saul Levi Mortera had buried his own daughter, Simcha, just a few years earlier; perhaps Mortera was able to offer Menasseh some words of comfort for a grieving father.)

Menasseh may have tried to distract himself from the loss of his baby daughter through work, although it is unclear how successful he was. He had put the finishing touches on his own *Sefer Pene Rabbah* the summer before she died, and did not print anything until the *Sefer Elim* a year later. That was the only book he published over a period of almost two years. There were his congregational duties for Neve Shalom to keep him busy, the teaching and occasional preaching, but this is not where he derived his true satisfaction.

By the spring of 1630, though, Menasseh's energies were back in full force. Within the next three years, he brought out, as publisher, no fewer than five Spanish and Hebrew prayer books; two of the Hebrew Bibles and the *humash* with Targum and *megillot* financed by Laurensz; and the *Tratado del Temor Divino* (Treatise on the Fear of God), a compilation of selections from the sixteenth-century kabbalistic work *Reshit Hokhma* (The Beginning of Wisdom) translated into Spanish by David de Isaac Coen de Lara, one of Menasseh's fellow students under Rabbi Uziel who would himself go on to become *hakham* in

Hamburg. Menasseh was able to produce all of this in addition to his massive undertaking of a two-volume annotated Mishnah!

Menasseh had also decided it was time to get started on his own religious and philosophical writings: not just concordances or commentary to rabbinic literature, but original treatises on topics of theology, metaphysics and ethics. It is hard to imagine a more audacious start to this than the work that would first bring him to the attention of the wider—and especially non-Jewish—world.

This was titled the *Conciliador*, a book ostensibly devoted to scriptural exegesis but that in fact has a much more ambitious goal. The author is identified on its title page as *Theologo y philosopho Hebreo*.[2] Menasseh boldly claims in his preface to the reader that "I present to you the reconciliation of all the places of Holy Scripture that appear to contradict each other."[3] His aim was to show that all those passages of the Hebrew Bible that seem incompatible, either because they narrate one and the same event in different ways (Was woman created at the same time as man [Gen. 1:27] or after him [Gen. 2:21]?) or because of some minor discrepancy in details (Were the Israelites in Egypt for four hundred years [Gen. 15:14] or four hundred and thirty years [Exod. 12:40]?), can all be shown to be entirely consistent. Since the Bible comes from God and is "in the highest degree true," there cannot be any real contradictions in it. Truth can never conflict with truth.

The reason why the Bible might *appear* to be full of inconsistencies to the unwary is because of a lack of understanding of how properly to interpret it. Menasseh notes that readers tend to treat all the passages of Scripture in the same way, either literally or metaphorically. The trick, in fact, is to know when to read a passage literally and when to read it only figuratively. Thus, Menasseh's preferred solution to one of the more glaring narrative incongruities in the Bible—"If in the beginning the Lord created male and female together in one form that he called 'Adam,' why does this other verse say that from one of his ribs he made Eve?"—is that God did indeed create man and woman at the same time.[4] However, God created the woman attached to the man's back, "such that Adam's figure was double," male in the front, female in the rear. God then separated the two sides and thereby created man and woman. The words 'God took one of his ribs' should thus be read metaphorically, as 'one of his sides.' This answer, Menasseh says, "appears to be the most probable," and he backs this up by appealing both to rabbinic commentaries ("the ancient Sages") and rational arguments.[5]

As for Creation itself, Menasseh considers the problem that arises when the statement "And God saw all that He had made, and behold, it was very good" (Gen. 1:31) is taken together with God's recognition that "it is not good for man to be alone" (Gen. 2:18).[6] How can it be that God judged everything he saw to be good if he also perceived something to be not good? The solution, Menasseh says, lies in distinguishing between the things created by God in a perfect condition right from the start and things that, though created by God, did not enjoy perfection at the beginning of their existence. The stars and the heavens were created "finished and perfect." The human being, on the other hand, had, at his creation, not yet "fulfilled the end for which he was created."[7]

In Exodus, there is the confusion raised when, in 33:11, it is said that "the Lord spoke to Moses face to face," but just a few verses later (33:23), God says to Moses "you shall see my rear parts but you shall not see my face."[8] Menasseh approves of the solution to this conflict offered by Maimonides and Abraham Ibn Ezra, that the phrases "face to face" and "rear parts" are to be taken figuratively to mean that Moses as prophet was afforded a direct and unmediated communion with God, but as a mere mortal he could not possibly apprehend the Divine Essence itself.

The first volume of the *Conciliador*, all two hundred pages of it, takes the reader through the entire Pentateuch. This meant reconciling not only problematic passages in the stories of Genesis and Exodus, but also apparent inconsistencies in the legal material of the other books. (Why, for example, does it say in Leviticus that twenty species of birds are unclean while in Deuteronomy twenty-one species are listed?)[9] Menasseh would need another two decades to complete three more volumes of this enormous exegetical project covering all the writings of the Hebrew Bible. It was, in the end, the work of a lifetime, and would be his crowning literary achievement.

At this point, though, Menasseh was not even sure that he would obtain permission from the Amsterdam Sephardic community to publish the first volume. As insurance, and using the same tactic that served him nicely with Delmedigo's treatise, he turned to a foreign rabbinate—in this case, Frankfurt—and asked its members to approve the work so that he could publish it in their city if necessary. Rabbi Shabbetai Sheftel Horowitz and his colleagues readily gave their endorsement. Menasseh soon gained the approbation of his fellow Amsterdam rabbis as well, however, with the kabbalist Abraham Coen de Herrera providing the necessary letter of certification and praising all of Menasseh's writings as being "as serious as they are elegant in style." Menasseh dedicated Part 1 of his treatise to the Amsterdam *parnassim* and had it printed (possibly in Frankfurt) in 1632.[10]

Menasseh wrote the *Conciliador* in Spanish, "to benefit the members of my nation who, for the most part, lack an understanding of the Hebrew language." He felt it was especially important to address an audience of conversos recently returned to Judaism. These new Jews, now reading the Hebrew biblical canon for themselves, primarily in Spanish, and struggling to make sense of it without the intercession of Catholic priests, might find it an appallingly puzzling, even indecipherable text. With Menasseh as their guide, their perplexities might be eased and their faith in the holiness of the work and their commitment to the coherence of Jewish law preserved.

Still, Menasseh obviously had grander ambitions than helping former conversos navigate the text of the Bible. He knew that his book would be of great interest to a broader public and could bring him some reputation—and perhaps some income—in the world beyond Vlooienburg. Non-Jewish readers, especially Hebraists and Bible scholars, would surely want to know how Jews resolve these long-troubling textual issues. A book written in Spanish, though, would be less accessible than one in Latin, the international language of the learned world. Thus, a translation was needed.[11]

Menasseh could read Latin with ease, judging by his broad familiarity with the works of classical antiquity, the Church Fathers, and early modern humanistic scholarship. But he seems to have been fairly uncomfortable writing in Latin.[12] One of his acquaintances noted that Menasseh was "not so expert in the Latin language that he could easily write or speak extemporaneously."[13] Later in life, while writing to gentile friends, including prominent Dutch scholars, Menasseh often opted for Spanish. Perhaps he feared that even minor mistakes in Latin grammar would open him to ridicule as a Jew who lacked a proper education. If the *Conciliador* was going to reach Latin readers, then, Menasseh would have to find a helping hand, almost certainly a non-Jew. Fortunately, a willing collaborator was close by.

The patriarch of the Vos clan was Gerrit Janszoon Vos, better known in the Republic of Letters by the Latinized form of his name, Gerardus Joannis Vossius. Vossius was a skilled classicist and philologist, expert in Latin and Greek and celebrated for the grammars he wrote for those languages. In the early stage of his academic career, he was primarily a theologian, and he put his humanistic scholarship to work for religious ends. Unfortunately for him, those religious ends were Arminian. Although not a Remonstrant, Vossius appeared sympathetic to that cause, which put him on the wrong side of the religious and political tracks when he was regent of the Theological College in Leiden.[14] Soon after the Synod of Dort, when the Counter-Remonstrants gained the upper hand throughout Holland, he was forced to give up that position. He was allowed to stay on at the University of Leiden as a faculty member, however, teaching rhetoric, history, and philology. At one point he was offered a chair at Cambridge University, but for family reasons he opted to stay in the Netherlands. By 1631, he was in Amsterdam, where, within the year, he would take up the post of professor of history and statecraft at the newly established Athenaeum Illustre for the extraordinary annual salary of twenty-six hundred guilders.

In the absence of a university, the Athenaeum functioned as Amsterdam's institute of higher learning. It offered public lectures for adults in the mornings before they went off to work and served as a preparatory school for advanced studies at a university. Young men around the age of sixteen who had completed their classical education in a Latin school might spend a year or two at the Athenaeum reading philosophy, history, and other disciplines. From there they could go on to one of the faculties in Leiden, Utrecht, or Franeker. Vossius quickly became a popular teacher at the Athenaeum—he led classes in philosophy, history, philology, and political theory—and a well-known figure in Amsterdam intellectual circles.

By 1632, and perhaps some years before, Vossius had come to know Menasseh. He was a great admirer of the rabbi, in spite of his general suspicion of Jews.[15] He believed them to be an "obstinate" people who refused to see the "truth"—that is, Christian truth. The Jews, Vossius insisted, were too resistant to the efforts at conversion that he regarded as essential for their salvation. "I have often seen what a light cloak the Jews use to evade our weapons."[16] He granted—and this was a major concession—that the Talmud "contained many things not unworthy of being known," but cautioned that it was also "covered with lies and falsehoods."[17] At the same time, he recognized the importance (and intellectual rewards) of engaging with Judaica, especially the classics of rabbinic literature. An understanding of Jews was essential if one was going to engage them in debate and convince them of the error of their ways.

His contempt for the Jewish people, however, did not prevent Vossius from admiring particular Jews. His affection for Menasseh was real. Writing to his friend Simon Beaumont in December, Vossius noted that "although it is the way of most Jews to be hostile to us, this man is quite a bit more friendly. Indeed, he can be of much use to Christians." He calls Menasseh "a learned and upright man"—no small praise, in this period, for a Jew by a gentile of high standing—adding the caveat "if only he were a Christian."[18] Menasseh was, Vossius told another correspondent, a man who, "if you except his religion, lacks nothing."[19] Over the following decade, the two men became not just scholarly colleagues but friends. Menasseh, abandoning all formalities, would drop in at Vossius's office at the Athenaeum, and even at his home on the Oudezijds Achterburgwal, unbidden, just for a visit.[20] Vossius played an important part in Menasseh's growing reputation in the gentile world, as he introduced the rabbi to a number of prominent and influential Dutch scholars.

Vossius was especially eager to take advantage of his relationship with Menasseh and learn what he could from him on Jewish matters. His elder son Dionysius, who had already been studying Hebrew, shared this enthusiasm, so Vossius sent him to Menasseh not just to perfect his skill in that language but also to study "talmudic and rabbinic books." A gifted linguist who was fluent in a number of classical and modern languages (including Arabic), the young man made impressive progress; he was soon translating into Latin one of the tractates of Maimonides's *Mishneh Torah*, the *Hilkhot Avodah Zara*, commonly known as the *Treatise on Idolatry*. This was among the very first Latin translations of a complete part of Maimonides's monumental compendium of Jewish law, a work that, after centuries of neglect, had become of great interest to Christian Hebraists.[21]

When Menasseh wanted a Latin version of Part 1 of the *Conciliador*, then, he needed only to ask his twenty-year-old student to do the work. Dionysius, who knew Spanish, readily agreed. The translation appeared in the summer of 1633 and quickly found an eager audience in learned circles. Dionysius's brother Isaac, who did not share their father's high opinion of Menasseh (or his brother's knowledge of Hebrew), nonetheless admired both Menasseh's treatise and Dionysius's elegant translation. Sadly, Dionysius died of smallpox shortly after the book's publication, and it was left to his grieving father to see his other literary achievements—his translation of Maimonides, a commentary on Caesar—into print.

The Latin translation of the *Conciliador* represented Menasseh's first publication for non-Jews and the beginning of his career as "an apostle to the gentiles."[22] Part of his goal was to show off Jewish learning—his own, of course, but more important, that of the Jewish sages of antiquity and the Middle Ages. The book is full of citations from rabbinic sources—not just the Talmud and *midrashim*, but medieval commentators and philosophers such as Rashi, Maimonides, Gersonides, Nachmanides, Ibn Ezra, Judah and Isaac Abrabanel, and many others. It is both an exhibition and a defense of Judaic erudition for an audience that was still learning that it had much to gain from a familiarity with Jewish intellectual traditions.[23]

Over the next two decades, Menasseh's grand literary project was, in essence, Jewish apologetics to the non-Jewish world. His works were devoted to explaining and justifying Judaism and its tenets to a European public that was at best tolerant of Jews, and at worst extremely hostile. He would try to show that the Jews are neither blasphemers nor heretics; that far from Jews being enemies of Christians, many of the fundamental doctrines of the Jewish religion are quite close to and compatible with those of Christianity.

Among the many themes that recur throughout all of Menasseh's writings are those that he expects will strike a chord with gentile readers and allow them to see what the two religions have in common. The existence of one true Creator, the divine origin and essential truth of Scripture, the immortality of the soul, the wisdom and justice of God's providence—these, he believes, are doctrines shared by Jews and Christians.

Above all, Menasseh rejects the particularism often defended by Jewish thinkers and argues that God's salvation is universal, directed at all righteous people regardless of their creed. The pious, whether they are Christian or Jewish, will enjoy reward in the world-to-come (*olam ha-ba*), an earthly paradise ushered in by the arrival of the Messiah (although, in an inversion of the present state of the world, that paradise will be ruled and dominated by the Jews).[24] Menasseh believes, with some naïveté (or perhaps disingenuousness), that Jews and Christians are in fact anticipating the same ultimate event. The difference, he insists, consists only in the timing.[25] In his dedication of Part 2 of the *Conciliador* to the directors of the Dutch West Indies Company, Menasseh insists that when it comes to matters of fundamental beliefs, there is "no difference between Christians and Jews."[26] His own works, he hoped, would convince Christians of this, "win universal approval," and thereby earn good will toward the Jewish people. This should not only ease their lives in the societies in which they dwelled but also allow for their settlement in nations from which they had been banned.[27]

Menasseh wanted to dedicate Dionysius's Latin version of

the *Conciliador* to the States of Holland. He probably thought this an astute move, since the imprimatur of this body might have allayed suspicions about the work's acceptability to Dutch readers. He may also have feared that his association with Remonstrants like the Vossius family could bring him some trouble from the more orthodox Calvinist camp, and "protection" by the province's governors could serve him well in case of any attacks. Ironically, that association may be precisely what worked against him gaining the States' permission to dedicate the work to it.

When the provincial magistrates in The Hague received Menasseh's request, they were unsure how to proceed, so they sought the advice of the theology faculty at the University of Leiden. The recommendation that came back from the academic experts was to reject the proffered dedication. The theologians were put off by some of Menasseh's solutions to alleged contradictions in the Bible—for example, the "fable" about God initially creating man and woman as one being.[28] But what really troubled them was that the book seemed to be an attack on Christianity itself. Menasseh's "reconciliations ... take away from Christians the arguments for the Trinity and Christ's divinity that have rightly been brought out of the five books of Moses. He does the same with predictions of Christ's coming in the flesh, of his spiritual kingdom and of his doing away with the ceremonies of the Old Testament, etc."[29] The fact that the work's translator came from a family known for its Remonstrant sympathies—something that could not be overlooked by Gerardus's former theological colleagues in Leiden—certainly did not help matters. The States of Holland, dominated by relatively liberal regents who might otherwise have welcomed the dedication but wished to avoid stirring up trouble with conservatives, accordingly said to Menasseh, "no, thank you."

It could have been a minor irritant, an affront from the province's governing body and nothing more. After all, Menasseh did not need their permission to publish his books. But in the volatile theologico-political environment of the Dutch Republic, with the Remonstrant/Counter-Remonstrant clash among ecclesiastics still infecting the civic realm, ostensibly small matters could quickly grow all out of proportion. In fact, this affair over the proposed dedication of the Latin translation of the *Conciliador* would soon cause a good deal of trouble for Menasseh, for his non-Jewish friends, and even for the Republic's entire Jewish community.

When Menasseh took his dedication offer to the States of Holland in The Hague, he brought along a letter of recommendation signed by two professors at the Amsterdam Athenaeum. One was the holder of the chair in history and father of the book's translator, Gerardus Vossius. The other was a man who would prove to be Menasseh's greatest defender among the gentiles, much to Menasseh's eventual detriment.

Caspar Barlaeus was, like Vossius, a Remonstrant sympathizer. He had also been vice-regent—right-hand man to Vossius—at the Theological College in Leiden, but he too was dismissed from his position because of his religious views (which, unlike Vossius, he was not shy about expressing). After a brief exile in France to study medicine, Barlaeus followed his former colleague to Amsterdam, where he joined him as one of the two founding professors at the Athenaeum. He was given the chair in philosophy and, because he had a way with words, was selected to give one of the institute's inaugural lectures. Barlaeus's real passion, however, was for poetry. He was already famous for his Latin verses well before his arrival in the city. Like Vossius, Barlaeus had a general antipathy for the Jews. "I do not defend Judaism," he told one correspondent, "I am abhorred by it."[30] But that did not keep him from developing a friendship with at least this particular Jew. He may have first met Menasseh at one of the intellectual gatherings that he occasionally held in his home, where, in addition to Vossius and Hugo Grotius, he was likely to be hosting such celebrated poets as Pieter Cornelisz Hooft and Joost van den Vondel.[31]

By the fall of 1634, Menasseh, Barlaeus, and Vossius *père* enjoyed enough of a social relationship that Menasseh could invite them to join him at the synagogue on the Simchat Torah holiday to observe the festivities. They were accompanied that day by the Remonstrant theologian Simon Episcopius (Simon Bisschop), who wrote in his diary for October 14: "I, D. Barlaeus and D. Vossius, with other friends of ours, were brought to the Jewish synagogue and well entertained by M. Menasseh ben Israel."[32] Thus, it was only natural that when Menasseh wanted some help in making his case to the States of Holland, he asked Vossius and Barlaeus for a letter that he could present to Cornelis van der Myle, former emissary of the Dutch Republic to Venice who was now a member of that assembly. As Vossius and Barlaeus explained to Van der Myle in their letter, they "could not say 'no'" to their Jewish friend. They went on to praise Menasseh for "writing well about Christians" and attested to the "utility" of a Latin version of his *Conciliador*, "since it is a most illustrious and serious thing to reconcile contentious scriptural passages. How could a Jew be of greater value to Christians, than by collecting and laying out in one work whatever all the Hebrew sages once wrote?"[33]

When Barlaeus heard that the States had, at the recommendation of his former colleagues in Leiden, declined Menasseh's offer, he was greatly annoyed. He took it quite personally, and well he should have, since they had ignored his own endorsement of Menasseh's book. Barlaeus felt that it was now incumbent upon him to come to his friend's defense. In a letter to his friend Van der Myle, he wrote that he could not now abandon Menasseh, "for no other reason than that I have sympathy for this man who is in equal parts humble and learned."[34]

Menasseh did not deserve to be treated the way he was. The *Conciliador* may not have defended Christianity, Barlaeus told Van der Myle, but neither did it attack it.

It was only fitting that the occasion for Barlaeus's vindication of Menasseh—as well as of his own judgment—would be the rabbi's next book. Unfortunately, his strategy, as innocent as Barlaeus may have thought it at the time, backfired, and he ended up defending Menasseh in a way that only magnified the whole affair over the failed dedication of the *Conciliador* and brought more trouble upon both their heads.

After the success of the *Conciliador,* Menasseh embarked upon another ambitious project that he envisioned as a contribution to Jewish-Christian rapprochement. Rather than reconciling conflicting passages in the Bible, however, he now proposed to resolve a number of straightforward philosophical and theological questions concerning God's creation of the world.

De Creatione Problemata XXX (Thirty Problems About Creation), which Menasseh himself printed in early 1635, appeared only in Latin—it was almost certainly written by Menasseh in Portuguese (or possibly Spanish) and translated by one of his gentile friends—and was supposed to constitute another defense of Judaism for a gentile audience.[35] Lest any reader miss this point, he began the work with an enumeration of Maimonides's thirteen principles of the Jewish faith. He then went on to use scriptural passages, ancient Greek thinkers, rabbinic and kabbalist sources, Christian authors, and straight rational argumentation to defend an account of creation that, he believed, Jews and Christians should all agree on. He showed that, contrary to Plato and Aristotle, most (but not all) of the Jewish and Christian sources concur that God—whose existence, unity, incorporeality, and eternity Menasseh demonstrates—created the cosmos *ex nihilo.* In fact, Menasseh insists, the entire validity of the Law depends on the world having its origin out of nothing. How else could one establish that there is a people originally chosen by God who have their beginning in Adam?

Some of the questions addressed by Menasseh in *De Creatione Problemata XXX* might have seemed quite practical to any religious community in the seventeenth century. Is the observance of the Sabbath a requirement only for Jews or for all people? Other topics are matters of abstract philosophical and theological speculation that would have had little import for the person in the street. Why, for example, did God create the world? In what month did he create it? (September, Menasseh argues, because it is clear that the creation must have taken place in the month in which the days are equal to the nights; and it could not be March since it also has to be a month in which things reach their full beauty and maturity—trees bearing fruit, green grass in the field, etc.) Was the world created in six successive days or all in a single instant? Were there other worlds before this one? (While this was an opinion condemned by Maimonides, Menasseh says, some Jewish thinkers accepted the idea; Menasseh suspends judgment, claiming that the important thing is just to recognize that our world was created out of nothing and that the human race begins with Adam and Eve.)[36] When were demons and angels created? (Menasseh, in fact, devotes quite a number of the questions to angelology.) Were all human souls created at the beginning of the world, or is each one created at the time its body comes into being? (He argues that all the souls that will ever exist were created on the first day of creation, with light, since as spiritual beings they are themselves like light.)

De Creatione Problemata XXX—with its dry scholastic style, abundance of quotations from a hodgepodge of sources, and markedly arcane topics (even for the seventeenth century)—is not Menasseh at his finest.[37] The work might have passed relatively unnoticed, with little fanfare or controversy, if not for a short poem that opens the book.

The verses, in Menasseh's honor, were composed by Barlaeus. His "Epigram to the Most Illustrious Menasseh ben Israel" appears innocent enough to the unsuspecting eye. Its praise of Menasseh for his "piety of faith" and for his account of the "hand that created the heavens and the earth, the vast waters of Nereus and the immense riches of the globe, and that commanded the sudden birth of the world that theretofore was sunk in shadowy depths" is tempered by an acknowledgment that what Menasseh does in his book is mainly bring forth the wisdom of his ancestors and of the Talmudic sages.

Of course, admiring a Jewish author for his "piety" and complimenting him for a work that "conforms to the truth" was a risky business in the 1630s. What really set Dutch Reformed teeth on edge, however, were the final four lines of the poem:

> Though we think differently, we live as friends in God,
> And may a learned mind have its value recognized everywhere.
> This is the highest expression of my faith. Believe this, Menasseh.
> Just as I am a son of Christ, so you are a son of Abraham.[38]

What Barlaeus appeared to his critics to be doing here was not just equating the wisdom of a Christian and the wisdom of a Jew, which was bad enough, but putting their religious faiths on the same level.[39] As Gerardus Vossius wrote to Grotius, the problem was that "my colleague Barlaeus" was being attacked because he "prefaced a little work on creation by Menasseh the Jew with a poem in which he even acknowledges piety in a Jewish man and confesses that he [the Jewish man] even serves God."[40]

The first to pounce was Gisbertus Voetius. The theologian, a raving anti-Semite, was an influential professor at the University of Utrecht and the leader of a coterie of young scholars. Although this intolerant firebrand did not limit his animosity to Jews—Catholics, members of dissident Reformed sects, and atheistic libertines were all targets of his venomous attacks—he was especially sensitive when it came to the dangerous influence of Jews in the United Provinces. The fact that Menasseh was dedicating books written in Latin to Christians only confirmed his worst fears.

In 1636, a year after the publication of Menasseh's book, Nicolaas Vedelius, a theologian in Deventer and one of Voetius's more devoted followers (as well as a skilled Hebraist in his own right), published a pamphlet in which he accused Barlaeus of a host of sins, including, somewhat incoherently, being a Jew, a Socinian, and an atheist.

Voetius himself entered the fray that fall with a series of disputations in Utrecht. The advertised subject for these public academic performances was *De Judaismo* and *De Generali Conversione Judaeorum.*[41] Among the topics he addressed was whether Jews should be permitted to hold public worship in their synagogues and even observe their ceremonies outside them, "which scandalizes Christians."[42] More pointedly, he asked "whether the Jewish religion can be said to have God as its source."[43] Voetius's complaints included the fact that, without any censorship by the civil authorities, Jews were free to publish their writings and infect the minds of Christians with their false ideas. They were aided by Christian co-conspirators willing to translate these corrupting works into Latin and even glorify them with adulatory poems! It was all Satan's work, Voetius insisted.[44] When he turned to the means by which the Jews, a stubborn people, might be converted, Voetius considered a number of peaceful overtures. But he also posed the crucial question: Should they, in fact, be killed? Mercifully, he cited only a negative response to this option.[45]

Voetius held Menasseh in particular—that "conciliator of the Jews of Amsterdam"—responsible for spreading Jewish messianic ideas and thereby trying to convert Christian readers. The problem was that, with his printing press, Menasseh seemed to be able to print whatever he wished.[46]

It was not just the *Conciliador* and *De Creatione Problemata* that incited the onslaught by Voetius. In early February, months before the Utrecht disputations, Menasseh had published yet another book, this time simultaneously in Spanish and Latin. The Spanish edition, *De la Resurreccion de los Muertos libros III* (The Resurrection of the Dead in Three Books) was published "at the home and expense of the author"; the Latin version, *De Resurrectione Mortuorum Libri III*, also translated by one of Menasseh's friends, was printed by Johannes Janssonius and dedicated by Menasseh to a pair of Christians: Laurens Reael, a former governor-general of the Dutch East Indies Company, and Albert Coenraedsz Burgh, a physician and a member of a prominent Amsterdam family who would go on to become one of the city's burgemeesters. Both men were curators of the Amsterdam Athenaeum Illustre, and Menasseh's dedication of the book to them was more than just a gesture of tribute. He had a plan.

Menasseh wrote that the main purpose of the treatise—his contribution to a long tradition of rabbinic writing on the topic of resurrection and which he probably began writing in 1633—was to refute latter-day "Sadducees . . . an abominably perverse sect who denied that the bodies of the dead would be resurrected and reunited with their souls at the end of time"; the subtitle of the book emphasized that it also contains a proof of the immortality of the soul. With his revival of the ancient term "Sadducees" he was clearly referring to contemporary heterodox individuals, including some members of the Amsterdam Sephardic community, who were agitating against a pair of doctrines at least one of which (the resurrection of the body) Maimonides had made into one of the thirteen essential precepts of Judaism.[47] One person in particular stands out.

Uriel da Costa, a former converso born and educated in Portugal and now living in Amsterdam, was disillusioned by the Judaism he found being practiced and preached in the Vlooien- burg quarter. This rabbinic religion was not what he expected from his reading of the Hebrew Bible as a young man in a Catholic environment. He had trouble with the ritualistic be- havior demanded of him and the theological doctrines he was supposed to endorse. He had in fact recently earned a *herem* (ban or excommunication) from the Portuguese *parnassim*—his second—and it is clear from Da Costa's own testimony that among the reasons for his recurring falling out with the com- munity were the arguments against the immortality of the soul that he first presented in a book published (in Portuguese) in 1624.[48] In the *Exame das tradições farisaicas* (Examination of the Pharisaic Traditions), Da Costa claimed that "the most dis- tressful and wretched time in my life was when I believed that eternal bliss or misery awaited man and that according to his works he would earn that bliss or that misery."[49] The soul, ac- cording to Da Costa, is nothing but a part of the material body, a vital spirit in the blood that animates the organism. It is there- fore essentially mortal and dies with the body.

(Da Costa's own bodily existence came to a sad end in 1640. The religious, social, and economic isolation enforced by his *herem* was too much to bear, so he expressed a desire to re- join the Portuguese-Jewish community. However, the condi- tions set for his rehabilitation were extremely harsh: a whipping while lashed to a pillar in the synagogue, then lying prostrate at the building's entry while the congregants walked out over his body.[50] He was so humiliated and distraught by the experience that, after going home and composing his memoirs, he killed himself.)

The immortality of the soul was taken quite seriously by Amsterdam's Portuguese Jews—perhaps because so many of these families had once been Catholics—as well as by their Dutch Calvinist hosts. The rabbis and *parnassim* thus made a concerted effort to ensure, and to make it well known, that their community was no haven for heretics who would deny such an important religious doctrine.[51] All of Amsterdam's Sephardic rabbis in this period delivered sermons and wrote treatises defending the immortality of the soul. Saul Levi Mortera's *Ha-Sharut ha-Nefesh* (On the Immortality of the Soul) was most likely written in 1624, around the time that Da Costa published his essay, while Isaac Aboab da Fonseca composed his *Nishmat Hayyim* (The Breath of Life) in 1636, just as Menasseh was printing his own treatise on resurrection and immortality.[52]

Appealing to Scripture, ancient and medieval authorities, and rational argument, Menasseh in *De la Resurreccion* offered an extended case for the immortality of the soul and the resurrection of the dead. The work, in fact, provides insight into Menasseh's own eschatological views, which he anticipated would be embraced by both Jewish and Christian readers. However, he cautioned that, except for those things that he was able to demonstrate through reason alone, much of what he said should be taken as mere conjecture. Only the prophets know the truth about these matters, and they are not willing to say much about them.[53] Nor is there a single rabbinic view on such speculative, non-halakhic topics, despite the attempt by Maimonides to make resurrection, at least, a matter of Jewish dogma.

The soul, Menasseh argued, is an immaterial spiritual substance. It is therefore incorruptible, since only things made out of matter—bodies—are subject to corruption and decay. Thus, the soul naturally and necessarily survives the demise of the body, which is "reduced to dust and ashes." However, at a certain time the bodies of the dead will once again be reanimated by the same souls that they had in life and enjoy "a second life of the body in this world." These resurrected and revivified individuals will then be rewarded or punished by God according to their desserts, with the virtuous enjoying a felicity from which the vicious are cut off.

Menasseh claimed that this resurrection would be general, applying to Jews and gentiles alike. And in the end, all who deserve it, regardless of the religion to which they belong, will receive their rightful place in the world-to-come. Contrary to Maimonides, for whom the world-to-come is a purely spiritual realm of disembodied souls, Menasseh insisted that this future world would be the period of the resurrection of the dead, which in turn is identical with the Days of the Messiah. This "new world" where final judgment is meted out on the reunited body and soul is not some supernatural domain. Rather, it is "of the same perfection and excellence as the first world," that is, Adam's worldly paradise in the Garden of Eden. Not everyone who is resurrected, though, will have a place in the world-to-come. Among those who will be excluded from a future life are those who deny the existence of God and those who do not acknowledge the resurrection of the dead. Also permanently barred from the world-to-come are Jews who reject Mosaic Law.

With this last claim, Menasseh entered a debate that was raging within the Amsterdam Jewish community just as he began writing *De la Resurreccion*. It was a theological battle that divided the congregations and left a good deal of bad blood among the members of the local rabbinate.

In the early 1630s, some members of Neve Shalom and Beth Jacob had been going around proclaiming that every Jew will, as a matter of both right and fact, eventually enjoy a portion of eternal happiness in the world-to-come. After all, the Mishnah says that "all Israel has a place in the world to come" (Sanhedrin 11.1), and these congregants took those words literally. No Jews will ever suffer eternal punishment, no matter what their sins. This view would have been most sympathetically received among Amsterdam's Sephardim, many of whom still had family back in Spain and Portugal living as Catholics and thereby committing one of the gravest sins a Jew can commit—denying their Judaism.

Rabbi Mortera was quite disturbed by this development. He worried that such a loose interpretation of the Talmudic sages, whereby there was ultimately nothing to fear before God, would lead to wanton licentiousness. As a stranger to the converso experience, Mortera did not share his congregants' concerns about the eternal fate of the souls of their apostate relatives. Consequently, he insisted that the ancient rabbis meant to exclude certain types of sinners permanently from the world-to-come; only the righteous who follow the laws of the Torah can expect entry into paradise. There is no guarantee that just because a person is Jewish he can avoid eternal punishment for his sins.

Mortera's response, delivered in some of his sermons to the Beth Jacob congregation in 1635, only inflamed the passions of his opponents, who were allegedly encouraged in their views by Menasseh's colleague in Neve Shalom, Rabbi Aboab. The debate grew so heated that the leaders of the community, still insecure in their grasp of the fundamentals of normative Judaism, had to appeal to the rabbis of Venice for advice. While the Venetians were reluctant to get involved and encouraged the Amsterdam congregations to find a peaceful resolution on their own, they eventually ruled in favor of Mortera. A resentful (and argumentative) Aboab went on to compose his *Nishmat Hayyim*, in which he not only attacked Da Costa's denial of immortality but took direct aim at Mortera as well when he addressed the questions "Is there eternal punishment of souls or not? And what did our rabbis, of blessed memory, intend by saying 'The following have no share in the world-to-come'?"[54]

Likewise, by writing a treatise on resurrection and immortality in Spanish, Menasseh was not just responding to Da Costa but taking a stand on an intense debate within the Amsterdam

Portuguese community. Menasseh's throwing in his lot with Mortera would, after the disagreeable affair over his publication of Delmedigo's *Sefer Elim*, be yet another sore spot in his relations with Aboab.[55]

But the work, as with so many of Menasseh's writings, was not only for intramural Jewish consumption. With the Latin version *De Resurrectione Mortuorum*, he was also, once again, offering an *apologia* for Judaism to non-Jewish readers.[56] In his Latin dedicatory letter to Real and Burgh, Menasseh reminded them (as well as his gentile readers) that "we all worship one God, we are subject to His commandments, and we anticipate a better life after the difficulties of this life."[57]

It was bad enough that Menasseh was spreading Jewish ideas with his printing press. But the intolerant camp led by Voetius would have been even more appalled by rumors that Menasseh was part of an international conspiracy to convert Christians to Judaism. Menasseh himself, not one to be circumspect in conversation, apparently contributed to such gossip. To a guest in the synagogue from Portugal, he bragged that in 1632 he had sent "two chests of books" containing copies of the *Conciliador* to Spain and Brazil, no doubt with the expectation that conversos in both places would profit from his scriptural exegesis. And then there was the report to the Inquisition by one Feliciano Dourado, originally from Brazil but now living in Portugal, who visited Holland in 1636. When interrogated by the Inquisition upon his return to Lisbon, Dourado testified that when he was in Amsterdam he was

> in the company of two Jews, one of whom called himself Manasse ben Israel, being the rabbi among them; the name of the other he does not recall. Among other topics of conversation, the said Jews made many complaints to him of the oppression that was done to them in Spain in order that they should not be Jews; and this is the first thing on which they

speak to Spaniards when they meet them. Continuing with the said subject, the said Manasse said to him, with much feeling and passion, that whatever they might do in Spain they would not prevent them from being Jews, because all the New Christians in Spain were Christians by violence, and that every year there went certain Jews from Holland to the capital of Madrid and to many other parts of the realm of Spain to circumcise the New Christians.

Menasseh's Jewish companion was concerned with the rabbi's careless chatter to this Portuguese-speaking foreigner, and warned him to keep quiet about such matters.

With this, the other Jew caught hold of his [Menasseh's] hand, intimating to him that he did wrong to reveal this before the deponent, because he would return to Spain and recount it, and might do harm to the persons in his Nation. After this warning, the said Manasse treated the matter jokingly, saying that he had not meant it seriously.[58]

This was just the kind of talk that could get one—and one's community—into serious trouble.

The series of events that began with Menasseh's offer to dedicate the Latin edition of the *Conciliador* to the States of Holland—the negative judgment by the Leiden theologians, the rejection by the States, the response by Barlaeus in the epigram to *De Creatione Problemata*, Menasseh's Latin *De Resurrectione Mortuorum*, the attacks by Voetius and his allies—did not make life any easier for the Republic's Jews. One immediate consequence of Menasseh's dedication offer was that, just two days after Leiden's theological faculty gave its advice to the States, the university created a special chair devoted to countering Jewish influence and providing the intellectual resources for converting Jews to Christianity. The first *Professor Controversiarum Judaicarum* was Constantijn L'Empereur, a learned Hebraist who also happened to be a close friend of Gerardus Vossius and, thus, probably acquainted with Menasseh himself.[59]

Even before the public harangues by Voetius, the regents of a liberal city like Amsterdam, with its growing Jewish population, had to be sensitive to what was being said in religious quarters and careful not to give conservatives an excuse for protest or even intervention. They knew of the judgment of the Leiden theologians and the backlash against Barlaeus's poem; they also knew that Menasseh was close friends with prominent Remonstrants. All of this may explain an entry in the record book of the Amsterdam burgemeesters for January 10, 1636: "The Lord Mayors and former mayors of this city resolved that the request of Manasses ben Israel to teach the Hebrew language in the Illustrious School and to have an honorarium . . . is denied."[60] Menasseh, who was already giving Hebrew lessons to students preparing to enter a university, had applied for a formal (and remunerative) position to do this at the Athenaeum Illustre. His dedication of the Latin *De Resurrectione* to two of the school's curators, Reael and Burgh, was probably intended help his case, but in the end it did little good. The Amsterdam burgemeesters must have felt that in the current climate an institution like the Athenaeum had to be beyond theological and moral reproach, that it could not afford to get caught up in a scandal by hiring a Jew, and a controversial one at that.

Menasseh was not unaware of the risky position in which he was putting himself and his community with his writings and his friendships. In a letter from November 1639 to Johan van Beverwijk, a physician in Dordrecht and a former student of Gerardus Vossius, he expressed his concerns about Beverwijk's proposal to take an essay Menasseh had recently written (probably in Spanish) and publish it in Latin.

> You think that this pamphlet might be dressed up in a Roman toga for the public good. I am of a somewhat different opin-

ion. I see that there are two or three men of non-negligible
authority who are doing everything they can to make our
nation [i.e., the Jewish people] hateful before all the people
of this country. To do such a thing without publishing any
writings is a great crime. These men even consider it an offense by this republic of Amsterdam to allow my writings to
appear in Latin. What would happen if they were translated
into Dutch?

Menasseh did not tell Beverwijk (who, in his Latin correspondence, went by the name Beverovicius) not to go ahead with the
Latin translation, but he asked him to keep his name out of it.[61]

As careful as Menasseh hoped to be about not antagonizing
the Dutch, especially those who were opposed to allowing Judaism to flourish in the Republic, the Amsterdam Jews were
just as worried about his ecumenical projects and his personal
contacts with Christians—especially Remonstrants. They, too,
were concerned that his endeavors and connections would in-
cite their enemies to new restrictive measures, or worse. His
relationships with the other rabbis and with the community's
lay leaders would, over the coming years, be quite rocky, and
Menasseh's outreach to the gentile world was in no small part
responsible for this. There is even some evidence that at one
point the *parnassim* or their agents began intercepting Menasseh's correspondence.[62] As Gerardus Vossius told Simon
Beaumont, after describing how Menasseh, unlike his Jewish co-
religionists, was especially friendly and useful to Christians, "for
this reason he suffers some problems among his own people."[63]

Vossius was reporting this in 1632, when Menasseh's only
published treatise beyond Bibles and liturgical compendia was
the Spanish *Conciliador*. By the end of the decade, with several
of Menasseh's theological and philosophical works circulating
in Latin among Christian scholars, the Portuguese-Jewish leadership must have been even more concerned. The irrepressible
rabbi was now widely recognized, for better or for worse, as a

learned and accessible Jewish authority. His circuit of gentile acquaintances, Dutch Reformed or otherwise, had expanded in significant ways. He became, for a lot of people, the go-to person for all things Jewish.

Gerardus Vossius, for one, did not hesitate to take advantage of Menasseh's services. He was also happy to refer others to him. It was no doubt on Vossius's recommendation that his friend Claude Saumaise, a French humanist scholar who was now professor at the University of Leiden, chose to consult with Menasseh in the late 1630s on some finer points of Jewish law. Saumaise was at the time writing a series of books about monetary interest, and so, using Gerardus's son Isaac as a go-between, he wrote to Menasseh to ask about the nature of usury in rabbinic tradition. Menasseh replied that it was difficult to find in Scripture a coherent set of rules governing usury, but various texts suggested that any form of usury is prohibited not only between the rich and the poor but between all Israelites. Saumaise was also curious about the status of Jewish laws and customs "once Judea lost its autonomy" and was reduced to a Roman province. He thus followed up with a second letter containing some queries about the Sabbath Year (*Shmita*)—when all debts are to be forgiven—and about whether the ancient Hebrews, as Roman subjects, allowed polygamy. Menasseh satisfied him on all counts. He told Saumaise that the practice of the remission of debts on the Sabbath Year continued only until the time of Hillel; and that according to the ancient historian Josephus there was polygamy among the ancient Hebrews—just as today, he adds, it is practiced in some European countries (but, he is careful to note, certainly not in Holland).[64]

Menasseh boasted around this time that "I have replied to more than 150 letters from learned men from all over Europe on many excellent doubts and questions."[65] Vossius, himself a prolific letter writer, was certainly impressed by the extent of

Menasseh's correspondence. He later wrote: "I do not think that there is anyone among the rabbis more expert than him or who is more often consulted by Christians through letters— not only in this land but also in Germany, France and other places. The integrity of his soul matches his remarkable erudition, which is surpassed by no other members of his people."[66] It was his admiration of Menasseh that led Vossius to recommend him to yet another friend, a gentleman of high scholarly standing in the international Republic of Letters but now in deep political trouble in his native land.

Hugo Grotius was a major figure in philosophy, jurisprudence, theology, and politics in the seventeenth century. He is perhaps most famous for his writings on natural law and on the morality of war, and his classic work *De iure belli ac pacis* (On the Law of War and Peace) was published in 1625. However, Grotius's personal fortunes had by then taken an extremely unfortunate turn. This man whose opinion was once respected enough to be asked by the States of Holland for advice on whether to allow Jews to settle in the province was now living in forced exile.

Grotius was a pensionary of Rotterdam and still one of the city's representatives in the States when, in 1618, the clash between the Arminians and their opponents reached its climax. In the wake of the Synod of Dort, and because of his defense of the Remonstrants—he was opposed in principle to the repression of ideas and conscience—Grotius was stripped of his offices and sentenced to life imprisonment. With the aid of his wife, he was able to escape from prison and flee to Paris. He enjoyed a temporary rehabilitation in 1631 and returned to the Netherlands to take up the governor-generalship of the Dutch East Indies Company. But his peace was short lived, and less than a year later he was on the run again, never to return to the United Provinces.

There is no reason to think that Grotius ever got to meet

Menasseh in person. It would have to have been when he was back in Holland between periods of exile; but references to Menasseh in his later correspondence show no trace of a personal acquaintance. Still, after his second departure from Holland he became familiar enough with Menasseh, both from Vossius's letters and through reading the rabbi's books, copies of which Vossius had been sending him.[67] Grotius was especially taken by the *Conciliador* and claimed to regard Menasseh as the better scholar when it came to the Bible and its interpretation. In a series of letters during the summer and fall of 1638, and using Gerardus Vossius as an intermediary, he asked Menasseh to clarify some biblical passages and to explain to him "the judicial system of ancient Israel," naturally a topic of great interest to this celebrated legal scholar. Menasseh responded— citing the Bible, the Talmud, and the *Mishneh Torah* of Maimonides, among other sources—with an account of the establishment of the Sanhedrin, the qualifications of its members, the order of courts and judges, and their method of rendering judgment and dealing with appeals.[68]

Grotius was quite satisfied by the rabbi's responses. In a letter to Vossius that October, he said: "I wish Menasseh good health. He is a man who is useful in both public and literary matters. I desire at times to learn various things from him."[69] It took Grotius some time finally to express his gratitude to Menasseh himself, however, as he was rather busy with diplomatic affairs. Writing to Menasseh in October of 1639 from Paris, where since 1635 he had been serving as the ambassador for Sweden, Grotius told him:

> The things you have responded to me about certain passages of sacred scripture and history gratified me very much. Nor do I think that there is anyone who could have responded to me any better. I myself have read many commentators [on Scripture], but, as numerous as they are, they are few com-

pared to those whom you know, have read, and have mastered. For this reason I am not only very grateful to you, but also emboldened by this courtesy to turn to you again if in the future further doubts of such a kind should occur.[70]

Grotius informed Menasseh that he was not the rabbi's only admirer in the French capital. He had recommended his works to numerous acquaintances in Paris, and they had been very well received. "They are read by many here not without pleasure and utility."

Menasseh's relationships with gentile scholars involved more than just intellectual exchanges on legal, theological, and philosophical topics. Menasseh moved easily in the gentile world and enjoyed good social relations with quite a few of his correspondents. In addition to accompanying non-Jews on their visits to the synagogue and having the occasional beer with them in a tavern, Menasseh would come by their homes and receive them in his own.[71] In a letter to Isaac, then in Rome, Gerardus Vossius told his son that "Menasseh is arriving as I am writing this, and he told me to give you his greeting."[72] Later in life, Menasseh would reflect back with pride on the fact that "I have held friendship with many great men, and the wisest, and most eminent of all Europe; and also they came to see me, from many places, at my house, and I had many friendly discourses with them."[73] For a Jew in the seventeenth century to be able to count men like Grotius and Vossius among his admirers and friends was rather remarkable.

Menasseh also enjoyed a warm relationship with the cloth merchant Gerbrand Anslo, the son of a Mennonite preacher and once one of his students in Hebrew and rabbinics. Anslo wrote a dedicatory poem, in Hebrew, for Menasseh's *De Resurrectione*. He called his former teacher "most learned of the rabbis" and praised the book as "a light for the righteous."[74] Menasseh later returned the favor by dedicating a work to Anslo.

No one will wonder that I call you most erudite; but many, of this and that religion, will [wonder] that I call you dearest friend [*amicissimum*], even though both [religions] believe in the one God of Israel. This is because they deny that there can be any friendship except between those whose minds are sworn to the same divine things. What a great error.

He took pleasure in reminding Anslo—and revealing to his readers—that "you visit my home, and you regard it as a sign of honor that I frequent yours. For this reason it matters little to me whether I have many friends; it suffices to have good ones."[75]

For every Voetius, then, there was a Vossius, a Barlaeus, a Grotius, or an Anslo. To be sure, the motives of Grotius and other Christians who sought Menasseh's Judaic expertise and with whom he was on friendly terms were not entirely innocent. For many of them there was an agenda, and it involved the eventual conversion of the Jews. They believed that this event was necessary for the (second) coming of their Messiah and the beginning of his thousand-year reign, the Millennium. Their quest for a deeper understanding of Judaism, while in some cases a matter of authentic scholarly curiosity, was often in the service of this conversionist program. In order to get the Jews to acknowledge their blindness and accept the truth of Christianity, one needed to engage them intellectually, and this required knowing something about their laws, their traditions, their texts, their language, and their history. One cannot refute something with which one is not familiar. For just this reason, most rabbis were unwilling to engage Christians intellectually to the degree that Menasseh did. They were reluctant to teach Hebrew to non-Jews and to study Judaica with them out of fear that such cooperation only gave their enemies tools with which they might turn on them.[76]

Menasseh was aware of what his gentile acquaintances were up to, of course. He was no fool, and he was very well read in the conversionist literature. Indeed, he figured that two can play at that game, and in the coming years he would cleverly try to co-opt the overtures of conversionists and put them to use for his own Judaic purposes.

Nevertheless, the close relationships that Menasseh enjoyed with Vossius, Barlaeus, Anslo, and others were genuine. What made this possible may have been that which, despite religious differences, they all had in common. They were all, in their respective communities, controversial figures. Just as Menasseh's activities were frowned upon by leaders of the Jewish community, so most of the gentiles with whom he associated were themselves not in especially good standing with the dominant orthodox faction of the Dutch Reformed Church. Grotius was in permanent exile, while Barlaeus would be harassed by his theological critics until his death in 1648. Remonstrant sympathizers like Vossius, Mennonites like Anslo, and other religious dissidents among the Calvinists continued to be suspect and even persecuted throughout the 1630s and 1640s. Menasseh and his closest non-Jewish friends were, in a sense, all in the same boat.

Menasseh was confident that he could manage his competing engagements and constituencies without much danger to himself or to his community. Perhaps he was *too* confident and a lower profile on occasion might have been wise. And yet, as much as his sorties into the Christian world irritated his Jewish colleagues, he was not without his supporters along the Houtgracht and the Breestraat. The *parnassim* still allowed him to publish his writings and he continued to receive book commissions and financial support for his printing business from influential Jews both within and beyond Amsterdam.

The output of Menasseh's print shop had, in fact, increased dramatically since publishing his Mishnah in 1633. Besides his own works, he had put out a collection of Hebrew blessings according to Ashkenazic and Polish ritual; several Sephardic prayer books in Hebrew, as well as a bilingual *siddur* in Hebrew and Spanish; some Hebrew Psalters; two Bibles with vowels; and a volume of daily prayers and readings from the Bible, the Mishnah, and the Talmud. In 1635, he published the *Zekher Rav*, an orthographically idiosyncratic retelling of the story of creation in verse—all the Hebrew word roots are used only once—by the physician and philologist Benjamin ben Immanuel Mussafia (who at the time was living in Hamburg but would later settle in Amsterdam, and who is said to have been related to Menasseh by marriage). He also put out an edition of Aisik Tyrnan's book of *minhagim* describing the seasonal religious customs in Poland, Lithuania, Ukraine, Bohemia, Moravia, and Germany. Two years later Menasseh's press issued Salomo Almoli's *Pitron Halomot*, on the interpretation of dreams, financed by Isaac Montalto (the son of Rabbi Mortera's late patron and a wealthy member of the Amsterdam Portuguese community) and an edition of the *Shevet Yehuda*, Solomon Ibn Verga's chronicle of the "various calamities, martyrdoms, dispersions, accusations, and exiles" of the Jews since the time of Solomon's Temple. The 1630s were, far and away, the most productive period in Menasseh's career as a printer.

He had also moved beyond printing and publishing to become an active retail bookseller. Menasseh's visit to the Frankfurt Book Fair in 1634 was an especially valuable step in this new dimension of his business, as well as a unique opportunity to expand the clientele for his own press.[77] The annual fair was begun in 1454 by the city's booksellers, and it soon became the largest and most important book market in early modern Europe. It allowed Menasseh to engage in acquiring and selling his primary and second-hand inventory on a scale he could not do from his home in Amsterdam. He also came away from the fair with some profitable commissions for publications. One of these was an advance order from a congregation in Dornum, in East Friesland, for copies of a Hebrew prayer book for German Jews.[78] Another involved financing from Jewish communities in Germany and Poland for large editions—on the scale of thousands—of various ritual books (daily and holiday prayer books, *humashim*).[79] The fair thus gave Menasseh entrée to the large market for Jewish books in eastern Europe. His publication of Tyrnan's book of customs in 1635 was probably meant for these Ashkenazic readers, while in 1638 two German booksellers ordered from him three thousand Pentateuchs, with Rashi commentary.[80] Menasseh also took advantage of the opportunity at the fair to network with other Jewish booksellers in Europe and acquaint them with the world of Hebrew printing in Amsterdam.

Closer to home, over the next several years Menasseh sold to the Amsterdam Municipal Library at least two caches of books, earning around three hundred and thirty guilders for a couple dozen volumes. These were mainly antiquarian books that Menasseh had acquired either on the open market (perhaps at Frankfurt) or at auction. Most of them were sixteenth-century editions of works in Hebrew, including a pair of midrashic texts published by Daniel Bomberg and a three-volume copy of Maimonides's *Mishneh Torah*, all produced in Venice.[81] The relationship between Menasseh and the municipal library probably began when Dionysius Vossius, his former student, was appointed librarian in 1633, and continued after Dionysius's premature death that year, when he was succeeded by his brothers Matthaeus and Isaac. With the Vossius clan in charge of the library, Menasseh had an inside line for sales.

Rabbi, teacher, writer, printer/publisher, bookseller, correspondent, consultant—Menasseh's considerable energies seemed rarely to flag in this period. It is no wonder that for a brief time in 1639 he was too unwell to do much of anything, perhaps suffering from exhaustion. In a letter to Saumaise in October, he apologized for not having replied sooner to his inquiry. "Please do not blame me for not responding until now to your letter. I must say, in truth, that a serious and long illness prevented me for two months. Now that my health is a little better, I feel my-self ready to respond to you by doing my best."[82]

There may, however, have been another reason for Me-nasseh's indisposition in the fall of 1639—not so much injury as insult, given the way he was being treated by the Amsterdam Jewish community. Just as Menasseh's fortunes beyond the con-fines of Vlooienburg were on the rise, his standing in the neigh-borhood was about to take a serious fall.

5

—————◆◆◆◆◆—————

"I am not my own master"

Perhaps it was the rancorous dispute over the eternality of punishment between Rabbi Mortera of Beth Jacob and Rabbi Aboab of Neve Shalom. Or maybe there were recurring difficulties over the fair distribution of communal funds. Whatever the reason, by the late 1630s it had become clear to the lay leaders of Amsterdam's Portuguese Jews that having three congregations, each with its own *ma'amad,* all within the same neighborhood and all practicing the same Sephardic rites, just wasn't working. There were several community-wide agencies responsible for education, caring for the sick, taxes, charitable projects, and burials. But the Sephardim now numbered over a thousand individuals and needed a more centralized and efficiently structured organization. It was time for Beth Jacob, Neve Shalom, and Beth Israel to put aside their differences and merge into a single congregation.

After extended consultations and negotiations between the

separate groups of *parnassim*, and probably seeking the advice of the Jewish community in Venice, the *Senhores Quinze* of the joint board of *deputados* met in September 1638 to conclude the agreement to establish the *Kehila Kedosha* (Holy Congregation) *Talmud Torah*, named after the Venetian congregation. The merger agreement was approved by the members of the three congregations in the spring of 1639. It proclaimed that any Jew of "the Portuguese and Spanish nation" who was residing in Amsterdam in 1638 or who settled in the city after that year automatically became a member of the united congregation; Jews not of Sephardic background could not become members and were allowed to attend services only with special permission.[1]

The house on the Houtgracht belonging to the Beth Israel congregation was the largest of the three synagogues, so henceforth it would serve as the synagogue for Talmud Torah. One of many contemporary Dutch visitors to "the Jews' house of prayer" was impressed by what he saw there:

> The Portuguese have a fairly large place for which they have put together two houses; below, you enter a hall or large bare vestibule containing a water-butt that can be turned on with a tap. Upon it you will find a towel, for the Jews wash their hands before they enter the church; on either side there are stairways by which you reach their church; the women, who are separated from the men and cannot be seen by them, are seated high up in a gallery. At one end of the church there is a large wooden cupboard with two doors; it contains many precious things, among them the Books of Moses wrapped in rare embroidered cloths. Their teachers stand on a raised platform some three feet higher than the other congregants; the men don white shawls over their hats which hang down over their shoulders and trunk and each holds a book in his hand, all of which are in Hebrew.[2]

An etching from the period by the Dutch artist Romeyn de Hooghe shows the synagogue's exterior with a beautiful, ornate two-story facade, much like any upscale mansion along one of the city's canals. There is nothing to indicate that the building was a Jewish house of worship (just like the *schuilkerken*, or hidden churches, of the local Catholics, and no doubt much to the relief of the Reformed consistory).[3] Another print, by Jan Veenhuysen, shows that the synagogue interior had a wide central aisle flanked by large columns that offset two narrower side aisles. The ceiling had four vaults running parallel to the building's main axis: two over the main aisle and one directly over each of the women's galleries on the second tier above the side aisles. At the far end of the building stood the imposing *tevah* or ark for the Torah scrolls, while the *bimah* or reader's platform was in the center of the hall, in keeping with Sephardic practice.

The more delicate problem arising from the merger was what to do with the rabbis. On the one hand, it was clear that Mortera, as the senior and most experienced (and arguably most learned) *hakham* in the community, would be the chief rabbi for Talmud Torah and principal for the school. He was to offer three sermons a month and give Talmud lessons to the most advanced students. For this he would be paid six hundred guilders a year (along with one hundred baskets of turf for his heating needs). David Pardo, the son of Joseph Pardo, from Beth Israel, would be second in rank and receive five hundred guilders annually. His responsibilities would include serving as administrator of the Beth Haim cemetery.

That left Menasseh ben Israel and Isaac Aboab, and this is where things became awkward. The two men were practically the same age and had both been students of Rabbi Uziel and rabbis for Neve Shalom. Officially, Menasseh was appointed third in rank, preaching on one Shabbat each month—but, notably, not assigned any formal teaching duties—while Aboab was ranked fourth, teaching in the upper level of the school and giving evening sermons to students.[4] The problem was that

Aboab was to be paid four hundred and fifty guilders a year, while Menasseh was allotted an annual income of only one hundred and fifty guilders—fifty guilders less than he was earning as rabbi of Neve Shalom earlier that year, before the merger![5] There is no explanation provided for this wide discrepancy in responsibilities and salary. Menasseh, of course, took it as a sign of disrespect, which is probably how it was intended. Whether there was jealousy over his popularity in the gentile world, or misgivings about his various activities, or simply personal dislike, the *parnassim* made it clear that Menasseh was not to enjoy a high status in the united congregation. It was a blow to the rabbi's pride, not to mention his purse.

While the negotiations for the congregations' merger were going on, Menasseh continued to run his printing and bookselling operations. His main occupation in 1639, however, was finishing another treatise of his own—one that, of all his works, was certainly the most interesting philosophically but perhaps the most dangerous theologically.

In 1634, Johannes Beverwijk (Beverovicius), the Dordrecht physician, had canvassed a number of leading intellectuals for their opinions on the following question: "Can a human being influence the duration of his life?" Beverwijk was concerned that medicine and other practices that contribute to good health would be pointless if the time of a person's death was unalterably fixed by God. He wrote to Barlaeus, Simon Episcopius, Gerardus Vossius, Marin Mersenne (a Catholic priest and close friend of Descartes), and others, and published the responses he received as a book, *Epistolica quaestio de vitae termino, fatali an mobili?* (Epistolic Question on the Term of Life: Fated or Modifiable?).

The topic, as Beverwijk knew, had significant ramifications for a number of hotly contested theological issues that, while originating in antiquity, had acquired a particular urgency in the tumultuous religious world of the Dutch Republic. For orthodox Calvinists, one's fate—both the length of one's life and one's eternal condition—is determined irrevocably by God. While there is a sense in which human beings enjoy free will—they are able to will what they desire and so act voluntarily—they do not have the liberty to desire, and thus to will and act, otherwise than as they do; and they certainly do not have the power to alter the course and length of their lives and their ultimate fate. An individual is predestined to either eternal felicity or eternal damnation. It all depends on whether one has been granted the free and unmotivated gift of efficacious divine grace. God chooses, prior to creation, who will be saved and who will not, regardless of an individual's works or merits.

Although Beverwijk had collected a variety of Protestant and Catholic opinions for his volume, he realized that a certain perspective was missing. He wrote to Menasseh to find out "what is the opinion of the rabbis and the cabbalists" on the subject. Rather than give Beverwijk something for the next edition of his book, Menasseh opted to compose his own treatise on the subject, *De Termino Vitae* (On the Term of Life).

Menasseh agreed that a person's life ordinarily has a certain and definite term. It is set by a number of factors: astrological, according to how the stars and the heavens influence a person's actions; physical, since the proper proportion and harmony of the elements composing the human body are essential for the continuation of life; and divine, in so far as God has determined that human lives in different historical eras should be of different lengths.

At the same time, Menasseh (following Maimonides) rejected the idea that these factors "precisely and unalterably" fix the term of one's life. Any person has the power to increase or decrease the duration of his life through the exercise of virtue. "Life," he says, "may be shortened by sin and, on the other hand, it can be prolonged by virtue."[6] Citing a variety of sources, including the Bible, ancient philosophy, and the Talmud, Menasseh argued that through good diet and spiritual exercises—such as the study of Torah—one can escape a death that might have occurred through the vicissitudes of fortune and the ordinary course of nature. If this were not the case, then prayer, caution, and medical intervention would all necessarily be useless. Even the influence that the cosmos has on a person's fate can be transcended by right living. "The force and efficacy of virtue is much greater than that of the stars and planets."[7] By meditating upon and observing God's commandments, as well as caring for one's body, one can take advantage of divine providence to prolong one's life. This is because God will come to the aid of the pious and give them the means to lead longer lives than they might otherwise lead. Once a person willingly embarks on a virtuous course of action, God, "king of heaven and earth," will lend assistance and support by "disposing all things wisely, without any impediment to free will," so that they are in one's favor. God will arrange external circumstances such that they provide more opportunities for virtuous action and allow for the results that the pious individual (and God) desires.[8]

The "Jewish" answer to Beverwijk's question, then, at least according to Menasseh, is that there is no predestination. Human beings are endowed with free will, and the proper exercise of that freedom can alter the length of their lives and their ultimate fate. Why else would God issue commands that we are expected to follow if it were not within our power to obey or not obey them as we choose? Either God is unjust, or a person is free "either to obtain life through virtue or . . . through vicious actions, to bring ruin upon his head."[9] Not even an omniscient God's foreknowledge of how a person will act—what he will or will not choose to do in actual circumstances—destroys that freedom. "God has known, from eternity, all future contingent things ... Nonetheless, there remains for man a liberty by which he can make his life longer or shorter."[10]

Menasseh was explicitly, and not without some trepidation, rejecting the doctrine of divine predestination so dear to the Dutch Reformed Church. He did claim that nothing he said on this question "contradicts the Christian religion," and insisted that "most [Christian] scholars did not hold an opinion that is different from most of the rabbis."[11] Still, he must have known that he was essentially siding with the Arminians against their orthodox opponents. Although the only extant version of *De Termino Vitae* is in Latin, Menasseh would have written the work in Spanish, and he warned Beverwijk that a Latin translation would bring some risks. "If someone, without my knowledge, translates me into Latin, I cannot fault him, if it is even a fault; but if I am the instigator of the translation, it will be said that I am disturbing the republic."[12]

The publication of *De Termino Vitae* could not have helped Menasseh's standing in the Sephardic community. He was no longer only the rabbi of one congregation among several but one of four rabbis representing the united community. Its leaders must have received his venture onto Calvinist theological terrain with some anxiety.

Still smarting from the insult he had received from the Amsterdam *parnassim* in the merger, Menasseh began seriously to consider leaving the community altogether and taking his services elsewhere. In fact, there was a Sephardic congregation in a Dutch colony on the other side of the Atlantic Ocean that was looking for a new rabbi.

By the early 1630s, the Dutch, through the power of the West Indies Company, had conquered from the Portuguese substantial portions of northeastern Brazil. Under the new regime, New Christians living in the now Dutch colony of Pernambuco were allowed to return to Judaism. The Jewish community there grew rapidly as Sephardim from Amsterdam and elsewhere also came to settle in the province, especially its capital, the port city of Recife; contemporary reports suggest that Jews might even have constituted a majority of the city's population. As growers, brokers, and merchants, they played a major role in the trans-Atlantic sugar trade during the seventeenth century. (Sadly, they also profited from the trafficking of African slaves, both as traders and as plantation owners.)[13] These Sephardim cultivated and milled cane in Pernambuco and managed transportation networks for the exporting of sugar (as well as tobacco and wood) to northern Europe. They worked closely with relatives and partners in Amsterdam, where by the 1630s there were several dozen sugar refineries.[14]

In 1636, the Jews of Recife established their own congregation, the first in the New World, called Tsur Yisrael (Rock of Israel). Menasseh knew many of the members there, since they were from Amsterdam families, and he thought that perhaps they might show him more appreciation than he was receiving at home. Thus, almost immediately after the merger of the three congregations in Amsterdam, Menasseh was considering moving to Brazil, possibly to become the rabbi at Tsur Yisrael but certainly to try to increase his income. Gerardus Vossius wrote to Grotius in January 1640: "Menasseh is thinking [of taking himself to] Brazil ... perhaps to act as rabbi but primarily to engage in trade. He loves his studies very much, and thirsts for glory. But as I told you, his family affairs [i.e., finances] persuade him [to do this], for he is not thriving in this respect."[15] Grotius replied that he would be unhappy to see Menasseh go. "With all my soul I hope that all things go well for Menasseh, and I am sorry that, by the urgency of his affairs, he is obliged to go so far from us. I would willingly repay him for his services if I could." Grotius was not unaware that behind Menasseh's desire to relocate was the treatment he had received from his congregants in Amsterdam, especially his low remuneration. "I used to think that the men of the Amsterdam synagogue were both wealthy and liberal. Now I see that I was wrong about this. I am unsure whether they speak the truth or want to be thought poorer than they are in order to avoid taxes."[16]

The "trade" in which Vossius described Menasseh as engaged was the business partnership that he set up around this time with his brother Ephraim and his brother-in-law Jonah Abrabanel. It was yet another effort to supplement his meager income as a rabbi, which he believed would not only relieve the pressure on the family budget but also allow him to devote more time to study. "Since the remuneration provided by our synagogue is not particularly splendid, I have sent my brother Ephraim to Brazil, to see if perhaps, through him and by trade, the torch of some fortune might shine on me, so that I can devote myself a little more freely to divine literature."[17] He also saw it, however, as just one more blow to his dignity. As he told Beverwijk,

> Now, as if in total neglect of myself, I am engaged in trade; which is not only difficult and full of trouble, but also costs me a good deal of time that I would otherwise devote to my studies. But what else am I to do? I have neither the wealth of Croesus nor the soul of Thersites.[18]

There is no extant record of the goods with which the firm dealt, but—given the fact that their initial center of operation was Brazil, where Ephraim relocated in 1639 to serve as their agent—it most likely began with sugar or tobacco.

As if things were not bad enough in Menasseh's relations with the leaders of Talmud Torah, in the spring of 1640 they deteriorated even further. It was his business partnership with Jonah that, more or less, led to a confrontation with the *ma'amad* in which he came out the loser.

In early 1640, according to a report in the community's record book, some anonymous individuals had "put up certain posters or defamatory papers on the doors of the synagogue, on the bridge, at the market and in other places."[19] The placards, which the report says touched on "the subject of Brazil," were apparently impugning the business practices and character of certain members of the community involved in the South American trade. Most likely they were directed at merchants who did not appreciate any new competition and so were making things difficult for others seeking to enter the market. Dishonorable behavior in commerce was one thing, and it would be dealt with, but publicly shaming fellow congregants was yet a more serious violation of the community's regulations. This kind of insolent behavior could not be tolerated. "It is well understood by all that this deed is abominable, reprehensible, and worthy of punishment." And so, on February 9, 1640, the members of the *ma'amad* issued an at-large punishment on the unknown culprits.

> We put under *herem* and announce that the person or persons who have made such papers and posted them are cursed by God and separated from the nation. Nobody may speak with them or do them a favor or give them assistance in any way.

A *herem* was an act of banning or ostracism (sometimes translated as "excommunication") often used by the Amsterdam *parnassim* to punish congregants who had violated communal regulations and generally to keep people in line. It was a form of religious, social, and economic isolation. A person under *herem* was usually forbidden from participating in synagogue services, as well as from socializing and conducting any business with members of the community. It was an effective measure for maintaining Jewish discipline and social order among relatively new Jews still getting used to an orthodox life.[20]
One could be put under *herem* in the Amsterdam Portuguese-

Jewish community for a wide variety of offenses regarding religious and devotional matters as well as more mundane activities. One would receive a ban for buying non-kosher meat (or meat from an Ashkenazic butcher), gambling, or lewd behavior in the street; for failing to pay one's communal taxes, showing disrespect to the *ma'amad*, or insulting the rabbis. Congregants were forbidden to engage gentiles in theological discussions, and Sephardic women were warned, with a threat of *herem*, not to engage in sexual relations with gentile men or to cut the hair of gentile women. (Sexual relations between Sephardic men and gentile women, on the other hand, while against both Jewish and Dutch law, were generally overlooked.) Needless to say, one could also earn a *herem* for espousing unorthodox theological views. In 1656, the young Spinoza received the harshest expulsion ever issued by the *parnassim* for his "abominable heresies and monstrous deeds." Unlike most of the bans issued in this period, which were usually lifted after the offending party apologized and paid a fine, the *herem* against Spinoza was never rescinded.[21]

In the case of the libelous posters, the *ma'amad* quickly learned who the guilty parties were—Daniel Rachaõ and Israel da Cunha—and the ban was applied to them the very next day. (It was lifted on Rachaõ a week later after he expressed contrition for his actions.)

However, a short time later, the *ma'amad* discovered that Jonah Abrabanel and Moses Belmonte were also involved in the "Brazilian matter," either as participants in the original escapade or by circulating new posters again suggesting that certain Portuguese-Jewish merchants were less than honorable. Abrabanel and Belmonte were each given a *herem*, but were soon back in good standing after expressing deep and sincere remorse for their behavior and paying their fines.

Menasseh, however, was incensed by the way in which his brother in-law had been treated. He, of course, as Jonah's part-

ner, shared his sentiments about the merchants who were seeking to monopolize the Brazil trade, and he may even have been
involved in distributing the offending material. But even more,
Menasseh felt that the *ma'amad* had shown great disrespect to
Jonah when the whole affair was made public in the synagogue
during services, not least by failing to accord him the honor-
ific title *senhor* when his name was read out. (It could not have
helped matters that the original *herem* had been pronounced by
Rabbi Aboab.) Menasseh lost his temper and protested loudly
from the rabbis' bench. According to the report of the *ma'amad*,
"Menaseh came from his place and, with loud voice and all
worked up, complained that his brother-in-law was not called
'*Senhor*'—giving him the title that was owed to him." The congregation's *gabbai* responded that Abrabanel did not deserve
the title, as it was to be used only with sitting members of the
ma'amad. This only made Menasseh madder.

> A large part of the assembly left its place, whereupon Me-
> nasseh turned on them, without being willing to calm him-
> self, as he was continuously warned to do, until finally two
> *parnassim* of the synagogue stood up in order to make him be
> quiet, and indeed, since they could not do it with sufficient
> words, used the punishment of *herem*. They ordered him to
> stop and to return to his house. He countered with a loud
> voice: he would not. Then the *parnassim*, who were in the
> synagogue, came together, and since the disturbance contin-
> ued further, they confirmed the punishment of the *herem* in
> order to make him [Menasseh] stop, and they ordered as well
> that no one speak with him.

The members of the *ma'amad* retired to their chambers, whereupon Menasseh followed them, burst in, and

> raising his voice and pounding on the table, said in a serious
> fashion all the unbridled thoughts that came into his mind,
> so that finally one of the *parnassim* apprised him that he is

the cause of various disturbances . . . the *parnassim* told him
to leave the chamber and that they regarded him as cut off.
He responded to that with loud voice that he was putting
them under *herem* and not the *parnassim* him, and other such
shameful things.

It was an impressive display of righteous indignation. Out
of respect for his position and years of service to the community, the *ma'amad* took some pity on him. Menasseh's ban, recorded on May 8, 1640, and imposed "for the insubordination,
the scene, and the curses, which he had spoken four times," was
in place for only one day.[22] From sundown to sundown, he was
forbidden from entering the synagogue and communicating
with any members of the community. On top of that, however,
"to serve as an example to others," he was suspended from his
rabbinical duties for a year. It was a heavy penalty for what was
regarded as a serious breach of decorum. Unlike his brother-
in-law, there is no indication that he ever expressed remorse for
his behavior.

This treatment at the hands of the *ma'amad*, deserved or
not, must only have strengthened Menasseh's resolve to leave
Amsterdam and go to South America. In early 1641, he was still
considering "departing this most flourishing land of Batavia for
the distant parts of Brazil."[23] To help his case with the Recife
congregation, Menasseh dedicated Part 2 of the *Conciliador*—
which, nine years after the printing of Part 1, he had finished,
taking him through the Book of Kings—to the governors of
the Dutch West Indies Company. As an added, and hopeful,
touch, he inserted a letter of praise to the *nobilissimos y magnifi-
cos señores* of Tsur Yisrael in Pernambuco.[24]

In the meantime, Menasseh suffered another painful loss
to his family, one that would likely also affect his business prospects. On November 23, 1640, "Efraym Sueiro," Menasseh's
brother—he kept the old family name for business purposes—

was buried in the Beth Haim cemetery in Ouderkerk. He died in Amsterdam while on a return from Brazil. Besides Menasseh, donations in Ephraim's memory were made by Jonah Abrabanel and by two of Menasseh's colleagues: Rabbis Mortera and Aboab.[25]

Menasseh's letter of praise for the *parnassim* in Recife in Part 2 of the *Conciliador* did not help his case for the congregational job in that colony, primarily because the *ma'amad* there did not see it before selecting their new rabbi. In the end, the position went to Menasseh's nemesis, Isaac Aboab. Perhaps the Recife community had a preference for a kabbalist like Aboab. Or maybe they knew Menasseh all too well and were afraid that he would be a rather difficult personality for their delicate colonial position. Either way, their choice gave Menasseh yet another reason to resent Aboab.

On the other hand, Aboab's departure for Brazil in May of 1641 meant that he would be out of the way, far away.[26] It also meant that there would be more opportunities for Menasseh in the congregation and, importantly, a higher annual salary. He took over some of Aboab's classes in the school—including the lowest of the upper levels, "grade six," teaching "grammar and first lessons in *gemara* [Talmud]"—and received a raise to six hundred guilders.[27] If he harbored any hope of teaching the most advanced students in Talmud, however, he was to be disappointed. The directors of the community's education had little confidence in Menasseh as a Talmudic scholar. This really was Mortera's domain. Moreover, within just a few years Menasseh would be relieved of his teaching in grade six—and the supplemental salary this brought—and replaced by Rabbi Jacob Judah Leão, who moved from Middelburg to Amsterdam in 1643.[28] (Rabbi Leão would later be better known by the moniker that his son, Solomon, added to the family name—Templo—to honor his father's fanatical devotion to studying the ancient

Temple in Jerusalem and the scaled reconstruction of it that he paraded around Europe. The rabbi was proud of his model and gained an international reputation for his traveling exhibit.)

The continuing work on the *Conciliador*, the new business venture in Brazil, and the bookselling, all on top of his teaching and other rabbinic duties, meant that Menasseh had little time for his printing operation or starting new scholarly projects. Between the summer of 1639, when he published *De Termino Vitae*, and the spring of 1642, not a single book came off Menasseh's press. (He handed over the publication of Part 2 of the *Conciliador* to the Dutch firm of Nicolaes van Ravesteyn.) His days were quite full, as he told a correspondent a few years later:

> Two hours are spent in the Temple every day, six in the school, one and a half in the public academy, and the private one of the Senhores Pereyra, in which I have the office of President, two in the corrections of my printing press, which all pass through my hands. From eleven to twelve I give audiences to all who require me for their affairs and visits. All this is precise, in addition to which comes the time for domestic cares and to reply to the four or six letters which come every week, of which I keep no copy, for the time fails me.

Menasseh especially begrudged his time in the classroom. He complained that "I am not my own master," and that because of the hours he had to spend teaching he did not have the opportunity to do the intellectual work that he much preferred. "I am lost to myself in order to advance others, forcibly preventing me, after having conceived the finest works, from making of these grapes more wine of this sort." He called his work in the school a "troublesome occupation."[29]

The recipient of this letter, Manuel Fernandes Villareal, was a Portuguese New Christian living in Paris and serving as Portugal's consul general there.[30] He had written to Menasseh to seek his opinion on some questions of biblical chronology, including the duration of the captivities in Egypt and Babylonia. He also enclosed a "Table of the Kings of Jehuda and Israel" that he had compiled, which Menasseh found "very well ordered." Unfortunately, when Villareal returned to Lisbon, he was denounced by a rival as a secret Judaizer and arrested by the Inquisition. On the basis of his confession—under torture, of course—he was convicted and put to death in 1653. It is possible that his correspondence with Menasseh bore some responsibility for his tragic fate.[31]

The "public academy" to which Menasseh referred in his letter to Villareal was the recently established Ets Haim seminary, the community's institution for advanced students and especially the training of rabbis. The "private one of the Senhores Pereyra," on the other hand, was a yeshiva founded in 1644 by a pair of wealthy brothers recently arrived from Madrid by way of Venice. Along with Menasseh's friend the physician Ephraim Bueno, Abraham and Isaac Pereyra endowed this association for adult study and appointed Menasseh as its principal. It was a nice feather in his cap, and may have helped relieve his feelings of being underappreciated. The additional income was welcome too, particularly since Menasseh's enterprise in Brazil was not going well. Partly this was because his business-savvy brother was no longer around to manage things. More important, by the mid-1640s the West Indies Company was losing control of Recife and the surrounding area, after an uprising by Portuguese planters.[32] In the end, Menasseh took a major financial hit. As he later told Villareal, "I lost my estate in the varying fortunes of America."[33]

The appointment as head of a yeshivah was not the only honor that Menasseh received in the early 1640s. Overall, his standing in the community seems to have rebounded somewhat after the departure of Aboab.

On May 22, 1642, Menasseh enjoyed what was probably the

greatest day of his life as a rabbi. Henrietta Maria, queen consort of Charles I of England, was visiting the Netherlands. She
was accompanying their daughter, Mary, to see her future husband Willem. Young Willem was the son of Frederik Hendrik,
the Prince of Orange who had been appointed stadholder of
Holland and other provinces in 1625, after the death of his half-
brother Maurits of Nassau. (Both were sons of Willem I, or
Willem of Orange, the great leader of the Dutch revolt against
Spain, also known as Willem the Silent.)

There were, at least officially, no Jews in England—they
had been expelled in 1290 by King Edward I—and Henrietta
Maria had expressed a desire to see the synagogue in Amsterdam and observe the Jews in prayer. Her entourage, which included the Stadholder, was given a most proper welcome by
the Sephardic community. The *parnassim*, dressed in their finest, received the royals with all due pomp, and Jonah Abrabanel
read out some poems that he had composed for the occasion.
But the true honor of the day belonged to Menasseh. He,
rather than the chief rabbi, Mortera, had been selected to deliver the official welcoming address. He marshaled all his rhe-
torical skills and gave a warm and congratulatory speech, one
that, crafted to flatter the Stadholder, was generous in its praise
for the Dutch Republic, the province of Holland, and especially
Amsterdam.

> We Portuguese—exiles deprived of our property and having
> first taken our refuge as if in your bosom—bear testimony
> [to your justice]. Now we live, now we have been saved and,
> like everyone else, enjoy the freedom here. This is a great
> sign of your virtue, and an even greater sign of your courage.

He compared Frederik Hendrik's father to the ancient Jewish
priest Mattathias ben Yohanen. Just as Mattathias and his fight-
ers during the Maccabean revolt "delivered the land of Judah
from slavery under King Antiochus," so "your father Willem

liberated Holland from the tyranny of Spain. And as Judah Maccabee after [Mattathias], through his bravery, succeeded in repulsing a great power, so has your brother the invincible hero Maurits [repulsed his adversaries]." The current stadholder himself was said to enter "this powerful city of Amsterdam" just as Alexander the Great entered Jerusalem.

The biblical allusions were calculated to appeal to a Dutch audience that saw itself as God's new chosen people and the Republic as the New Israel. It was a common enough trope in contemporary Dutch political theory, as well as in the art and literature of the period. If Moses led the Israelites out of Egypt, the land of many gods, so the House of Orange liberated the United Provinces from the idolatrous Spanish Catholic overlords. Now these independent northern lands, having suffered under repressive regimes, offered refuge and protection to the people of Moses. "We are protected by almighty God from all dangers," Menasseh continued, "and in the same way are we obliged to Your Highness and the most illustrious States of Holland for our freedom. . . . We no longer consider Castile or Portugal our fatherland, but Holland. We do not think of the Spanish or Portuguese kings as our lords, but the States of Holland and you."[34]

Just a few days later, a proud Menasseh had his welcome address published in Dutch, Portuguese, and Latin versions. In a letter enclosed with copies of the pamphlet, he told David de Wilhem, a counselor to the stadholder, that he composed the speech in a rush, just one hour before delivering it. Nonetheless, he was confident that "everyone seemed to like my address." He added, with a bit of exaggeration, that "those of my nation (among whom I occupy the highest place, with a reasonable stipend) gave me many thanks."[35]

The choice of Menasseh to preside on this grand occasion must have rankled Rabbi Mortera. The two men had been at odds for months, and by this point were probably not on speaking terms. According to an entry in the *ma'amad*'s record book on June 2, "some unfortunate matters have arisen." Although no specifics are mentioned, it seems the two men were using their sermons to snipe at one another, with each accusing the other of not knowing how to interpret the Torah.[36]

That Menasseh and Mortera had very different, even incompatible ideas about how to read Hebrew Scripture—and thus some further insight into what was probably behind the unpleasantness—emerges from an unusual conversation that took place in the synagogue just a year or two later.

Among the frequent gentile visitors to the Jewish community was a man named Jan Pietersz Beelthouwer. He was a rather eccentric character, religiously about as marginal a figure as one could be in the Dutch Reformed Church. A schoolteacher and *ziekentrooster* ("comforter of the sick"), Beelthouwer was associated with the Collegiants, a dissident sect whose members, meeting in "colleges," ran the gamut from devout pietists to spiritually minded freethinkers; the Counter-Remonstrants were not fans. Beelthouwer himself had strong Remonstrant sympathies. What really got him into trouble, though, were his Socinian (i.e., anti-Trinitarian) tendencies. The church council of Enkhuizen, where he was born, would eventually excommunicate him as a heretic and ban him from the town.[37] However, Beelthouwer was also a skilled Hebraist and deeply interested in problems of biblical interpretation. Writing in 1660, he recalled that starting in 1643 he entered into a series of discussions on Hebrew vocabulary and grammar with Menasseh and Rabbi Leão and "various Jews." On one occasion, the conversation turned to the difficulty of interpreting a passage from the prophet Zechariah (11:12–13). Beelthouwer says that

> I asked a Jew, and then a Jewish rabbi named Jacob, whether they would translate the Hebrew words of Zechariah 11:12–13 into Dutch, and I showed them the Hebrew Bible printed in

Amsterdam by Rabbi Menasseh ben Israel in 1635 and 1636;
and they translated these words for me just as they are in our
printed [Dutch] translation. Rabbi Isaac Montalto and Rabbi
Aron said to me that Zechariah wrote these words around
four hundred years before the birth of Christ. I asked Rabbi
Menasseh in their synagogue about the meaning of these
words. He said to me, within earshot of many Jews, there is
no one under heaven who can explain these words literally.
There is, to be sure, among us a rabbi who has written a literal explanation of them, but it is without much foundation.

Beelthouwer's curiosity was piqued, so he insisted on getting a
literal interpretation of the passage.

[But] Rabbi Menasseh said there are over thirty interpretations. I asked him for the primary ones, and he said (and it
really isn't much): "Some would say that it speaks of the time
of Judah Maccabee, how the priests, who are clean as silver,
were sold; and others would say something else; Zechariah is
difficult to understand, so he must be understood somewhat
metaphorically." I said that Christians do know of a literal
meaning. Rabbi Menasseh was silent, but one among the mass
of Jews shouted "Yes, the fable they [the Christians] teach
about that wretch who is said to have been sold for thirty
pieces of silver!" Soon some Jews came out of the high synagogue and said to me "Come, go now with us, and it shall be
explained to you literally." And there sat Rabbi Hakham
Mortera with the eldest youths [?], and he had before him
that book that Menasseh told me was hardly convincing in
its explanation. But I cannot now in truth say how it explained the verses literally, so tortured were they.[38]

Menasseh was open to a plurality of meanings of biblical passages, many of them metaphorical; Mortera, by contrast, preferred literal readings. Neither of them thought very highly of
the other's approach, and they were making that clear in their
respective sermons.

Such skirmishing between its rabbis would surely set a con-gregation on edge. The *parnassim*, perhaps fearing another rift in the community like the one over eternal punishment just a few years earlier—or worse, like the schism that led to Beth Is-rael breaking off from Neve Shalom in 1618—decided to put the men on warning. They ordered them to submit their sermons to the board in advance of services, for review and approval.

The forced truce in the rabbinate would be only temporary.

When Salom Italia arrived in Amsterdam sometime in 1641, he did not know a word of Dutch or Portuguese. He was, however, an expert draftsman and engraver, and he hoped that these skills would serve him well enough. He had been born in Mantua, Italy, in 1619, but the family fled with the rest of the Jews of that city in 1630, when it was invaded by the Austrians. They settled in the ghetto in Venice, where Salom began work-ing as an artist, primarily on paper. Printmaking ran in the family—it was his father's line of work, and his uncle Eliezer had run a Hebrew press in Mantua. There was a lot of compe-tition in Venice, though, so when he heard about the prosperous community of Portuguese Jews on the Amstel River, he must have figured that such well-off and cosmopolitan merchants and professionals would be in need of someone—Jewish—to do portraits, book illustrations, and other personal and religious projects.

It was a smart move. Italia's business flourished in the Vlooienburg quarter, with commissions for illuminated prayer books, Passover *haggadot*, and marriage contracts (*ketubot*).[39] His major work was a series of illustrated Esther scrolls for mem-bers of the community.[40] The biblical Queen Esther, who had to conceal her Jewish identity as consort to King Ahasuerus, was an especially significant figure for former crypto-Jews now living openly Jewish lives in Amsterdam and other European cities. Like them, she had led a double life, albeit courageously revealing her true heritage when it was necessary to save her people from destruction.

Italia also did portraits of the community's rabbis. His engraved image of Jacob Judah Leão depicts him above a rendering of the ancient Temple, which he devoted his life to studying, and serves as the frontispiece for Leão's book. From Italia's engraving burin we also have our only authentic portrait of Menasseh ben Israel. Italia made Menasseh's acquaintance soon after his arrival in Amsterdam. He was no doubt already familiar with the books bearing Menasseh's imprint—the press had many clients in Venice—so the rabbi's home on the Nieuwe Houtmarkt, as his base of operations, was a natural destination for Italia when he landed in the city. Books needed frontispieces, decorated title pages, printer's marks, and other pictorial features.

From Italia's engraving, done in 1642, we can see that the man who stood before the Stadholder and his royal guests that spring wore his dark hair just below his ears, with bangs cut short over his forehead. His cheeks were full and clean-shaven, but his mouth was surrounded by a long mustache and goatee. He had light-colored eyes, probably green, although they did not serve him well. In his letter to David de Wilhem about the welcome address, Menasseh complained about "my poor eyesight"; he was near-sighted, since on that glorious day he could not see well enough across the synagogue's gallery to identify someone.[41]

The English clergyman Thomas Pocock, who translated *De Termino Vitae* into English in 1699, wrote that Menasseh "was of a middle Stature, and inclining to fatness. He always wore his own Hair, which (many years before his Death) was very Grey; so that his Complexion being pretty fresh, his Demeanor Graceful, and Comely, his Habit plain and decent, he commanded an aweful Reverence which was justly due to so venerable a Deportment."[42]

In Italia's engraving, Menasseh's visage is surrounded by a banner on which appears his motto, *Peregrinando quaerimus* ("Through our wandering we seek"), and the title *Menasseh ben Israel Theologus et Philosophus Hebraeus*. Below it is a poem in Latin:

> His learning and his modesty wanted to be depicted here.
> Can this sheet present both?
> See these eyes, this face. They agree perfectly on both sides:
> Learning expressed its aspects, & modesty its own.[43]

Menasseh used the print to publicize his writings, and he sent it to his friends and correspondents as a kind of calling card. One recipient, the Christian kabbalist Abraham von Francken-berg, who praised Menasseh's writings as providing an "excellent understanding of Holy Scripture," says of the rabbi's face that "the light of your countenance is God, and the lamp for your feet is his Word, and both remain with you as you wander on the paths of truth through life."[44]

Menasseh, inspired by Rabbi Leão's book on the Temple, may also have wanted the portrait to serve as a frontispiece for the work he was about to publish.[45] *De la Fragilidad Humana, y Inclinacion del Hombre al Peccado* (On Human Weakness and Man's Inclination to Sin) appeared that spring, with the desired "approbation" and dedicated to the *parnassim* of Talmud Torah—perhaps as a peace offering from Menasseh after receiving his *herem*. A Latin translation followed just a few months later, dedicated to his former student—and, not coincidentally, a Remonstrant—Gerbrand Anslo.

De la Fragilidad Humana, Menasseh informed his reader, was yet another entry in his ongoing project "to offer in several works the sum of all our theology."[46] As the modified subtitle in the Latin edition indicates, Menasseh's topic this time concerned the doctrines of original sin and divine grace—"all questions of the highest nobility that occupied many Greek and Latin authors. Nonetheless," he insisted, "I am the first of our nation to treat them in a learned manner." Once again Menasseh had decided to address a theologically contentious, potentially dangerous set of issues that divided Jews from Christians and even Christians among themselves. And yet, he said, "I would like my works to receive universal approval," and he hoped that everyone will find his account "most gratifying."[47]

Menasseh was either deluding himself or being disingenuous—almost certainly the latter. He could not have been unaware that his account of the nature and origin of human sin and the means to salvation would not be acceptable to his more orthodox Reformed readers in the Netherlands. Menasseh unambiguously rejected original sin, as he must, having taken on the role of explicator of Jewish doctrine to the gentiles. His desire to find common ground between Judaism and Christianity could take him only so far. Just as Menasseh's commitment to freedom of the will led him to argue against predestination in *De Termino Vitae*, so it forced him to place the ultimate responsibility for sin on each individual. Still—and this is the most he was willing to concede to the Christian camp—human weakness is such that all people, even the most virtuous, do, at some point, commit a sin.

Jewish thinkers long struggled to reconcile astral or natural determinism with free will.[48] They generally agreed that the stars and planets are not without their effects on bodies and minds in this world. But, with a few exceptions, they did not think that such influence ruled out the human capacity for making free and uncoerced choices. Freedom from external constraint was the only way to preserve moral responsibility and divine justice. Menasseh fully concurred with this philosophical position.

The view defended in *De la Fragilidad Humana* is that the human being is, by his nature, "inclined to vice." Menasseh followed the rabbinic tradition according to which every individual is endowed from birth with two basic urges: *yetzer ha-tov*, or the inclination toward good, and *yetzer ha-ra*, the inclination toward evil. In the Garden of Eden, Adam originally had perfect control, through reason, over all of his passions and urges; he always and naturally chose what was good. But after Adam's sin, the human power over the evil inclination was weakened. The rational side of human nature was no longer able to resist the desires generated by the baser urge. This is the "fragility" of human nature. "It is impossible," he wrote, "for God, if he considers the entirety of human actions, to find a human being who is totally innocent. . . . Everyone naturally sins."[49] There never has been, and never will be, a person so just, so on his guard, so chaste and so humble that he has never committed a sin—even if the sin has been done by accident, by ignorance, or just in thought.

This does not mean, however, that a person is determined or destined to sin, much less that sin is inherited. Rather, human nature, corrupted by the matter in which it is embedded, is weak, and so a person will be led to sin, albeit through his own free choice. The will is inclined but not constrained to a vicious action by the evil urge and its concupiscent desires.

Menasseh cited a wealth of textual material—from a variety of religious traditions and philosophical orientations—to support his account: Scripture, rabbinic authority, medieval Jewish thinkers and kabbalah, of course, but also Plato, Aristotle, Cicero, Renaissance humanists such as Giovanni Pico della Mirandola and Marsilio Ficino, Machiavelli, and even Christian theologians like Augustine, Jerome, Origen, and Thomas Aquinas. (It is telling, and somewhat remarkable, that this rabbi referred to Church Fathers as "our theologians.") All these authorities agree, according to Menasseh, that we are not born sinners; but they also confirm that no one reaches the end of his life without ever having sinned.[50]

Most people do end up choosing, freely and through their

own natural powers, to do some good. Menasseh absolutely rejected the rigorous Calvinist doctrine of grace, where no human
being can possibly act well without God's aid.

> While a human being can be contaminated by all these
> causes, that is, a harmful planet, a deranged temperament,
> the region of his habitation, still, {the human will is not, for
> all that, determined with necessity, such that it succumbs
> always to sin}. Man can nevertheless overcome all these ob-
> stacles, acquire knowledge and virtue, and conquer nature
> through his effort alone.[51]

However, for salvation in the world-to-come it is not sufficient to have performed virtuous actions, even if they constitute the majority of what one does in this life. One must also
repent for one's evil actions. Everyone will have to undergo
some period of punishment in hell (*infierno*), since everyone
sins and a just God not only rewards virtue and the perfor-
mance of *mitzvot* but also punishes wickedness. "Hell is destined for the purgation of sins and the punishment is propor-
tionate to their quality and quantity. Then, once these have
been purged, the souls ascend to paradise to receive the reward
for their works."[52] (In a later work, the *Sefer Nishmat Hayyim*,
he clarified that in order to attain a place in the world-to-come
one need not observe *all* six hundred and thirteen commandments of Torah; indeed, it is enough to observe just one *mitzvah*, as long as one does it "with love"—with all one's heart and
all one's soul.)[53]

Menasseh was willing to concede to Christians that there is
such a thing as "divine grace," but it is not some unearned gift.
On the contrary, it is entirely deserved, since it is simply that
additional support and opportunity that God provides to the
virtuous for the good works that they have already freely undertaken. Once a person begins to accomplish a *mitzvah* or pious
deed, God helps this person to achieve his goal and thereby

sustains him in his virtue. Citing the kabbalistic treatise *Reshit Hokhma* (The Beginning of Wisdom), Menasseh noted that "just as, when a man is in the process of lifting up a burden and cannot do it, there comes along another person to help put it on his shoulders, so when someone begins a good action and encounters material difficulties in completing it, God helps him so that he brings his action to its end."[54]

Menasseh was perfectly aware that "the Hebrews treat this matter of grace or aid very differently from the Greeks and Latins."[55] So were his Dutch Calvinist readers. None would have been surprised that a Jewish author would reject their views on free will and the necessity of divine grace.[56] But that did not stop the more conservative Reformed theologians from seeing Menasseh as lending support to the Remonstrant cause. In the eyes of some, the book on human weakness was an Arminian treatise and deserved to be censured as such.[57]

The two members of Talmud Torah delegated to review Menasseh's book and who gave it their approval at the end of May—Daniel de Caceres and Aaron Sarphati—were friends of his. They were certainly impressed by what they read. One can easily imagine, though, that the members of the *ma'amad* themselves were not so happy to see Menasseh once again confronting orthodox Reformed theology in such a direct way.

Nor would they have been pleased to learn that Menasseh was engaged in debates with Christians. Beelthouwer's visits in the early 1640s to Montalto's home and to the synagogue to discuss matters of Hebrew grammar and the interpretation of the Bible were not motivated by pure scholarly curiosity. After all, the title of the book in which he told (in Dutch) of his discussions with Menasseh and others is *Schildt der Christenen Tegen alle On-Christenen* (A Shield for Christians Against All Non-Christians). These were disputations—and quite public ones, as Beelthouwer kept reminding his reader that the conversations were "within earshot" of "a crowd" of other congregants. The Collegiant was out to refute the Jews, if not convert them. (The heading of one of the chapters is "Refutation of the Jews That Their Books But Not Ours Are from God.") His goal with Menasseh and Leão was to show them that the Hebrew text of the Bible supports the Christian messianic reading of the "Old Testament." In his query regarding the passage from Zechariah, Beelthouwer was trying to find in the prophet a reference to Judas's betrayal of Christ, despite having been told that that would be impossible, given when Zechariah was writing. Among the other topics they covered was whether any of the words used by Jews to refer to God could also be read as referring to the Son of God, the Messiah, thus confirming the identity of God and Jesus.[58]

By engaging Beelthouwer as he did—and openly, in the synagogue!—Menasseh had really crossed a line. He was violating not only the Jewish community's regulation forbidding theological discussions with gentiles, but a condition laid down by the Amsterdam authorities in 1616 when they officially permitted the Sephardim to settle in the city.[59] The municipal regents made it perfectly clear that the Jews "were not to speak or write anything (and to ensure that nothing is spoken or written) that may, in any way, tend to the disparagement of our Christian religion." The Portuguese Jews were still very sensitive as to how they were perceived by their Dutch hosts, and their insecurities made them quick to punish those whom they believed, rightly or wrongly, to be putting their residence in Amsterdam at risk. It is somewhat surprising that Menasseh did not receive another *herem* for his disputations with Beelthouwer.

Menasseh, however, had more pressing matters on his mind in the mid-1640s than the annoyance of the *ma'amad*. Family finances continued to be a worry, especially with the failure of his Brazil enterprise. And now it seemed that even his printing business was in trouble.

Over the next seven years, until the end of the decade, Menasseh's press put out a slow but steady trickle of books—about a dozen in all, mostly in Hebrew and Spanish, including two editions of the Mishnah, a Rashi commentary, and an edition of the commentary on the Book of Daniel by his wife's presumed ancestor, Isaac Abrabanel. The catalogue now also included works in Yiddish, a natural move given the significant increase in immigration to Amsterdam by Jews from eastern Europe. These Ashkenazim represented not only an expansion of the local clientele, but, as Yiddish speakers, a pool of potential typesetters and correctors in that language. When in 1644 Menasseh's firm published the *Mizmor leTodah* by David ben Menachem Hacohen, a rhymed compilation of Bible stories and the first Yiddish book printed in Amsterdam, the compositors were Reuben bar Elyakim and Joseph ben Alexander of Witzenhausen.

Conspicuously absent from the publication list, though, are works in Latin. Perhaps the *parnassim* made it clear that they did not want books in that language—especially books that might offend orthodox Calvinists—coming from their community. Or it may have something to do with the fact that the business was no longer being run by Menasseh himself. In 1643, for reasons that remain obscure, Menasseh had turned the press over to another member of the community, Elijah Aboab. Was it a matter of financial exigency, with Menasseh no longer having the resources to subsidize projects? Did Menasseh simply decide to take a break from publishing, given all the other demands on his time? Or was it an involuntary sabbatical? Given the *ma'amad*'s concerns over Menasseh's activities as printer, especially in the wake of *De la Fragilidad Humana*, it is conceivable that the *parnassim* ordered him to stop publishing, at least for a while.[60] Menasseh did manage to stay involved, serving as editor and corrector for a number of books published by Aboab, including Hacohen's Yiddish text. And the deal with

Aboab was not a permanent arrangement, since in 1646 the business was back in the family, now under the management of Menasseh's son Joseph.[61]

Among the volumes with Aboab's imprint was Menasseh's own *Thesouro dos Dinim* (Treasury of Laws). A five-part work in Portuguese—published between 1645 and 1647—whose subtitle indicates that these are the laws "which the people of Israel are obliged to know and observe," the *Thesouro* was meant to be accessible to as broad an audience in the Amsterdam Sephardic community as possible. It offered a summary of the most important tenets of Judaism and the commandments of the Torah, and was essentially a practical guide to a halakhic Jewish life (and death) for new Jews. Part 1 of the *Thesouro* is devoted to blessings and prayers, and Part 2 to "moral precepts of the Divine Law." These included one's duties and obligations in the community (including charity to the poor and the redemption of captives), the synagogue, school, business and legal affairs, the home, the cemetery, and the street. Part 3 covers the observance of the Sabbath—including the lighting of candles and saying kiddush—and the festivals throughout the year. Part 4 presents the Jewish dietary laws, with a rundown of permitted and forbidden foods. There are separate chapters on butter and cheese, fruits, wine, "beer and other liquors," and many other items; a special section at the end is reserved for a "Treatise on Meat with Milk." The final part of the work, titled *Economica* and which Menasseh addressed specially to "the very noble and most honest women of your Portuguese nation," provides specific directions on demeanor, on marriage and conjugal relations (including instructions for men on their duties as husbands and fathers), and how to keep a kosher home.

There are few aspects of communal and private life not covered in the more than eight hundred *in-octo* pages of Menasseh's "treasury." As an aid for new converso arrivals from Iberia who needed to leave their old ways behind—including whatever "Jewish" practices they may have been following in a corrupt form for generations—and adapt to the Judaism being observed in Amsterdam (or Venice or Hamburg or Salonika), the *Thesouro* is arguably his most significant accomplishment as a congregational rabbi.

While Menasseh might have stepped away from printing and publishing, at least for the time being, he remained an active bookseller, even expanding the business into new markets. His clients now extended across Europe, from the British Isles to Poland and down to Venice and Rome. Menasseh dealt almost exclusively in Hebrew Judaica. A catalogue of his inventory that he put together in 1648—the first catalogue ever by a Jewish bookseller, and intended for prospective non-Jewish customers—is divided into two parts.[62] First, there are Hebrew books in a variety of editions and formats—Bibles, Pentateuchs and related items, including anthologies of the prophets and commentaries on particular biblical books; Talmuds, *midrashim* and other rabbinic writings; prayer books and liturgical companions; books of Hebrew poetry, philosophy, history, science, and "morals"; and grammars and dictionaries. It is a remarkable list of more than five hundred volumes. The second part of the catalogue contains books in Hebrew and Spanish that were printed by Menasseh himself. This much shorter list contains some of his own writings, including the Latin translations of the *Conciliador, De la Resurreccion,* and *De la Fragilidad Humana.*

Menasseh was still working out of his home in the Nieuwe Houtmarkt. The rooms must have been overflowing with books and other printed matter, making things tight for him and Rachel. (Their daughter Hannah had married her cousin Samuel Abrabanel—the son of Menasseh's sister Esther and his business partner/brother-in-law Jonah Abrabanel—in 1646 and was no longer living at home. Neither were their sons, Joseph and Samuel, now in their twenties, although both were involved in

Menasseh's publishing and bookselling business.) Thus, in April 1648, Menasseh submitted a request to the Amsterdam municipal authorities for permission to open a bookshop in which he could sell his wares. The response from the burgemeesters was short and definitive: "The request by Menasseh ben Israel to be able to open here in the city a shop for Hebrew books is judged to be denied and refused."[63] No reason was given for the rejection of Menasseh's request. It could have been personal—not unlike their refusal to allow him to teach in the Athenaeum— because of his known connections with Remonstrants and other unorthodox types. Or it could have been related to the edict enacted in 1632 that not only forbade Jews to engage in businesses governed by guilds but also excluded them from owning and operating open shops.[64]

Without a storefront of his own, Menasseh had to continue bookselling primarily by post and special orders. Besides his Jewish customers in Sephardic and Ashkenazic communities, there was the ever growing clientele among gentile intellectuals. These included celebrated humanist scholars (and old friends) like Grotius, Saumaise, and members of the Vossius and Huygens clans, but also lesser academics, clergy, politicians, and diplomats. Even ordinary businessmen with an interest in letters (including Hebrew texts and Judaic literature), the gentleman-scholars known in contemporary Dutch circles as *mercatores sapientes* ("wise merchants"), were familiar with his catalogue. In the summer of 1645, the wealthy Amsterdam *mercator* Isaac Coymans, who himself employed Menasseh's services, wrote to the Dordrecht pastor and scholar André Colvius to update him on a shipment of books from Menasseh that Colvius had been expecting and that was overdue.[65] Menasseh had not kept either client abreast of where the books were or when they were coming, but Coymans reassured Colvius that they would soon arrive.[66]

Among other new acquaintances and clients in the non-

Jewish world was the Frenchman Samuel Sorbière. A physician and philosopher, as well as a devoté and translator of the radical English philosopher Thomas Hobbes, Sorbière was one of those independent and eclectic minds—known to their contemporaries as *savants* or *érudits*—that flourished in the seventeenth-century Republic of Letters. Wherever he happened to be based—Paris, Amsterdam, London—Sorbière remained the center of an impressive literary network, facilitating correspondence among a diverse and widely dispersed cast of scholars.

Sorbière got to know Menasseh when he was residing in the Netherlands in the early 1640s. Even a man of his sophistication and cosmopolitan experience could not shake off the prejudices of the age. He was fascinated by the fact that such "a wise man" as Menasseh, with all his learning (and not just in rabbinics), could remain committed to a religion such as Judaism. Sorbière—who was born a Protestant but would later convert to Catholicism—was especially interested in what, if anything, bothered Menasseh about Christianity. They also talked about the remarkable persistence of the Jewish people throughout history despite constantly residing among enemies. Their survival, Sorbière noted, was "just like that bush surrounded by fire"—the bush that Moses saw that was "on fire but not being burned up" (Exodus 3:2).[67]

In his memoirs, Sorbière recalled that Menasseh, with whom he would visit the homes of mutual friends, was careful not to let his socializing with gentiles lead him to violate Jewish restrictions on food and drink. Once, when Menasseh was with Sorbière, Vossius, Barlaeus, and Episcopius during the time of Passover, he was offered a cup of wine. However, "he [Menasseh] excused himself because the cup, having also served for a drink of beer, might still contain some residue with atoms of leaven."[68] Sorbière found Jewish laws, and especially Menasseh's strict observance of them even in a relaxed setting of mixed company, an endless source of puzzlement.

For a rabbi, Menasseh was keeping some very interesting company indeed.

A bookdealer in the seventeenth century could not rely on random incoming orders alone. It was important for Menasseh to reach out to buyers and sellers. In 1649, he sent his older son Joseph off to Poland. Previously a teaching assistant in Talmud Torah's Ets Haim seminary, Joseph had taken over the printing operations from Elijah Aboab three years earlier. His mission in Poland was both to unload books from the firm's catalogue and acquire new books to sell. Joseph settled in Lublin, the site of an annual Hebrew book fair held in conjunction with a yearly convention of Jewish delegates from all over the Polish kingdom.[69]

It was not the first time that Menasseh had sent Joseph eastward on a book-buying and selling mission. A previous trip took him to Danzig, and although Menasseh worried greatly about his son's fate when the ship on which he was traveling was delayed coming back to Amsterdam, he returned safely. This time, however, tragedy did strike. Shortly after his arrival in Lublin, Joseph took ill. He died just a few days later.[70]

This was a tremendous blow to Menasseh. He may have felt some responsibility for his son's death, since it was his idea for Joseph to go to Poland in the first place. Beyond the deep personal loss, this also represented a major financial setback. The inventory that Joseph brought on this trip and any books he might have acquired while in Poland were now lost. With this, on top of the deterioration of whatever trade Menasseh was still carrying on in Brazil, he was once again in serious money trouble. Writing just a year or so later, in March 1651, he told Isaac Vossius that he was unable to afford certain publishing projects he was hoping to undertake—including a Bible that, he insisted, would be "of great use to all of Europe" and a complete Talmud that he was certain "there is no library in Europe that will not want to buy." The problem, he said, was that, "as you know, . . . my capital has been lost in Brazil and Poland with my son."[71]

This probably explains why, in 1650, Menasseh decided to sell a portion of his type to a Hebraic scholar named Christian Ravius. It could not have been easy to part with those pieces that he had ordered to be made specially for him by Nicolas Briot, way back in 1626, and with which he started the most important Hebrew press in Europe. But compared to the loss he had just suffered, it was nothing—just another concession to his unhappy fate.

6

The Hope of Israel

In the fall of 1644, a foreign traveler arrived in the Vlooienburg quarter with a very strange tale to tell about a faraway land.[1]

Antonio Montezinos—also known as Aaron Levi—was a converso from Villaflor, Portugal. In early 1642, he went to South America. Once there, he was conducted by a group of "Indians" led by a chief named Francisco into the mountains of the province of Quito, in New Spain (now Ecuador).[2] During the journey, Montezinos heard one of his escorts talk about "God's holy people" who lived nearby and whom the Indians had mistreated over the years. His curiosity was piqued, but he learned nothing further at the time and continued his travels. When he arrived in Cartagena, he was interrogated by the Inquisition and imprisoned for some months on the charge of Judaizing. However, the tribunal did not find sufficient evidence to convict him (despite the fact that the accusation was true), and he was eventually released.

While in prison, Montezinos reflected on what the Indians had been saying about a holy people in their territory, and began to wonder whether "the Hebrews might be the Indians." He returned to Quito, found Francisco, and asked him to lead him back to the mountains. On their way, Montezinos made what, within Spanish imperial dominions, was a brave, possibly reckless confession:

> Now when they were got out of the city, Montezinos confessed himself to be a Hebrew, of the tribe of Levi, and that the Lord was his God; and he told the Indian that all other gods were but mockeries. The Indian being amazed, asked him the name of his parents. He answered Abraham, Isaac and Jacob.[3]

Upon learning this, Francisco told Montezinos to follow him. After an arduous journey of more than a week, they came to a river. "Here," Francisco said, "you shall see your brethren." The guide then signaled to the other side of the river. Three men and a woman appeared out of the forest and came over in a boat. After Francisco spoke to the strangers and told them about Montezinos, two of the men approached the Portuguese visitor and recited, in Hebrew, the *Shema*, the central prayer of the Jewish liturgy from Deuteronomy 6 ("Hear O Israel, the Lord our God, the Lord is one"). They then told him that "our fathers are Abraham, Isaac, Jacob and Israel," and claimed to be descendants of Reuben.

Over the next couple of days, Montezinos had some difficulty getting further information from the men as to who they were and how they knew Hebrew and the Jewish prayer. Growing frustrated, he tried to reach the shore from which they came, but after a failed attempt (and nearly drowning) he was told in no uncertain terms that he was not to cross the river or "enquire more than we tell you." For the rest of the week, different men continued to appear on the distant shore and come over to where Montezinos was camped and repeat the exact same things that the first group had told him.

> There came and went about three hundred. These men are somewhat scorched by the sun, some of them wear their hair long, down to their knees, others of them shorter, and others of them much as we commonly cut it. They were comely of body, well accoutered, having ornaments on their feet and legs, and their heads were compassed about with a linen cloth.[4]

When there were no more interviews to be had, Montezinos asked Francisco to tell him what he knew about these people. The Indian replied, "Your brethren are the sons of Israel, and brought there by the providence of God, who for their sake wrought many miracles." Francisco's people had waged war against the tribe across the river several times, but always lost badly. In light of their inability to defeat these people, they concluded that "the God of those Children of Israel is the true God." From Montezinos's report, it appears that Francisco's people now saw themselves as "Hebrews" as well.

When Montezinos came to Amsterdam in 1644, he went straight to the Portuguese-Jewish community and, meeting with "the chiefs of the Portuguese nation"—the *parnassim*— told them about what he had found in the mountains of South America. Menasseh ben Israel recorded his story, and later added his certification that "the author Monterinos [*sic*] is a virtuous man and separate from all manner of worldly interests; and that he swore in my presence that all which he declared was a truth."[5] Because Montezinos was "a Portuguese and a Jew of our order . . . why should I not believe a man that was virtuous and having all that which men call gain?"[6]

In the sixteenth and early seventeenth centuries, following reports from European explorers on the people they encountered in the New World, speculation flourished among theologians as to where the native inhabitants of the Americas fit in the scope of biblical history. Were they, too, descendants of Adam and Eve, perhaps remnants of European peoples who had long ago migrated across the ocean? Grotius thought so, suggesting that their ancestors were the Vikings. The French Huguenot Isaac La Peyrère, on the other hand, thought that their lineage went back to a race of "pre-Adamites," people whom, he claimed, God created before he made Adam and Eve.[7]

The wondrous report of Montezinos only fueled these debates. Knowledge of his testimony before the *ma'amad* was for some years limited to those who heard it first-hand from Montezinos himself—not just the *parnassim* but anyone he might have spoken with during his sojourn in Amsterdam—or through word of mouth. A transcribed version did not appear in print until 1650. However, even foreign gentile visitors to the Jewish neighborhood of Amsterdam during the 1640s were able to glean rumors about a man who had encountered "Jews in America." This, at least, is how an Englishman named John Dury first came across Montezinos's tale.

Dury, a Calvinist minister from Scotland, had spent his childhood in the Netherlands, where his Presbyterian clergyman father was in exile. He reported that when he was on a return visit to the Low Countries, around 1644, he heard talk of "a Jew who came from America to Amsterdam" and who claimed to have met and conversed with Israelites in the New World.[8] Dury does not say who told him about Montezinos, but it was almost certainly Menasseh, whom he got to know while in Holland and whom he later asked for a written copy of the traveler's deposition. The story made a strong impression on Dury. Just a few years later, in 1648, when his friend Thomas Thorowgood asked him to read the page proofs of his forthcoming book *Jewes in America, Or, Probabilities that the Americans*

Are of that Race, it began to dawn on him that this discovery in the New World might have enormous significance. For Thorowgood had connected the question of the genealogy of the Indians of America with another mystery of biblical proportions.

According to Hebrew Scripture, in the late eighth century BCE, King Shalmaneser of Assyria "captured Samaria and deported its people to Assyria and settled them in Halah and on the Habor, the river of Gozan, and in the cities of Media . . . the Lord banished the Israelites from his presence, as he had threatened through his servants the prophets, and they were carried into exile from their own land to Assyria" (II Kings 17:6, 23). Shalmaneser "took them [several of the Israelite tribes] away into a strange country."[9] Only the people of Judah and Benjamin were left behind in the Promised Land.

By the mid-seventeenth century, the enigma of these "Lost Tribes" had long inspired a host of historical conjecture and theological speculation. What became of them? Where were they now? What would it mean if they should reappear?

Thorowgood did not know of Montezinos's adventure until Dury told him about it, well after he had finished writing his book.[10] But he knew where the missing tribes were. "There hath bin a common tradition among Jews, and in the world, that those ten tribes are utterly lost; in what place are they then like to be found if not in *America?*"[11] In his treatise, whose purpose was to stir up financial support for the missionary efforts of John Eliot in the New World, Thorowgood argued that the "Indians" in America were Jews—and not just any Jews, but the Ten Lost Tribes.

Reading all this in Thorowgood's pages was a stunning revelation to Dury. He then recalled what he had heard during his visit to Holland four years earlier and put it together with the prophecies of the Christian Gospels. He said that he initially found Thorowgood's thesis "strange and unlikely to have any truth in it." But, he told Thorowgood, as he reflected on the fact that

> all the Tribes of Israel shall be called to the knowledge of Jesus Christ, before the end of the world: and when I had recollected and laid together some other scattered and confused thoughts which at several times I have received, partly from the places of Scripture, which foretell the calling of the Jewes, and their restitution to their owne land, together with the bringing back of the ten Tribes from all the ends and corners of the earth ... I was so far from derogating anything from that which you have conjectured concerning the American Indians; that I beganne to stand amazed at the appearances of the probabilities which so many waies offered themselves unto me, to make out and confirme the effect of that which you have said.[12]

It was Dury who linked the reported recent discovery of "sons of Israel" in America with Thorowgood's hypothesis about the Ten Tribes and then placed it all in an eschatological framework.[13] He saw a connection between tales of heretofore unknown Jews living as a nation in distant lands and the ultimate destiny of humankind. The reappearance of the Israelite captives, if true, would herald the coming of a New Kingdom.

Dury was particularly interested in hearing a Jewish take on all this news, so he decided to inquire of the one person who he was certain could give him an informed opinion—someone who could even, perhaps, speak on behalf of Judaism itself. "Because I was not satisfied in some things, and desired to know how farre the whole matter was believed among the Jewes at Amsterdam, I wrote to Menasseh ben Israel, their cheife Rabbi [sic], about it, and his answer I have gotten in two letters."[14]

Dury was not the only Englishman seeking Menasseh's insight on the missing Hebrews at this time. While he was corresponding with Menasseh in the summer of 1649, two other theologians, Nathaniel Homes and Henry Jessey, also wrote to the Amsterdam rabbi to see what light he could shed on Jewish beliefs about the gathering of the exiles. These Puritans, possibly inspired by what Dury might have told them about Montezinos's story and his letters from Menasseh, wanted to know how to put together the news about the Lost Tribes with biblical prophecies about the coming of the Messiah.[15]

Whatever messianic portents Menasseh may have found in Montezinos's tale and legends about the Lost Tribes—and he was at first unaware that they had any such significance—would necessarily be quite different from what his Protestant friends saw. Menasseh, always seeking common ground with his Christian interlocutors, was unsure how to respond to Dury and Homes. He had to walk a very fine line between encouraging them and not conceding too much. The debate over the meaning of the discovery of the "Jews in America" really put his ecumenical instincts and diplomatic skills to the test.

Samuel Hartlib was German by birth, but he moved to England as a young man to study at Cambridge University. Like Menasseh's friends Vossius and Sorbière—like Menasseh himself—he was the center of a diverse (and dispersed) learned circle within the Republic of Letters. While Hartlib was, by profession, more a philosopher and scientist than theologian, a deep religious feeling and sense of mission informed much of his intellectual activity. He was a close and credulous reader of the Hebrew Bible and Christian Gospels, which he saw as a source not only of spiritual and moral inspiration but also of historical prognosis. Inspired by events over the previous century—the Reformation, the Thirty Years War, discoveries in the New World, various celestial phenomena—and numerological reckoning by latter-day prophets, Hartlib, too, was eagerly anticipating the (second) coming of the Messiah.

Dury, Homes, Jessey, and Hartlib were but a small cohort

within an international lobby of religiously like-minded individuals who firmly believed that although this momentous event was imminent, it would not happen until one very important and necessary condition was met: the conversion of the Jews. These "Millenarians"—so called because of their belief, inspired by the Book of Revelation, that the Last Judgment would be preceded in *this* world by Christ's Thousand-Year (millennial) reign over a restored Kingdom of Israel—whether they were based in England, Holland, or Germany, thus saw it as their calling to do what they could to promote that conversion.[16] In treatises, correspondence, and personal encounters they sought to spread the Good News (*Bonum Nuncium*) to the Jewish people and convince them that the time to acknowledge Jesus Christ as their Savior was near. Success in this endeavor, though, would require much preparatory work: educating Christians about Judaism, so that they might better engage Jews in debate, and teaching Jews about Christianity, making it more palatable to them and opening their eyes to the truth of the New Testament. In a 1642 pamphlet, Dury and Hartlib stressed the importance of making "Christianity lesse offensive, and more known, unto the Jews, then now it is, and the Jewish State and Religion as now it standeth more knowne unto Christians." They thought it to be "a special part of the endeavors of Protestant Reformation, to perfect within themselves that part of knowledge and learning, which is necessary to prepare a way for their [the Jews'] conversion."[17]

This educational project—if not its conversionist goal—would necessarily require Jewish partners. To this end, Dury and Adam Boreel, the leader of the Collegiants in Amsterdam and a friend of Menasseh's, collaborated with one of the Talmud Torah rabbis, Jacob Judah Leão, on an edition of the Mishnah to be published in both Hebrew (with vowels, for easy reading) and Latin.[18] These volumes, Dury told Hartlib, were intended to be accessible to "the common sort of Jews" so that they "might know what the Constitution of their religion is, and also that the learned sort of Christians upon the same discoveries might be able to deale with them for their conviction."[19] This Mishnah was, in other words, aimed at two distinct audiences, to be used by one as an instrument of conversion on the other. Boreel was told by Rabbi Leão, however, that if he wanted the work actually to be read by Jews, it should not have any Christian's name on it.[20] Thus, the title page of the Hebrew *Mishnayot* that appeared in 1646 did not make any mention of its gentile co-editors. It was published by Joseph ben Israel, and contained a preface by his father.[21]

That same year, Dury and Hartlib were hatching a plan to create a College of Judaic Studies in England. Far from being devoted to the disinterested academic study of Judaism, this institution, envisioned as part of a greater University of London, was to be tailored for the "conversions or correspondency of Jews."[22] The curriculum would consist in the study of "Oriental tongues" (Hebrew and two Aramaic dialects: Syriac and Chaldean) and the "Jewish mysteries." Christian students would thus gain a facility in communicating with Jews and engaging them on their own textual and theological turf.[23] (Naturally, there would be no Jewish students in this school.) Although the college never became a reality, it seems that Menasseh was among those whom Hartlib and Dury envisioned recruiting for the school's faculty. What his role there would have been remains unclear.

The outreach to the Jews, and to Menasseh in particular, by men like Dury, Homes, Hartlib, Jessey, and Thorowgood in England; Boreel and his fellow Collegiant Peter Serrarius in Holland; and the German mystics Paul Felgenhauer, Johannes Mochinger, and Abraham von Frankenberg—who wrote, a bit unfairly, that "Menasseh contributes not a little to the exit of the Israelites and the entry of the Gentiles"—has often led to their being called "philo-Semites."[24] But this is very misleading.

Christian conversionist efforts might have been motivated somewhat by a sincere and heartfelt concern for the well-being—the
eternal well-being—of the Jewish people and a sense of shared
hopes. Serrarius, for one, enjoyed warm personal relations with
Menasseh and insisted that

> what Jews and Christians are now anticipating so keenly is
> the appearance of the true Messiah in the glory of God. . . .
> We must show them love and respect because of the inheri-
> tance which was promised to them, and was, through grace,
> bestowed on us by the Lord Jesus, who is their Messiah and
> ours.[25]

The English and Dutch Millenarians, many of whom suffered
harassment, and worse, at the hands of the more orthodox factions of their denominations, were also generally more given
to religious toleration. They saw the Jews in their midst as an
opportunity, not a problem. In the end, though, their promotion of the study of Judaism and their friendly relationships
with individual Jews, however genuine, were ultimately in the
service of seeing them become Christians, and thus of abetting
the disappearance of their ancient religion.

Menasseh had no problem with serving as the Jewish contact for the Millenarian camp. As a teacher and a promoter of
interfaith understanding, he was more than happy to engage
with these messianic Protestants and find points of agreement.[26]
After all, many Jews of the time were likewise feverishly anticipating the arrival of the Messiah—especially Sephardic Jews,
who continued to mourn the catastrophe of their expulsions
from Spain and Portugal and who found comfort in various
kabbalistic divinations about the world-to-come. Menasseh also
saw these dialogues with relatively well-disposed Christians as
an occasion for building good will toward the Jewish people. As
much as Christians were awaiting the conversion of the Jews,
so were Jews on the lookout for signs of Christian benevolence

and an acknowledgment of their appointed role in the unfolding of God's providential plan.

Menasseh was a most tolerant man. He allowed that under the true Messiah there would be a place in the world-to-come for the righteous of all nations. As someone who was widely regarded by gentiles as the spokesman for the Jewish world, he felt an obligation to play along with the Millenarians and try to minimize the differences between their theological views.[27] However, he was not going to abandon the fundamental tenets of Judaism. Menasseh's messianic agenda certainly did not include the conversion of his people.

When, in the summer of 1649, Nathaniel Homes first pressed Menasseh for his views on what the purported discovery of the Ten Tribes in America meant in the grand scheme of things, Menasseh professed ignorance. As Homes later reminded him, "regarding the timing of the coming of the Messiah, you said you were uncertain."[28] It is not that Menasseh lacked an eschatological vision. Several of his works up to this point—the *Conciliador, De la Resurreccion, De la Fragilidad*—presented a fairly clear picture of what the world-to-come holds in store. When the Messiah arrives, the Temple in Jerusalem will be rebuilt and the gathered Israelites will enjoy "peace and tranquility" in the Holy Land.[29]

Still, Menasseh was not at this time seeing any connections between contemporary world events and the messianic era, and he was definitely not drawn to wondering when that "future world" would appear. He had not, in fact, given much thought at all to Montezinos's report since he first heard the adventurer's testimony. As far as we know, the converso explorer's American encounter did not even come up in a series of conversations that Menasseh had in the winter of 1647 with a Portuguese Jesuit who happened to be visiting Amsterdam, despite the fact that their talk focused on messianic themes and the return of the Ten Tribes.

It seems to have been a real meeting of minds—in the synagogue and over drinks in a tavern—with a bit of agreeing to disagree. Menasseh and Father Antonio Vieira, a confessor to the king of Portugal who had a genuine sympathy for the Jewish people, found that their religious traditions were in accord on some essential points regarding the return of the exiles—it would be "triumphal"—and the redemptive role of the Messiah.[30] Vieira was aware that there were also irreconcilable differences, among them the "errors" of the Jews that the Messiah is not the son of God and that he has not yet in fact come. "The Messiah in which the Jews believe is very different from the Messiah in whom we Christians believe."[31] For just this reason, though, Vieira told the Inquisition when he returned to Portugal, he was convinced—by Menasseh—that the Christian view according to which the Messiah has already come does not rule out the Jewish view that their Messiah has yet to come. There may just be two Messiahs!

Even the wide-ranging conversations with Vieira, though, seem not to have fully opened Menasseh's eyes to the import of Montezinos's discovery. It would be very strange indeed if Menasseh did not say anything about the story to Vieira, although the Jesuit does not mention it in his testimony about their conversations to the Lisbon authorities. If Menasseh did introduce the subject, he did not make much of it. It had not yet occurred to him that the discovery of Jews in the New World might be an indication that the Messiah's arrival was imminent. Even the correspondence with Homes in the summer of 1649 did nothing to move his thoughts in that direction.

However, a lot can happen in six months. Later that year, with Dury, Homes, and Jessey all asking him for his opinion on the Millenarian implications of finding lost Jews among the

American natives—and with Homes even suggesting that Menasseh go back and read the prophecies of Daniel—the rabbi's own messianic convictions were awakened. He was starting to put two and two together. On November 25, he wrote back to Dury saying that he now had a response to the Englishman's queries, but a mere exchange of letters would no longer do the trick. "What I was hoping to complete in a page or so has grown into a complete treatise."[32]

The book that Menasseh ended up writing to satisfy the curiosity of his Christian friends would prove to be the most influential of all his works. He called it *Miqveh Yisrael, Esto es, Esperança de Israel,* after a verse in the prophet Jeremiah: "O hope of Israel, their savior in time of trouble" (14:8). It was published in Spanish and Latin in January of 1650, and in an English translation, *The Hope of Israel,* later that year.[33]

In *The Hope of Israel,* Menasseh finally confronted the meaning of Montezinos's discovery. If there were indeed Jews in the Americas—and on that point Menasseh was inclined to believe Montezinos, with whom "I talked in conversation for the six months that he lived here"—then deliverance must be near at hand.[34] But that left open the question of who these American Jews were and where they came from.

Menasseh accepted the claim of Montezinos that some of the Ten Tribes were the "first inhabitants" of America, but he did not believe that *all* of the lost Jews ended up there. Nor, contrary to Thorowgood, did he think that the Indians (the term he used was *Indias*) now in America bore any relationship to those Jewish tribes that did settle there. While "the Spaniards living in the Indies on the whole consider that the Indians have their origin in the Ten Tribes, they are clearly wrong."[35]

His preferred theory was that the ancient Israelites, "being conquered at several times," were then "carried into several places." Besides Europe, some were taken to China or other Asian lands, some to Ethiopia, some to the Levant, and some to the West Indies and the Americas. What was plausible, he noted, and what Montezinos's testimony strongly suggested, was that "Sons of Israel" who ended up in Tartary (central Asia) eventually made their way across the Pacific Ocean (or a land bridge) to South America.[36] What Montezinos found was, in all likelihood, a remnant of the tribe of Reuben that had "hidden itself behind the Cordillera Mountains." They were forced there by the Indians that had migrated from the Indies to the American continent and "made war upon those inhabitants the Israelites, just as formerly the Britons were forced by the Saxons into Wales."[37] (As for the Indians themselves, Menasseh rejected La Peyrère's pre-Adamite theory. The Indians of New Spain and the Caribbean were, like Europeans, descendants of the first man and woman.)

The manifestation of even just a part of one of the Lost Tribes was, Menasseh claimed, of great significance. He quoted Isaiah: "I will bring you seed from the East and will gather you from the West. I will say to the North, give up; and to the South, keep not back; bring my sons from afar, and my daughters from the ends of the earth" (43:5–7). Eventually, the Messiah, descendant of David, will gather *all* twelve tribes "from all quarters of the earth" and bring them to Jerusalem to dwell under his rule in the Fifth Monarchy (the successor to the kingdoms of Babylonia, Persia, Macedonia, and Rome).

Menasseh did not know for certain when all this would happen, and he remained reluctant to speculate. "It is given to no one to know the time thereof . . . the time of the Fifth Monarchy shall be hid until the time when it shall begin."[38] Still, the appearance of Reuben's descendants in New Spain, and the fact that "our synagogues are found in America"—he may have been referring to the Jewish community in Recife—was proof that the tribes are now "scattered through all the corners of the world."

Recent events only added to the mounting body of evidence.

Menasseh took note of the tribulations of Jews in various parts of Europe and elsewhere. He was especially concerned with the continued suffering of conversos in Spain, Portugal, and their colonies.

> What shall we say of that horrible monster, the Spanish Inquisition, what cruelty has not daily been used against a company of miserable ones, innocents, old men and children, of every sex and age, who were slain, because they could not divine who was their secret accuser?[39]

The fate of relatives and friends still living in Iberia—the martyrs burning on the pyres of *autos-da-fé*—was never far from the minds of Amsterdam's Sephardim.

Such evils, Menasseh insisted, could only be signs that "though we cannot exactly show the time of our redemption, yet we judge it to be near."[40] As he said in a letter to Dury just a few weeks before publication, with this new book "I prove by many things that the day of the promised Messiah draws near to us."[41]

Menasseh was nervous that these exchanges with Christian Millenarians over messianic questions—perhaps even the fact that he was engaged in any kind of speculation over the timing of the Messiah's arrival—would unsettle his fellow rabbis and the lay leaders of the Talmud Torah congregation. (The theological conversations with Vieira, in the synagogue no less, would not have pleased the *parnassim*. Vieira also tried to engage Rabbi Mortera in a similar discussion, but Mortera would have none of it.) He was afraid of prying Jewish eyes finding out what was going on—with some justification, since earlier letters had been intercepted and opened. As a postscript to one of his letters to Dury, Menasseh asked the Englishman to send any future correspondence not to him directly but to his friend Johannes Moriaen, a German minister then living in Amsterdam. "There will be less of a danger of them falling into treacherous hands or eyes. For your first ones were not delivered to me; your second ones were delivered, but read by some Jew, I know not who."[42] The level of trust between Menasseh and his community had reached a low point.

Menasseh was fully aware, of course, that the Jews were not in fact "scattered through all the corners of the world." There was still at least one very important place where they were not living, at least officially. His London-based correspondents knew this as well, and they were concerned that until this situation changed, their longed-for Millennium would not arrive. In the 1650s, England and messianism—and the connection between these—would come to dominate Menasseh's interests, for better or for worse.

With the opening of lines of communication with English associates and the publication of *The Hope of Israel*, Menasseh was embarking on the most important project of his life—one that he believed would be of great consequence both for this world and the next. Sadly, he would not be able to see it to completion.

The year 1650 was one of those signature years in the political history of the Dutch Republic. Periodically, and very quickly, the balance of power would get totally turned around. The party that was ruling the major provinces and towns would, all of a sudden, now be on the sidelines while the party that was in opposition assumed control. Typically (but not always) nonviolent, marginally constitutional, such radical changes in governance, called *wetsverzettingen*, were usually occasioned by some crisis: a military defeat, partisan overreach, even doctrinal developments in the Reformed Church. Moreover, the political inversions almost always had corresponding ramifications in the social, cultural, and religious life of the United Provinces.

In 1648, just before eighty years of war with Spain came to

a formal conclusion with the Treaty of Münster, Stadholder Frederik Hendrik, whom Menasseh had so graciously welcomed to the synagogue years before, died. His son, Willem II, Prince of Orange, assumed leadership of the major provinces. The new stadholder was opposed to the peace agreement that his father had forged, but there was little he could do about it. The States of Holland, dominated by the pro-peace regents of Amsterdam, effectively controlled the States General and, thus, the political direction of the Republic.

The end of the war was good news for the Dutch economy, and especially for the Sephardim of Amsterdam. Spain and its colonies, especially in the Caribbean, were now open to Dutch shipping. And while Jewish merchants would have to work under Spanish or Dutch aliases to hide their Jewish identity— the Inquisition did not care about peace treaties—they managed to control a significant portion of the traffic with the Spanish realm. They brought timber and grain from northern Europe to Spanish territories, and in return they imported wine, fruit, raisins, olive oil, and almonds. This went a long way toward making up for the serious decline of the Brazil trade, which suffered as the Portuguese were close to expelling the Dutch from Pernambuco and regaining full control of the province.

The stadholder did not like being overruled by the States on matters of national policy, and was not one to give up easily. Willem II may not have matched his father in charisma, culture, or diplomacy, but he was a sly politician. He was able to drive a wedge between Holland and the other provinces—not just on the question of peace, but on a host of political, economic, and religious matters. He also earned the support of conservative Reformed leaders by backing a measure, opposed by the province of Holland, that excluded Catholics from lands controlled at-large by the States General. Those orthodox Calvinists, in turn, saw in the stadholder someone who would support their campaign against Remonstrants and other dissident sects. Behind these particular issues, however, lay the more general question of what kind of polity the Dutch Republic should be. The States Party, led by Holland and its major towns, favored a federation of quasi-sovereign provinces. The Orangists, on the other hand, looked for a more centralized sovereignty, with supreme authority vested in the States General and the stadholder.

Eventually, things came to a head. After the States of Holland voted to disband a number of units of the Republic's army, Willem and States General troops marched into the province. They received an especially rude welcome in Amsterdam. The stadholder, already inclined not to show leniency toward his enemies and now insulted by this treatment, put the entire city under siege and had the leading regents arrested.

Unfortunately for the Orangist camp, Willem died of smallpox in November 1650. Whatever changes he had tried to impose in Holland did not take root, and by the end of the year Amsterdam and other towns were back in the hands of the regents and their Arminian ecclesiastic allies. Thus began what would end up being a twenty-two year period without a Stadholder, the so-called Era of True Freedom. Political power devolved to the provinces, and by 1653 de facto leadership of the Republic at-large would fall to Johan de Witt, the liberal pensionary of the States of Holland.

With the States Party now effectively running things, the more intolerant elements of the Reformed Church—Voetius and his allies—saw their influence over public policy (and private lives) wane. This was good for dissident sects, especially Remonstrants. It was good for the Republic's economic, social, and cultural life. And it was good for the Jews. In early 1651, a Great Assembly was held in The Hague to discuss, among other things, the issue of religious toleration. During these meetings, the orthodox Calvinists fulminated against Catholics and dissenting or non-Reformed Protestants (especially Lutherans) in the land. But they saved their real venom for those "blasphem-ers against Christ," the Jews, who, they argued, should not be allowed to practice their religion openly. The Assembly made some minor concessions to the Calvinist conservatives, agree-ing that "in the future [unorthodox Reformed or non-Reformed congregations] will not be permitted in any places other than those where they are already practicing." The Jews, on the other hand, were left alone.

While De Witt and his associates may have brought peace and prosperity to the United Provinces and salvation to the Republic's liberal faction, as long as the Messiah had not yet arrived, Menasseh still needed to make a living. And in the ab-sence of a substantial raise in rabbinic salary or in his stipend as director of the Pereyras' yeshiva, this meant publishing and selling books and finding wealthy patrons.

After the death of Joseph ben Israel, his brother Samuel had taken over the family printing business. One of his first projects, in early 1650, was to bring out the Spanish and Latin editions of *The Hope of Israel*. This was followed shortly by sev-eral prayer books in Spanish, and, by the end of the year, the next installment of his father's *Conciliador*.

The effects of Menasseh's conversations with Millenarians and his work on *The Hope of Israel* are evident in this third part of his masterwork. He pays much greater attention to messi-anic themes in quite a few of the biblical passages that he is try-ing to reconcile. Thus, the problem that Menasseh finds with two statements in Haggai 2:9—"The glory of this latter house shall be greater than that of the former says the Lord of Hosts" and "In this place I will give peace, says the Lord of Hosts"—is that if they refer to the building of the Second Temple in the late sixth century BCE, they are hard to square with the fact that during the Second Temple period the Israelites never ceased to see war.[43] "From the building of the Second Temple they en-joyed no rest." Menasseh concludes that "the prophecy properly applies to the Third Temple, whose honor and magnificence will be greater than the First." Only then, under a new Kingdom, will there be peace, "for although the final conflict of Gog and Magog will then take place . . . it will be succeeded by an everlasting peace, as prophesied by all prophets. . . . Just as now, out of devotion, many go to Mecca and Rome, so will the most principal of the noble people who are the desirable and envied of people hasten to Jerusalem."[44]

Samuel also took responsibility for publishing one of only two books that Menasseh wrote directly in Hebrew, the *Sefer Nishmat Hayyim* (The Breath of Life).[45] It is a dense work of philosophy, speculative theology, and biblical exegesis, with Menasseh's typical excess of citations from Greek and Roman antiquity (Galen, Plato, Aristotle), biblical and rabbinic sources, Church Fathers, Muslim theologians, Renaissance and early modern humanists, and Jewish rationalist and mystical authors. In this follow-up to the earlier book on the resurrection of the body, Menasseh once again argues for the soul's natural immortality as a purely spiritual substance, unaffected by the decay that affects bodies. All the souls that will ever exist were created by God on the second day of Creation, when he made light. They were then introduced into human bodies over time. Upon a person's death, the soul will return to the divine realm, although not always directly; it may first have to go through a process of reincarnation, a wandering from body to body referred to as *gilgul* (the Hebrew word means "wheel" or "cycle").[46]

Guided by kabbalistic literature, Menasseh also takes up a number of questions about the supernatural, including demonic possession (as well as sexual relations between demons and living human beings), prophetic dreams, communications with the dead, transmigration of souls, witchcraft, and sorcery. All of these phenomena, purely spiritual in nature, are taken for proof that the soul is something different from and independent of the body.

Menasseh's exploration of mystical topics is not without an eschatological angle. A book on immortality cannot but address the eternal fate of the soul. For the most part, there is little here that he has not already explained in earlier works. There is a future life—he calls it both "paradise" and the "world-to-come"—in which the resurrected of Israel who have observed the Mosaic law, as well as the righteous among the gentiles, their bodies now reunited with their souls, will receive their reward. Those who have not led a life of virtue will be cut off, either for a period of time or forever, depending upon the nature of their sins. Menasseh also added some color to his earlier accounts of what lies in store for the wicked.[47] Although life in the world-to-come for the virtuous is a pleasurable embodied existence, the souls of the vicious will suffer in a rather nasty hell. "For the same god who created the righteous and created the wicked also created paradise (*eden*) and hell (*gehinnom*)."[48] In this eternal inferno, there are seven grades of punishment, for which reason Menasseh feels compelled to explain how a spiritual thing like a soul can nevertheless suffer from something material like fire.[49]

Sales of the new book on immortality were never going to be very large, since it was written in Hebrew and thus aimed at a very particular Jewish audience. Given the level of Hebraic skill among the Amsterdam Sephardim, Menasseh must have known that it would not be widely read in his own community; in fact, it has rarely been cited by Jewish authors.[50] It certainly did not enjoy the popularity of the *Conciliador, The Hope of Israel*, or even the earlier treatise on resurrection. If Menasseh's finances were going to improve, it was not going to be through his work as an author.

What he really needed were some major bookselling deals—even better, perhaps a permanent commission as an official supplier to a wealthy patron. And who better to cultivate as a client than an erudite queen?

Christina Augusta was the daughter of King Gustav Adolphus II of Sweden.[51] When her father was killed in battle in 1630, she assumed the throne. She was only four years old at the time, and did not actually start ruling until she turned eighteen. Much of her youth until then was spent studying—languages, mathematics, philosophy, theology, art, alchemy. For a woman of the seventeenth century—indeed, for *anybody* in the seventeenth century—she was extraordinarily well educated, earning the nickname "Minerva of the North." Seeking to create a kind of intellectual academy in Stockholm, she brought scientists, philosophers, poets, and artists to her court. The most famous—and the most reluctant—of these was Descartes, whom she lured from his cozy retreat in the Netherlands in late 1649 to be her philosophy tutor. He was not used to the frigid Swedish winter or the early morning hour at which he was expected to attend the queen. He died of a cold just a few months after his arrival (although there have long been unsubstantiated rumors that he was poisoned by a jealous rival).

A bookish monarch with a retinue of foreign scholars and the ambition to create a Scandinavian "Athens" needs a well-stocked library. Not just an intimate little collection of classics to adorn the walls of her study, but everything an omnivorous and progressive-minded reader who chose learning over marriage and who wanted to make her court a major European center of learning would require: from ancient poetry to medieval theology to the latest works of science; printed books, codices, and manuscripts, all in a wide range of languages. The collection would certainly have to include various editions of Scripture in its original language and masterpieces of rabbinic literature. After all, the queen read Hebrew.

What an opportunity for an enterprising bookseller specializing in Judaica. Fortunately, Menasseh had a connection. Isaac Vossius, the son of his old friend Gerardus, had been appointed librarian to the Swedish court in March of 1649, just before his father's death.[52] The thirty-year old Isaac was himself an accomplished humanist scholar, having studied with Claude Saumaise in Leiden. At the time of his appointment in Stockholm, Isaac, a devoted bibliophile, had been serving as city librarian for Amsterdam, succeeding his late brother Dionysius in that post. During his tenure there, he too purchased Hebrew books from Menasseh for the city's collection. Menasseh figured that Isaac could repeat the favor, on an even grander scale, now that he was working for the Swedish queen. After allowing Isaac some time to settle in to his new post, Menasseh decided it was time to make an overture.

On January 10, 1651, Menasseh wrote to Isaac in Stockholm to let him know about some verses he had composed, in Hebrew and Spanish, in Christina's honor, inspired by a portrait of her that he had seen in Vossius's house. Since he was on the verge of completing Part 4 of the *Conciliador*, he also offered to dedicate a single-volume edition of the entire work to her, as well as "a book of great value dealing with the immortality of the soul" that he was about to publish (presumably, the *Sefer Nishmat Hayyim*). He mentioned, too, that he had charged Michel Le Blon—an engraver, art dealer, and diplomat who was Christina's agent in Amsterdam—with delivering to the queen both his poems and a complete set of his own writings. (Le Blon had earlier tried to get Menasseh to sell him, for Christina, twenty old manuscripts, including one titled *Magia Cabalistica*; for some reason Menasseh turned down the deal, "courteously.")[53]

As if these less than subtle pleas for support were not enough, Menasseh finally came directly to the point. Writing in Spanish, he let Vossius know that

> since you are the librarian to the Court, let me tell you that I have the opportunity, with the help of a person whom I have sent to Poland, to obtain very rare Hebrew books. In-

asmuch as there is no one to whom this is better entrusted, I shall, if it should please Her Majesty to enlarge her book collection, seek out the best editions and the best works, with the assurance that I shall serve her faithfully and rigorously.[54]

Isaac did not share his father's high opinion of Menasseh. For one thing, he did not think the rabbi had very much to teach gentiles about rabbinics. When, in the late 1630s, he discovered that his tutor Saumaise was consulting Menasseh on Jewish law, he wrote to the Frenchman that "no doubt you have now received those things that [Menasseh] can gather from the rabbis. But I doubt whether they add much to what you already know. For I do not think that he has seen anything that you have not already seen."[55] In fact, Isaac Vossius held rabbis generally in low esteem. Unlike his father and brother, Isaac was no Hebraist.[56] But his lack of familiarity with rabbinic learning did not keep him from denigrating its value. "Can humane letters be successfully treated when the rabbis reign and where no theology other than rabbinic is cultivated?" Where his father and brother respected Jewish expertise, Isaac dismissed it as useless. He especially resented it when Christian theologians consulted rabbis on textual and theological matters—even when these concerned Hebrew Scripture. "Do not the deceitful Jews rightly laugh when they find so many fatuous sorts among Christians who . . . freely acknowledge Jews as teachers."[57]

Still, Isaac had warm feelings for Menasseh himself, perhaps from fond boyhood memories of the rabbi visiting their home. Menasseh, he told a friend, "is after all a very good man." He added that "like most Spaniards [sic] he is eager for fame, while he does his utmost to be counted for something among scholars."[58] Isaac was willing to help out an old family friend, especially if it would further the ambitions of his royal employer (and, not incidentally, his own standing in her court). He was thus receptive to Menasseh's offer to serve as Queen

Christina's book purveyor. The queen herself seems to have approved the idea.

Things were not moving forward very quickly, though, or at least not quickly enough for Menasseh. In a second letter to Vossius just two months later, he reminded the royal librarian that since he had now finished his Spanish translation of Johannes Jansson's four-volume *Nieuwe Atlas ofte Werelt Beschrijvinge* (New Atlas or Description of the World), he had plenty of time to devote to procuring Hebrew books for Christina.[59] He promised to do so with all due diligence, assuring Vossius that he was the right man for the job, "since no one has more knowledge of Hebrew books." After asking for some clues as to the queen's taste in literature, he offered to go to Frankfurt personally to purchase for her some manuscripts, as well as to take advantage of his business connections in Poland. "You can count on me to find the cream of the crop, the very best editions and specimens in good condition." Moreover, he let Vossius know that he was at work on printing a Spanish Bible with commentary, a book that "will be in great demand" in so far as the famous Ferrara edition (lacking commentary) was no longer available. Would the queen be interested in providing a subvention for this project? "This work is worth being printed at Her Majesty's expense, because it will be of great value to the whole of Europe and it will bring more fame to her than the Biblia Regia printed by Plantin brought to [King] Philip II [of Spain], because it will generally be read avidly and with pleasure."

To sweeten the pot even further, Menasseh offered Christina a major deal, one that would allow him to help her expand the royal library in a more than piecemeal fashion. He was at her majesty's service "in case [she] should now decide to put together a beautiful Hebrew library." With enough money, he could arrange to deliver a large cache of Hebrew books. He would even provide her with the annotated guide to rabbinic literature on which he had been working, the *Bibliotheca Rabbinica*—"a book that all Christianity desires, since it deals not only with the lives of authors but also the subjects they treat, along with my critical opinion"—so that she could use it as a catalogue. "Such a library," he added, "could be put together for six or seven thousand florins [guilders]."

Menasseh closed the letter with one final—and rather sad—allusion to his financial situation, in case Vossius had not fully grasped his seriousness of purpose and dire need. He informed the young man, who was not much older than Joseph was when he died on a business trip, that he did not have enough money to publish the Spanish Bible and Talmud that he had been working on, "since my wealth has perished, as you know, in Brazil and Poland, with my son." With this emotional appeal, Menasseh seemed rather desperate to be put on Christina's payroll.

One year later, Menasseh was still waiting for his commission. Writing once again to Vossius in Stockholm, he offered "a reminder concerning my affairs."[60] Despite Le Blon's assurance that the books he was charged with delivering made it to the Swedish court, Menasseh was still uncertain as to whether the queen herself had received them, since he had not heard a word from her. He would like Vossius to follow up on that, and to remind Christina that the single-volume edition of the *Conciliador* that he might dedicate to her is still in the works, as is the "book about the immortality of the soul," a Latin summary of which he enclosed for her perusal. Still hoping that she might take him up on his offer to be her supplier (on retainer) of Hebraica, he told Vossius of his plan to travel to Germany and Italy to do some bibliographic research to make sure that the *Bibliotheca Rabbinica* he was offering the queen would be complete. This was, however, an empty boast meant to impress, since Menasseh never made any such trip; indeed, he never finished (and, as

far as we know, never really started) the catalogue. He closed
the letter with yet another plea for royal support.

> I would be appreciative if I might receive from the Most Se-
> rene Queen in one form or another a commission to pur-
> chase some rare items for her, which I may be able to obtain
> for a favorable price. I petition Your Grace to recommend
> me to Her Most Serene Majesty, may God protect her, with
> the kindness that you have always shown to me, and I shall
> always be thankful and indebted to Your Grace, may the out-
> comes of your efforts always be favorable, according to the
> wishes of your devoted friend and servant.

The formal, even obsequious tone of these letters to Vossius is
striking. Isaac was the son of a recently deceased close friend.
Menasseh had known Isaac since he was a little boy, when he
was visiting their home to meet with his father and giving Hebrew lessons to his older brother. Even in a period when epis-
tolary relationships were governed by certain conventions of
propriety, one would expect a little more familiarity in the exchanges between a senior rabbi and a younger man of long
acquaintance.

Unbeknownst to Menasseh, there was in fact little that
Vossius could do for him at Christina's court at the moment,
since he was not in Stockholm. Just before Menasseh sent this
third letter, in February 1652, Vossius had left Sweden for what
was supposed to be a brief visit to Holland. Even worse for Menasseh's long-term ambitions, during this trip abroad Vossius
fell out of favor with the queen. The librarian had made the
mistake of crossing Saumaise, his former tutor and Menasseh's
one-time correspondent, who was also a member of Christina's
circle of learned courtiers and, not coincidentally, one of her
favorites.

The conflict began with a simple dispute over money.[61]
Saumaise's son had borrowed money from Vossius, and after

waiting some time for repayment Vossius began pressing Saumaise to cover the debt. Saumaise replied that it was none of his business, that it was a matter between Vossius and his son, and that moreover Vossius was a fraud since the queen had already repaid the money. One thing led to another, insults were exchanged ("imposter," "commoner"), and Vossius sued Saumaise and wrote to the queen herself to impugn his character. The relationship between the two scholars deteriorated to the point that they were no longer on speaking terms. Rumors soon reached Christina that Vossius was now saying offensive things not only about Saumaise but about the queen herself—something to the effect that while he could live without the queen, the queen could not live without him.[62] Christina resented the implication, but was especially angry about the way in which Vossius had treated Saumaise, whose company she preferred. As one spectator of the affair—who actually saw a letter that Christina had sent to Vossius—reported to a friend, "she was amazed at his impudence (this word she used more than once) toward so great a man [Saumaise], whom he [Vossius] should have esteemed and respected if only for her sake."[63] The queen was not to be mollified until Vossius apologized to Saumaise. She went so far as to forbid him from returning to Sweden until Saumaise himself told her that all was forgiven. Saumaise refused to make that concession, and so Vossius was stuck in Amsterdam.

This exile in his homeland did at least allow Isaac to spend some time in Menasseh's company. Thus we find him with the rabbi in the synagogue one autumn day in 1652, along with a number of learned gentile friends. One member of the group was Pierre Daniel Huet, a young French scholar of Catholic stock. Huet would go on to become a prolific author, editor, and translator—he enjoyed some renown later in life as a hostile critic of the new philosophies of Descartes and Spinoza—and, in 1689, after a midlife career turn taking holy orders, the

Bishop of Avranches. In the spring of 1652, Huet had traveled to Christina's court in the company of his former tutor Samuel Bochart—he wanted to inspect a rare manuscript in the queen's collection—but half a year in the Swedish capital was more than enough for this native of Caen. He was now in Amsterdam, one leg of an intellectual itinerary through Europe, and, in the company of Vossius and others, on a visit to the house of prayer on the Houtgracht. Many years later Huet recalled how

> I found myself in Amsterdam, and I wanted to examine more carefully the rites and mysteries of the Jews, of whom there are many in these parts. As a result, I was taken to meet one of them who was then considered the most expert and most to be consulted on the whole of Jewish knowledge. We discoursed for a long time and in detail on our respective doctrines.[64]

Huet's interlocutor was, of course, Menasseh. The two men must have hit it off, since they spent "a whole month meeting, conferring, and discussing." In his career as an ecclesiastic, Huet would show himself to be no friend of the Jews. While not quite at the level of hatred of a Voetius, he still held them in general contempt. Even as a young man, in his discussions with Menasseh, he accused the Jews of "deforming God's holy testament" with "senile fables and most rotten inventions."[65] Yet, like so many gentiles of his ilk, he had a soft spot for this unusual rabbi. Menasseh, in his eyes, was not your "normal" Jew.

> Rabbi Manasse ben Israel was a Jew of the first order, head of the synagogue in Amsterdam. I knew him intimately, and I had long and frequent conferences with him on matters of religion. . . . He was otherwise a very good man, of gentle spirit, agreeable, rational, free of the many Jewish superstitions and the empty dreams of the Cabbala. Through long study and meditation he acquired a profound knowledge of the letter of Holy Scripture.[66]

Huet, who was impressed by Menasseh's knowledge of the writings of the Church Fathers—even if Menasseh was too focused on the negative things they had to say about the Jews—said that he, Huet, has "profited greatly from our conversations" and would have been happy to continue them had he not had to return to France. He found Menasseh to be "stubborn," like his co-religionists, but that did not diminish his respect for both his learning and his demeanor.

Huet reported that during the visit to the synagogue he was "paying great attention to the ceremonies," and so accidentally stepped on a corner of the ark of the Torah. This caused a bit of a stir among the congregation, "as if it were intended as a sign of disrespect to their religion." However, Menasseh came to the rescue of his guest. "The good Manasse immediately alerted me [to what I had done], and the modest and submissive promptitude with which I withdrew my foot and returned to a respectful posture appeased them."[67]

Menasseh would have received Vossius and his friends in the synagogue with mixed feelings. While always happy to be an ambassador to non-Jews wanting to learn more about Judaism and even see Jews engaged in worship, he must have been disappointed to learn that Vossius could not, at present, be of any help to him in currying royal favor in Stockholm. Before his falling out with the queen, Vossius was at least able to arrange a one-time purchase of a collection of Hebrew books from Menasseh. It was a substantial order, worth nine hundred guilders. The books were sent from Amsterdam, but what eventually became of them—and of Menasseh's expected compensation— would end up being a rather contentious matter entangled in breakdowns in communication, court politics, religious turmoil, and international affairs.[68]

Menasseh was certainly not idle as he waited—in vain, given Vossius's current status—for word from Stockholm about a more permanent commission as purveyor of Hebrew books to the Swedish crown, an appointment that would alleviate his financial worries. With new friends and new projects, Menasseh found numerous outlets for his considerable energy in the early 1650s. Even as he neared the age of fifty, he managed to maintain an extremely active agenda both within and beyond the Amsterdam Jewish community. There was his mission as Judaica expert to the gentile world—in person and in writing— classes to teach in the community's school, lessons to prepare for the Pereyra yeshiva, and, not least, sermons to be written. Menasseh was extremely proud of his sermons, or *predicaciones*, and claimed at one point that he had delivered more than three hundred and fifty of them, which, he says, "were very gratefully received and applauded."[69]

And then there were books to be published. In 1652, after several years running the printing press on the Nieuwe Houtmarkt, Samuel ben Israel Soeiro turned the business back over to his father. Although nothing was published for two years after Samuel's final project—two indexes (in a single volume) to biblical citations in the Babylonian and Jerusalem Talmuds— Menasseh got things going again in 1654 with a Spanish Pentateuch.

However, his heart was no longer in it. The publishing house of Menasseh ben Israel would, in his lifetime, issue only three more books, including one final treatise by Menasseh himself. Was there not enough time to devote to an old passion? Did he simply no longer have the inclination? Or was it that, with his realization that the arrival of the Messiah might be near, there was another, much more important and consequential project that demanded his attention?

7

$\longrightarrow$ •◆•◆ $\longrightarrow$

The English Mission

THINGS WERE GOING DOWNHILL in Netherlands Brazil, and the Jewish community in Recife was extremely worried. The uprising against the Dutch West Indies Company by Portuguese planters that began in 1645 was now, in the early 1650s, gaining momentum. If Portugal retook Pernambuco province, the Sephardim in the port town and the surrounding countryside would have to flee, and rather quickly, before the Inquisition moved in and began its search for former New Christians now living as Jews.

The rebellion was taking a serious economic and psychological toll not only on the Jewish colonists but on their sponsors in Amsterdam as well. The city's Portuguese Jews had put a lot of capital into the Brazil trade, and it was all disappearing as the Dutch gradually lost control over their territory there. A panic was setting in on both sides of the Atlantic as investments failed, fortunes were lost, and lives were endangered. When

Recife finally fell to the Portuguese in 1654, the Dutch colonial governors, the directors of the West Indies Company, and the Amsterdam Sephardim were all faced with a crisis that was both financial and humanitarian.

For the Jews of Amsterdam, the fall of Recife posed an especially serious refugee problem.[1] The Sephardim who relocated to Brazil in the early 1640s had been departing the country for some time now, an exodus of almost a thousand individuals between 1645 and 1650.[2] Most of these returned to Holland—over six hundred persons, according to one estimate—with some going to Dutch colonies in the Caribbean.[3] With the final reconquest by the Portuguese, the flow of emigrants from Brazil to Amsterdam—along with new arrivals from Spain, where there was renewed persecution of New Christians, and from Venice, mainly for economic reasons—increased significantly. They swelled the ranks of the nearly two thousand Sephardim that were already in the city. The community in the Vlooienburg quarter was overwhelmed. It lacked both the space and the resources to absorb all these returnees and newcomers. Moreover, with the municipal regents unwilling to revise the regulations on Jewish business activities, including restrictions on guild membership, there were only so many opportunities for the new arrivals to make a living.

One solution was to relocate them elsewhere. According to one historian, a new colonization movement brought about a fundamental transformation of the Sephardic diaspora. While Amsterdam remained the "hub of the western Sephardic commercial network," the city's Portuguese-Jewish community became a major sponsor of Sephardic migration to the Caribbean, North America, Italy, and eventually—it was hoped—England.[4]

Among the Jewish returnees from Brazil, there was one who, at least in Menasseh's eyes, was not especially welcome: their rabbi. By the fall of 1654, Isaac Aboab de Fonseca, who twelve years earlier had left to serve the Recife community, was back in Amsterdam. Menasseh could not have been happy to see his old rival return to the community. Although it did not mean a demotion in rank for Menasseh among the congregation's rabbis, Aboab was given some of Mortera's duties as teacher in the highest class of the community's school and one of the chief rabbi's monthly sermons.[5] He was also reinstated at his old salary, four hundred and fifty guilders a year.[6] As this required a decrease in pay for the other rabbis—the annual salary of Mortera, the chief rabbi, was cut by two hundred guilders, to four hundred—it could not have been easy for Menasseh to accept.[7]

As if there was not enough drama on the rabbi's bench in the Houtgracht synagogue, the sniping between Menasseh and Mortera in their sermons that, ten years earlier, occasioned a reprimand from the *ma'amad* had recently resumed.

Things had been quiet for several years. If the two rabbis were still at it, it was not happening in public—or at least not enough to warrant an intervention by the congregation's lay leaders. But on March 21, 1654, the following resolution was entered into the record book of the *parnassim*:

> On the 3rd of *Nisan*, the men of the *ma'amad*, having considered the past disputes between the esteemed Rabbis of this Holy Community—the esteemed Rabbi Saul Levy Mortera and the esteemed Rabbi Manace Ben Is[rael]—and [the fact that] once again they have fallen into a dispute, have agreed ... that said Rabbis should be suspended for two months from their rabbinical duties and giving sermons, and that during the said two months they would not earn a salary nor would they be paid in any way neither with any type of goods nor by any other means, nor with any type of luxury.[8]

Menasseh was ordered to pay an additional fine of twenty guilders for having exacerbated the situation. It seems that when the decision of the *ma'amad* was made public, Menasseh stood up in the synagogue and loudly and disrespectfully protested.[9]

It was not as if Menasseh and Mortera had not recently been warned again, several times. Just one year earlier, on February 10, 1653, the *ma'amad* had to step in with a rebuke and a brief suspension of duties. The entry in their book notes that "the men of the *ma'amad* [having learned of] some disagreements that have arisen between the esteemed Rabbis Saul Leui Morteira and Manose ben Israel that are in need of remediation . . . has determined that the said esteemed Rabbis should be suspended from going up to the ark of the Torah, giving sermons, and performing their duties for the amount of time that the men of the *ma'amad* see fit."[10] Then, less than a week later, the *ma'amad* had to caution "the esteemed rabbis Saul Levi Morteira and Manose ben Israel" yet again to restore a "good relationship and friendship" and "to always maintain a state of decorum that [the *ma'amad*] would find satisfactory." They added that "if between them there should be contrary opinions regarding matters of the Law, on no account should they make this public, either within the congregation or outside it without first coming to some agreement, and that neither within the congregation nor in public should they offend or contradict each other." Should any further discord arise, the two rabbis were to bring it to the *ma'amad* for adjudication, "so that they might make a reasonable judgment."[11]

Now, in April 1654, well after these earlier warnings and three weeks after the suspensions and fines levied in March, the *parnassim* wanted to make it clear to all concerned that enough was enough. In a final entry on the matter of "the differences between the esteemed rabbis," they proclaimed that the next time "the tension between the two men" breaks out, the person who initiates it and fails "to fulfill his obligation and best keep the peace" will be removed from his position—permanently?— and forced to pay a fine.[12]

It is still unclear what was being said by whom, other than the fact that there were "contrary opinions regarding matters of the Law." Such disagreements on matters of *halakha*, while of course not unusual among rabbis, would be a problem if the disputants were teachers in the same congregation. And the legal dispute was no doubt aggravated by mutual *ad hominem* remarks about the other man's level of intelligence.

Menasseh—feuding with one rabbi, resentful toward the other, and pretty much on probation from the *ma'amad*—must have found his situation in the congregation nearly intolerable. Perhaps that is one of the reasons why leaving the country at this point seemed to Menasseh not such a bad idea.

In the fall of 1650, some months after its publication in Spanish and Latin, *The Hope of Israel* appeared in English. The translator was Moses Wall, a Millenarian scholar and a friend of the poet John Milton. It was printed in Amsterdam—although not by Menasseh himself—and the translation (like the Latin version) was dedicated to "the High Court, the Parliament of England, and to the Councell of State."[13] Menasseh was out to curry favor, and he said so explicitly. "In dedicating this discourse to you, I can truly affirm that I am induced to it upon no other ground than this, that I may gain your favour and good will to our Nation, now scattered almost all over the earth." The operative word here is "almost," since at the time the scattering of the Jews did not include the British Isles. While acknowledging to the English authorities, somewhat disingenuously, "how much you have hitherto favoured our Nation . . . [and] your charitable affection towards us," Menasseh requested that they "still favour our good, and further love us." Lest the recipients of this warm dedication mistake his meaning, he alerted them to the fact that, as the Prophets had foretold, once "Israel [is] brought back to his own place, peace which is promised under the Messiah may be restored to the world."[14] If *The*

Hope of Israel was not originally conceived as an appeal to the English to allow the Jews to resettle on their island, the book and its messianic message had become an important tool in that mission.[15]

Menasseh claimed that the idea of the readmission of the Jews to England went back to his exchanges with Dury, Jessey, and others. Writing in 1656, he noted that "the communication and correspondence I have held, for some years since, with some eminent persons of England, was the first originall of my undertaking this design. . . . They affirmed, that at this time the minds of men stood very well affected towards us; and that our entrance into this Island, would be very acceptable, and well-pleasing with them."[16] But what may have moved him seriously to contemplate engaging on such a momentous mission was the execution of Charles I and his replacement by a potentially more congenial leadership.

Menasseh probably received the news of Charles's beheading in 1649 with mixed feelings. On the one hand, Menasseh had had the honor of officially welcoming Charles's wife, Henrietta Maria, to the synagogue on the Houtgracht; he could not have been without some sympathy for this woman whom he had so warmly received eight years earlier. On the other hand, he was not unaware of the way the Jews were historically treated by English monarchs, going back to Edward I's edict of expulsion in 1290. He could not help but feel a bit of *schadenfreude* as he learned of England's descent into civil war in the late 1640s. Writing to an acquaintance in London, he confessed:

> I cannot express the joy that I have when I read your letters, full of desires to see your country prosperous, which is heavily afflicted with civil wars, without doubt by the just judgment of God. And it should not be in vain to attribute it to the punishment of your predecessor's faults, committed against ours; when ours being deprived of their liberty under

deceitfulness, so many men were slain only because they kept close under the tenets of Moses, their legislator.[17]

His hope, expressed in the dedicatory letter of *The Hope of Israel*, was that Parliament would do better toward the Jews.

Menasseh was certainly not the first to raise the issue of allowing for Jewish resettlement in England; nor was it an idea percolating only in Jewish minds. In early 1648, a widow named Johanna Cartenright and her son Ebenezer Cartwright lobbied Thomas Fairfax, commander of the parliamentary forces during the civil war, so that "the inhumane cruel Statute of banishment made against them [the Jews] may be repealed, and they under the Christian banner of charity, and brotherly love, may again be received and permitted to trade and dwell amongst you in this Land, as now they do in the Nether-lands."[18] Johanna and Ebenezer had been living in Amsterdam, and were enlightened by the Sephardim there as to the virtues of having a thriving Jewish community in their own land—not least because "both they [the Jews of Amsterdam] and we find, that the time of hereall draweth nigh." That is, the Messiah would soon be arriving and it would be best to be prepared.

England was not totally devoid of Jews in the first half of the seventeenth century.[19] There were individual Jews, real and suspected, here and there throughout the country. There were also gentile Judaizers, Christians living according to Jewish law and custom—people such as John Thraske, who was, by contemporary accounts, "a Jewish Christian, observing the Sabath on Saterday, abstaining from swine-flesh and all things commanded in the law."[20] Thraske had his followers, but he was thrown into prison in 1618.

There were also prosperous Spanish and Portuguese New Christian merchants living in London by the end of the sixteenth century, much as there were some residing in Amsterdam around the same time. But whereas the Amsterdam conversos were soon able openly to return to Judaism—first tacitly, then with full legal acknowledgment—those in London who were secretly practicing Judaism had to continue to keep a very low profile, at least through the first six decades of the new century.

There were in fact a fair number of these Judaizers, enough to warrant a royal order expelling them in 1609. Still, a contingent of New Christians remained, one of whom was even serving as Queen Elizabeth's personal physician. By the late 1640s and early 1650s, with their numbers increased by new arrivals from Spain, Portugal, and France, they had become a well-organized if very quiet Jewish community, possibly several dozen families. Their leaders, among whom was the wealthy and well-connected merchant Antonio Ferdinando Carvajal, were careful to keep things relatively under wraps, although by this time it was no real secret among many Londoners that there was a small group of Jews living in the city. Their worship behind closed doors was condoned by the municipal authorities, so much so that Francesco Salvetti, the Tuscan ambassador to England, could, in 1655 (just as the issue of resettlement was being taken up at an official level), write to a senator back home that in London the Jews "organize their synagogues privately in some houses and [there] they hold their Jewish rites."[21]

Menasseh's own account of what led him personally to get involved in advocating for the readmission of the Jews to a nation from which they had been banned for almost four centuries is a mix of humanitarian concern, *realpolitik*, economic pragmatism, and messianic dreams. In September 1655, on the eve of his departure for England, Menasseh composed an open letter to "all the gentlemen of the Hebrew nation living in Asia and in Europe, principally the Holy Synagogues of Italy and Holstein," letting them know of his mission to see "conceded to us in the most flourishing Republic of England the public exercise of our religion."[22] (The letter was written in Portuguese, not Hebrew, so it was intended primarily for the Sephardic diaspora in Rome, Venice, and Hamburg.) Among the reasons he presented for this undertaking was "the affliction of those of our people who are today so oppressed, who could find refuge and remedy in that most powerful Republic." Menasseh was referring to the increasing number of New Christians, whether or not they were Judaizers, who continued to suffer under the Inquisition and who might find relief and freedom on the shores of Spain's enemy. (His concern here was not just for the welfare of the persecuted conversos in Iberia, but for the good of the Portuguese-Jewish community in Amsterdam as well. Better that any new refugees should settle somewhere other than Vlooienburg and the Breestraat, which could not accommodate more immigrants without great difficulty.)[23]

Menasseh was also conscious of the economic benefits that would accrue to the Amsterdam Sephardim by having business partners in London. With the ever shifting political and military alliances in the seventeenth century and the consequent uncertainties in shipping and trade on the high seas, it was good to have multiple bases of operations. If the Dutch were to be at war with Spain, or some other power—including the English!—commerce could be carried on through associates in England; if England were the one at war, then the merchandise could proceed under Dutch flag. Moreover, while the Sephardim of Amsterdam had unrestricted trade networks with Dutch colonial holdings in the Caribbean, lands in the West Indies under the English crown—such as Jamaica and Barbados—would, through their London agents, now be open to them as well.

And of course there is the matter of the restoration of all of Israel to Zion under a new king from the House of David. Writing in English after he had settled in London, Menasseh said:

> I conceived, that our universall dispersion was a necessary circumstance, to be fulfilled, before all that shall be accom-

plished which the Lord hath promised to the people of the Iewes, concerning their restauration, and their returning again into their own land, according to those worlds *Dan.* 12.7. *When he shall have accomplished to scatter the power of the holy people, all these things shall be finished.* As also, that this our scattering, by little, and little, should be amongst all people, from the *one end of the earth even unto the other.*[24]

He added, revealing a touch of a Moses complex, "And I knew not, but that the Lord who often works by naturall meanes, might have design'd and made choice of me, for the bringing about this work." There would be no Messiah until the dispersal of the Jews was complete, and it was Menasseh's God-given task to bring this about.

But why England? True, Jews were now—after Montezinos's report—known to be present in the Americas. And, as Menasseh said, there were Jews in Asia.[25] But there were plenty of other nations into which the Jewish people had not yet been "scattered." In Europe alone, Jews were still absent (at least officially) from the kingdoms of France, Spain, Portugal, and Sweden.

Aside from the geographical convenience of the land just across the North Sea and the political and economic advantages of London, there was in fact a compelling scriptural reason for pressing for settlement in England—or, at least, so Menasseh claimed. He said, with reference to the verse from Deuteronomy ("God will scatter you among all the peoples from one end of the earth even unto the other" [28:64]), that "I conceived that by the *end of the earth* might be understood this *Island,*" meaning the British isle.[26] The biblical text says that the Jews will be scattered to *ketzeh ha'aretz,* the corner or angle of the earth. And in medieval Jewish writings, that is the Hebrew term used for "Angleterre," "Angle-land"—that is, England.[27] The Torah itself, then, proclaims that until the Jews are in England, the Messiah's arrival will be on hold.

Jewish interest in readmission to England was certainly not matched by an equal enthusiasm on the other side. To be sure, there were many in England who had great expectations for seeing Jews once again in their midst. Hebraist scholars, Puritan theologians, and Millenarians all saw something to be gained by allowing resettlement. These were the people of the "Old Testament" bearing knowledge of the Holy Language. As one contemporary put it, the Jews were the "anciently beloved people of God, the seed of Abraham, Isaac and Jacob."[28] Millenarians—men such as Henry Jessey and John Sadler—argued that their conversion, so essential to the inauguration of the reign of Jesus Christ as King of Kings, would be facilitated by their presence in England. The "Calling of the Jews to Christ" was imminent—by 1658 at the latest, according to one reckoning—and it was up to England to do its part.[29] These Fifth Monarchy Men made their case by refuting some of the stigmas and libels historically associated with Jews. That there would also be economic benefits to allowing such successful and internationally well-connected merchants and professionals to settle in London was acknowledged among members of the English business class, although many feared the competition that the Jews would bring.

And then there was the simple moral matter of religious toleration. Roger Williams, back in England from the Rhode Island colony, insisted that "I humbly conceive it to be the Duty of the *Civil Magistrate* to break down that superstitious *wall* of *separation* (as to Civil things) between us *Gentiles* and the *Jews*, and freely (without their asking) to make way for their free and peaceable Habitation amongst us." These were, he noted, God's chosen people, and it was in his compatriots' own best interest to cease "the *unchristian oppressions, incivilities*, and *inhumanities* of this Nation against the Jews."[30] Similarly, in a 1648 pamphlet, Edward Nicholas urged his fellow countrymen to "show ourselves compassionate, and helpers of the afflicted Jews" so that England "may be an example to other nations that have done them, and continue to do them wrong."[31]

Menasseh's translator Moses Wall, for his part, though certainly no philo-Semite, argued that allowing the Jews to return to England was simply the right and humane thing to do. In his preface to *The Hope of Israel,* Wall warned the reader, "Do not thinke that I aime by this Translation, to propagate or commend *Iudaisme.*" Rather, he stated, his goal was "to remove our sinfull hatred from off that people."[32] In an appendix to the work, Wall reminded the opponents of Jewish settlement that "they have the same Humane nature with us; from this ground we should wish well to all men whether *Jew,* or *Gentile.*"[33] Still, conversion was never far from Wall's mind. The title of that appendix is "Considerations Upon the Point of the Conversion of the Jewes," while in the preface he reminded the opponents of settlement that it is the Jews "whose are the Promises, and who are beloved for their Fathers sakes; and who . . . we shall hear to be, ere long, reall Christians."

Unfortunately, the tolerant attitudes of Williams and Wall were not shared by most Englishmen, least of all by those in the theological profession. The Jews may have been the first to enjoy God's favor, but their law-bound religion had long ago been surpassed. As non-Christians, they were outside the new covenant. At least Catholics, problematic as they were in the eyes of England's established church, did not pose the threat to the faith and salvation of ordinary folk that Jews did. As Christians, they fell under the Agreement of the People, which in 1649 offered toleration only for those "who profess faith in God by Jesus Christ."[34] Even the "practical" arguments for readmission proffered by Millenarians—that it would expedite the Second Coming—did not move more conservative Protestants. The attitude of one royalist journalist, writing on the eve of the execution of Charles I, toward those who were arguing for Jewish settlement was not untypical: "No marvell, that those which intend to crucifie their King, should shake hands with them that crucified their Saviour."[35]

Despite (or perhaps because of) the opposition to Jewish settlement, the English translation of *The Hope of Israel*—a second edition was published in 1652—was quite a success. It found a wide readership, and served only to invigorate efforts by Millenarians and other supporters of the cause. Here, indeed, was a Jew—a rabbi!—who confirmed their opinion that the age of the Messiah would soon be upon the world and who was advocating measures that would hasten its arrival. Menasseh's dedication of the book to Parliament and his not-too-subtle plea for formal readmission made it practically impossible now to avoid the question of whether or not to admit the Jews and, if so, under what conditions.

In September 1650, a member of Parliament from Middlesex named Edward Spencer made his contribution to the debate. Spencer, having the read the Latin edition of *The Hope of Israel* and the plea to Parliament in its dedicatory preface, was not in principle opposed to readmission. He accepted the Millenarian arguments for the advantages of allowing Jews to settle in England. In his "A Breife Epistle to the Learned Manasseh Ben Israel," he claimed that "this little worke of mine . . . ayms at the conversion of the Jewes."[36] He confessed to Menasseh that "truely my bowells yearne after your conversion," and insisted that England was "the likelyest Nation under Heaven to doe it. For wee hate Idolatry as much as you." However, Spencer told the rabbi, while "my consent ye shall have, that you and your people shall live in England," he believed that there should be rather strict conditions imposed upon them, lest they be "burdensome to the State."

Spencer seemed to be obsessed with the rite of circumcision. Jews who had already been circumcised would be allowed into the country, he said in his recommendations, but "I doubt whether we may admit you to circumcise in our land."[37] To ensure compliance with this, a record would be made upon entry as to who is in fact circumcised; and every year "a search shall be made, whether any male childe be circumcised, and if done in England, or the Dominions thereof, a confiscation of halfe the parents estate shall ensue."[38] In consideration for their observance of this restriction upon such a fundamental element of Judaism, Jews would not be forced to be christened. However, any who did undergo christening and then reverted to Judaism should be punished. Unconverted Jews would be allowed to attend "praiers and sermons" in Christian churches—as long as they "behave themselves reverently and decently"—and should even be compelled to do so on Good Friday.

Spencer also recommended imposing severe financial penalties upon Jews. They could engage in business but not join or organize guilds, and they were to pay double the customs rate that Christians paid. The family of anyone who dies as a Jew would have to forfeit two-thirds of the estate, with one of those thirds going to "the maintenance of converted Jews," whereas the posterity of a convert to Christianity would get to keep the whole of the deceased's estate. Naturally, there would be no intermarriage permitted between Jews and Christians.

So far, it was all just talk, ideas being thrown around. Aside from the Cartwrights' petition in 1648, there had not yet been any formal proposal for or steps taken toward opening England up to Jewish settlement. But this was about to change.

In early 1651, a group of English diplomats arrived in The Hague charged with negotiating a treaty of alliance. Led by Oliver St. John, chief justice of the Council of State, their primary goal was to ease tensions between the two nations, which had been growing as a result of fierce economic competition. Rather than fighting with each other, they argued, England and the United Provinces should unite and turn their attention to limiting the ambitions of Catholic powers such as France and

Spain. The English also hoped to discourage the Dutch from lending support to Charles II in his quest to reacquire the English throne for the Stuarts. (The Royalist cause had many supporters living in exile in the Netherlands, thanks to the hospitality of the House of Orange.)

During their stay in Holland, the members of the English delegation traveled to Amsterdam, where—like the royal party a decade earlier—they paid a visit to the Portuguese synagogue. The congregation welcomed them with all due pomp and ceremony. Menasseh himself reported:

> my Lord St. John . . . was pleased to honour our Synagogue at Amsterdam with his presence, where our nation entertained him with musick, and all expressions of joy and gladnesses, and also pronounced a blessing, not onely upon his honour, then present, but upon the whole Common-wealth of England, for that they were a people in league and amity; and because we conceived some hopes that they would manifest towards us, what we ever bare towards them, viz. all love and affection.[39]

The St. John mission, as it came to be called, did not succeed in securing the treaty it had been hoping for. This was bad news not just for diplomatic relations between the two countries, which only deteriorated in the aftermath, but for Amsterdam's Sephardim as well. If the mission had been successful, the Jews of the Dutch Republic might have ended up with the same legal standing in England that they had at home. Settlement in London, with all of its economic advantages, could have followed as a matter of course.

At least one of the delegation's members, however—its secretary, John Thurloe (no doubt with the backing of compatriots who had read *The Hope of Israel*)—took advantage of the opportunity of being in Amsterdam to talk with Menasseh about formally making a request to Parliament for the readmission of the Jews to England. Menasseh took this as a very encouraging sign, and in October he submitted a petition to that effect. The matter was referred to the Council of State, which in turn handed it over to a committee, among whose members was Oliver Cromwell, at the time Lord General of the Parliamentary forces but who would soon become Lord Protector of England, Scotland, and Ireland. Neither the text of Menasseh's petition nor the deliberations of the committee are extant, but one year later, in November 1652, and then again on December 17, a pass was issued to "Menasseh ben Israel, a Rabbi of the Jewish nation, well reported of for his learning and good affection to the State, to come from Amsterdam to these parts" and begin discussions in earnest.[40]

However, it was not a good time for a Dutch resident to be seen cavorting with the English. In October 1651, just after the breakdown of the treaty talks, Parliament had passed the Navigation Act, an antagonistic piece of legislation practically guaranteed to worsen relations between the two countries. It set heavy restrictions on any nation seeking to trade with England and its colonies and effectively excluded all non-English ships from English ports in America and the Caribbean. This was a serious blow to Dutch commercial interests. Along with English interference with Dutch shipping in international waters and other insults to national pride, it was more than the United Provinces—newly sovereign since the Peace of Münster in 1648 had ended the long fight for independence with Spain—could bear. War broke out in the summer of 1652.

Menasseh, with his guarantee of safe conduct in hand, was, despite the hostilities, all set to go to England that December. He actually embarked on the voyage, and may have made it as far as the Dutch border, but did not get beyond that. He says that his family and friends persuaded him of the wisdom of postponing indefinitely any trip to enemy territory.

At that juncture of time my coming was not presently performed, for that my kindred and friends, considering the
checquered, and interwoven vicissitudes, and turns of things
here below, embracing me, with pressing importunity, ear-
nestly requested me not to part from them, and would not
give over, till their love constrained me to promise, that I
would yet a while stay with them.[41]

Some of the pressure to return to Amsterdam may have come
from the Jewish communal leadership. It would certainly not be
good for a member of the local Sephardic community—Iberian
foreigners whose loyalty to the Dutch Republic was always
suspect in the eyes of their enemies—to be seen traveling to
England at this time.

Undeterred, Menasseh was once again planning to cross
over to England the following fall, after submitting a new petition to Cromwell's "Little Parliament" (also known as the "Bare-
bone's Parliament" or "Parliament of Saints") that had been
installed in July 1653. This body, which around the same time
received a similar petition for readmission from a man named
Samuel Herring—who asked that "the Jewes should be called
into this Commonwealth, and have places allotted to them to
inhabitt in, and exercise there lyberty, for there tyme is neere at
hand"—did take up the question as to whether "the Jews might
be admitted to trade as well as in Holland."[42] It was Cromwell
himself who instructed his colleagues to do so, and alerted
them to the fact that "some think, God will bring the Jews
home to their station from the isles of the sea, and answer their
expectations as from the depths of the sea."[43]

Menasseh received a new "passe-port" in September 1653.
He even went so far as to give power of attorney over his affairs
in his absence to his son Samuel. However, his journey this
time got no further than the last, again because of the protests
of his family over the dangers of traveling in a time of war,

along with concerns about his health. "After having set out on the road on two occasions, I was persuaded by my relatives, for certain political reasons, to put off the journey for the time being."⁴⁴

It looked like there would be no progress on Jewish settlement in England until there was peace.

While biding his time for the right opportunity to go to London—it would, in the end, be another two years—Menasseh took care of some unfinished business with Swedish royalty; or, rather, *former* Swedish royalty. For in February 1654, the twenty-seven-year-old Queen Christina announced that she was converting to Catholicism and would abdicate the throne. She left Stockholm that summer—dressed in men's clothing to conceal her identity as she traveled through Denmark—and by August had settled in the Catholic city of Antwerp. Before her departure, she had had her librarian Isaac Vossius—now back in Christina's good graces—make a list of her favorite six thousand books from the royal library; they would later be packed up and sent to her in Flanders.

Christina had barely settled in at Antwerp when she was told that a rabbi from Amsterdam wished to meet with her.⁴⁵ It was a rather perilous trip for Menasseh to make. He was leaving the safe confines of Holland for territory still under the watch of the Inquisition. But the danger did not come from the Spanish alone. In 1644, Menasseh's own congregation had passed a regulation prohibiting "any circumcised Jew" from visiting "lands of idolatry." Anyone who violated this decree would be readmitted to the community only after he had publicly expressed contrition for his action; if the offender was a rabbi, he would also be suspended from his duties for four years.⁴⁶

Menasseh was willing to risk the ire of the Talmud Torah *parnassim*, so in early August he crossed the international border now separating Dutch-speaking provinces that, less than a century earlier, had all been a part of the Spanish Low Countries. Although his motives remain somewhat obscure, we can be fairly certain that what he was after in Antwerp was money. It was once thought that his goal was to press Christina in person finally to settle up her account and pay him for those Hebrew books that he had sent her a couple of years earlier (although it is still not clear that the shipment ever actually arrived at her court).[47] He may also have asked her, in lieu of payment, to return the books to him.

However, in a letter to Nicolas Heinsius on August 20, 1654—a week or so after Menasseh's meeting with Christina— Isaac Vossius, who was with the former queen in Antwerp, told his erstwhile librarian colleague back in Sweden that Menasseh *had* indeed been paid for the books. He knew this because he himself had paid him. Vossius was writing Heinsius because a "chest" filled with Menasseh's Hebraica that was supposed to have been forwarded to Christina had not yet arrived in Antwerp. The books were being held up in Stockholm by a man named "Dr. Eric," a Lutheran preacher who was highly critical of Christina for her conversion and who for some reason had them in his possession. Vossius wanted those books, not least because they were technically now his, since he had given Menasseh nine hundred guilders for them (although he hoped to have Christina reimburse him). Vossius thus asked Heinsius to urge another intermediary—Christian Meys, a merchant in Stockholm—to press this Dr. Eric "so that he might return the books that I asked D. Menasseh to send." Vossius said, "I see no reason why he [Dr. Eric] is holding for so long goods that do not belong to him." "As for those Hebrew books," he continued, "I have now satisfied Menasseh. And so those books should be sent not to him but to me, as long as I have not yet received that sum of money from the Queen."[48]

Menasseh was in Antwerp for two weeks, and probably spent time with the small community of "Portuguese merchants" there. These were in all likelihood Judaizers, and perhaps Menasseh led them in secret services and gave them some guidance on liturgical and other matters.[49] He may also have met with the French Millenarian Isaac La Peyrère, who was in Antwerp as the secretary of the prince of Condé and was a frequent guest at Christina's intellectual salon in-exile. La Peyrère, the proponent of the pre-Adamite theory, was also the author of a 1643 work titled *Du rappel des juifs* (On the Calling of the Jews), in which he argued for a return of the Jews to France where, without converting to Christianity, they might prepare for the coming of the Messiah. (He insisted, moreover, that the Messiah's herald and regent would be the king of France; English Millenarians begged to differ, as some believed that Charles Stuart, the future Charles II, was anointed for this role.) For La Peyrère the differences between Jewish and Christian messianic expectations could be reconciled by allowing that they were in fact hoping for two different saviors.[50]

As entertaining as these other engagements may have been, Menasseh's primary purpose in Antwerp was to meet with Christina. But if his business with her was not for payment for the Hebrew books, what was it?

Writing to Vossius in February 1655, six months after the visit, Menasseh reminded him of "the great zeal with which I have always tried to delight Her Majesty, in as far as my humble talent permitted me," but pointed out "how much time passed with the handling of those books. It is a certain fact that the absence of assistance has cost me twice their value." While this may seem like a complaint about not being paid, in fact—since Vossius had given him the money already—Menasseh must have been merely informing him that, between shipping the books and waiting so long to receive payment, the deal was a losing proposition for him. It was a loss, however, that could be compensated for if Christina would return the books to him or, even better, provide him with "assistance."[51]

In other words, what Menasseh was hoping for from Christina was, once again, financial support, either by putting him on retainer so that he might continue to serve as her procurer of Hebrew books, or in the form of a subvention for his publications. Menasseh even had a particular book project in mind. In his February letter to Vossius, he asked him to propose to Christina that she "support the commentary on a Spanish Bible which I am publishing." This must be the same "Spanish Bible with a commentary . . . [that] will be a book in great demand" and that "is worthy of being printed on Her Majesty's expense" about which he had written Vossius four years earlier when the royal librarian was still in Stockholm. At the time, Menasseh had proclaimed himself ready "to disengage from all other plans, for the sake of this project."[52] He now told Vossius that during his meeting with Christina in Antwerp she did indeed promise to "soon perform my request." He was therefore writing Isaac to press him to follow up with her, "to act favorably towards me in a matter as urgent as this, and to speak with Her Majesty, so that she will honor and help me."

Menasseh's Spanish Bible was never published, and it was unlikely that he would ever receive another *stuiver* from Christina.[53] A few months after their Flemish rendezvous, she formalized her conversion to the Catholic faith and would soon depart for Rome.

In the spring of 1654, John Dury was on an extended tour of the Continent. Cromwell, as Lord Protector, had dispatched him to Holland, Germany, and Switzerland to serve as a diplomat at-large. By April, Dury was in The Hague and Amsterdam. This gave him the opportunity to meet with Menasseh, who reportedly told him that after the two earlier, aborted attempts he still firmly intended to go to England to seek permission for the Jews to settle there.[54] With the signing of the Treaty of Westminster on April 5, the (first) Anglo-Dutch War

had come to an end. There were no longer any "political reasons" for Menasseh to delay his mission. Still, it would be another year and a half before he actually made the journey.

Perhaps Menasseh was already suffering the "long illness"
from which, in September 1655, he would still describe himself
as "not yet fully recovered."[55] His family may once again have
urged him not to travel, at least not until he was healthy enough
to do so. But the delay may also have been due to concerns
within the Amsterdam Portuguese-Jewish community, still
sensitive about how it was perceived by the Dutch, regarding
one of its rabbis heading across the North Sea to deal with the
English.

It is not that the Talmud Torah *parnassim* were opposed, in
principle, to the reopening of England to Jewish settlement.
Indeed, they encouraged it, and members of the community
privately lent the project moral and material support. English
readmission would obviously help relieve the pressure on the
community caused by the increased Jewish immigration from
west and east. And the Sephardim were certainly aware of the
economic advantages to be gained by having a sister community in London. As one member of the *ma'amad*, the merchant
David Nassi, noted at the time, the lay leadership of the community "exceedingly desires the common good that they may
have more enlargement, acknowledging that to plant themselves in that realme another congregacion" would bring "no
small profit" to both Holland and England.[56] It is even likely
that the initial impetus for negotiations on readmission came
from prominent families among the Amsterdam Sephardim.

What the *ma'amad* could *not* do, however, was officially
sponsor the effort. It needed to avoid the appearance that the
community was, so soon after the war, collaborating with England, and to reassure the Dutch that there should be no question as to where their loyalties lay. Jacob del Monte, another
parnas, made it clear that the *ma'amad* had no intention of for-

mally appealing to Cromwell on behalf of readmission. "It is a thing impossible to be done . . . it doth impugne our constancy, for, being subjects of the States [of Holland] who have allwaies protected us with the laws which you know, and (in this citty [of Amsterdam]) as their citizens, how can you desire that our nation [i.e., the Portuguese-Jewish nation] should write to cause gelousy in an other Potentate or Republic?"[57]

Such professions of non-involvement, though, while good enough to allow for plausible deniability before the Dutch, do not mean that the Amsterdam Jewish community did not have a great interest in seeing the England project succeed. As one historian notes, "to contemporary observers, the mission to London from Amsterdam in the autumn of 1655 was not in fact Menasseh ben Israel's mission . . . but the work of a substantial group of Dutch Sephardic Jews, acting not in defiance of, but without the official backing of, the Amsterdam *Mahamad*."[58]

Still, despite this behind-the-scenes cheerleading, and just because of its political anxieties, the *ma'amad* could not have been happy about seeing Menasseh, the community's most famous member, taking the lead in the endeavor. The *parnassim* may even have been among those who had discouraged Menasseh on his two earlier attempted departures. Lead it he would, however, just as soon as he was well enough—or free enough— to leave home.[59]

In the meantime, Menasseh decided that it would be good to have his son Samuel make a preliminary visit to England. The young man went in the company of a former converso from Spain named Manoel Martinez Dormido. Dormido had arrived in Amsterdam in 1640, whereupon he returned to Judaism and joined the Portuguese congregation. Now known as David Abrabanel Dormido, he quickly became a respected leader among the Sephardim; in 1654 he was elected one of the *parnassim* of Talmud Torah (and thus was among the men to whom Menasseh that year dedicated his *Thesouro dos Dinim*).[60]

The trip to England was, in part, a matter of business. Dormido had lost a good deal of money in the Brazil debacle and was now out to restore his family's finances. London offered as good an opportunity as any, especially since he had already established cordial relations with some members of the English ruling class—possibly through acting as a spy for England during the war with the Dutch.[61] Menasseh thought that sending Samuel along with Dormido would allow him not only to reconnoiter the political landscape and gauge the possibilities for readmission, but also to investigate their own business prospects there, whether by expanding their printing and publishing operations or, more likely, reentering the import trade.

Dormido and Samuel arrived in London in September 1655. By November, Dormido had submitted a pair of petitions—not to Parliament, but to Cromwell himself. Writing, openly and boldly, as a member "of the Hebrew Nation" and a "loyall subiect of Your Highnesse and this most noble Commonwealth," he asked Cromwell both to intercede on his behalf with the king of Portugal in order to recoup the losses he had suffered when the Portuguese reconquered Pernambuco, and to allow the Jews to resettle in England, "graunting them libertie to come with theire famillies and estates to bee dwellers heere with the same eaquallnesse and conueniences, which your inland borne subjects doe injoy."[62] Among the considerations that Dormido marshalled in favor of settlement was the fact that "busines will increase and the comerce will become more oppulant," with a concommitant "increasement to the states Revenues."[63]

Cromwell, always looking to gain the upper hand in the economic competition with the United Provinces, was sympathetic to both requests, which he forwarded to the Council of State for their approval. The council, however, declined to act on either matter, ruling that there was "no cause to make any order."[64] A frustrated Cromwell took it upon himself to send a letter to King João IV of Portugal asking him to make restitution with Dormido. On the question of readmission, though, he hesitated to act alone and without the council's support. In response to a follow-up appeal by Dormido in December, the council reinforced its decision and ruled that allowing Jews to resettle in England was "against the establish'd law."[65] It was now clear—to Dormido, to English Millenarians, and to Cromwell— that a more organized and powerful lobby would be necessary.

Back in Amsterdam, in Samuel's absence and as he waited for the right time to leave for England, Menasseh had reassumed control of the publishing house. His output was relatively meager, probably since much of his attention was focused on the readmission project, but he did manage to bring out a *humash*, in Spanish, and an edition of the *Sefer Mekor Hayim* (The Source of Life), a Hebrew commentary on parts of Joseph Caro's *Shulhan Arukh* by Chaim ben Abraham ha-Cohen.

In the year leading up to his departure, Menasseh had also been keeping rather unusual company, even for someone as tolerant and open-minded as he.

Paul Felgenhauer was a conversionist Millenarian from Bohemia who had been living in Amsterdam, off and on, since 1623. A religious mystic, he believed himself to be the prophet Elijah, whose mission was to announce the imminent arrival of "Our Savior." In December 1654, Menasseh was with Felgenhauer at the house of their mutual friend Peter Serrarius.[66] As Felgenhauer later recalled it, "our conversation, dear friend, although very brief, was about the Messiah."[67] In follow-up meetings at Menasseh's house, the three men continued reviewing points of agreement and difference. These messianic discussions, while cordial, must have been rather intense, even at times uncomfortable. We can imagine Felgenhauer pressing

Menasseh to serve as a model to his people and embrace Christianity. They would also lead to the strangest collaboration of Menasseh's career.

What especially interested Felgenhauer—and what was coming to occupy Menasseh's mind more and more—was the timing of the Messiah's arrival. Felgenhauer was certain that the momentous event was near, and something about his exchanges with an amenable rabbi only confirmed his intuitions.

Soon after his meetings with Menasseh, Felgenhauer set to work composing a book in which he recounted "the few but very certain signs announcing the Advent of the Messiah."[68] Among the celestial and terrestrial omens were "true vexations and great terrors"—such as comets, wars and pestilence—and the reappearance of the Ten Tribes in unknown lands.[69] The *Bonum Nuncium Israeli* (The Good News for Israel) is Felgenhauer's message "to the Jews in these new times about the Messiah," including the "redemption of the people of Israel from all their iniquities and their liberation from captivity." It is a conversionist tract, inspired by "love and solace," intended to move Jews to accept the fundamental truth of Christianity and do their part to bring about both their own political and spiritual redemption and the glorious End of Days.

Jews and Christians, Felgenhauer argued, both descend from Abraham. They are essentially one people and share equally in God's promise. Indeed, because God instituted his covenant with Abraham before he was circumcised, "when he was still like a gentile," Christians enjoy "the first blessing" promised to Abraham's seed.[70] The message is that faith alone, regardless of circumcision, is sufficient to be counted among God's chosen. There should thus be no reason not to unite in a single church. "We will all be one in One, Our Father the One God." There is but a single Messiah for Jews and Christians, Felgenhauer insists, and it is Christ. He counsels his Jewish readers with the words of the Psalmist: "If today you hear his voice, do not harden your hearts."[71]

Felgenhauer had sent to Menasseh the manuscript in which he laid out this messianic vision and ecumenical appeal. Menasseh responded with a letter to Felgenhauer in which he expressed his gratitude for "that good news delivered by you in these latest and most afflicted times for the people of Israel."[72] He added the wish, "would that your good news were true" and the messianic age soon to arrive. "After so many hardships over the centuries and with hopes put off for so long, I have never ceased ardently to wish for good news."

Menasseh claimed to have found some common ground with Felgenhauer, and much cause for hope.

> O good herald of good news, do you thus say it is now soon that our God, our Merciful One, will arrive, and that, as we have desired for so many centuries, He will shortly send our Messiah? Do you thus say that time is imminent in which God, who until now has been offended and turned away by us, will once again console his people and redeem them not only from this captivity greater than the Babylonian and from a servitude greater than the Egyptian in which it has now long languished, but also from its iniquities, in which it has almost been consumed?[73]

Menasseh was likewise keenly attuned to indications that the messianic era was near. He agreed with some of Felgenhauer's prognostications. The Messiah's coming, he conceded in his letter, would be preceded by "grand conturbations, tumults, seditions, intestine and most cruel wars," including the fall of the great empires—all of which, he argued, were reflected in the present bellicose state of the world. Felgenhauer's second sign, the spread of preaching about the reign of Israel over the whole world, was also confirmed by current events. Heralds in all countries, he claimed, were proclaiming the coming of "Israel's kingdom." However, Menasseh did not concur with the alleged third sign. He told Felgenhauer that the arrival of the prophet Elijah—who both Jews and Christians agree will immediately precede the Messiah but who, he reminded Felgenhauer, "must arise from our [Jewish] people"—had not yet occurred, so "we must suspend our hope until God will have revealed him to us." Menasseh was willing to allow in *The Hope of Israel* that "the day of the promised Messiah draws near to us," but he was not ready to commit to anything more specific; the prophetic writings were too obscure on this topic to allow for reasonable speculation. And he certainly could not agree with Felgenhauer's insistence that the inauguration of the Messiah's reign must be preceded by the Jews' acceptance of Christ.

Felgenhauer included Menasseh's letter to him in the *Bonum Nuncium*, which he published in Amsterdam in February 1655 with a dedication to Menasseh, "that most famous man, Hebrew philosopher and theologian . . . my friend, a man of true wisdom and lover of truth." He also included a poem of praise for Menasseh composed by Jacob Rosales ("Hebraic Mathematician, Philosopher, and Medical Doctor"), which was supplied by Menasseh himself; letters written to Menasseh from English, French, and German Millenarians (Jessey, Homes, La Peyrère, Abraham von Franckenberg, and Johann Mochinger); and a catalogue of Hebrew, Latin, and Spanish books "published by me" (Menasseh).[74]

Felgenhauer's name did not appear on the title page of the *Bonum Nuncium*. It is there at the end of the dedication, though, and the main chapters of the book are from his pen. But the book very much seems to be a joint enterprise between him and Menasseh.[75] To a suspicious reader, the rabbi could easily appear to have collaborated, as co-editor, on a book whose goal was to hasten the conversion of the Jews. He was, after all, given to handing out copies of the book to visitors to his home.[76] What Menasseh was thinking is anyone's guess. The *parnassim* in Amsterdam could not have been very pleased with this development. It is one thing to work for Jewish-Christian rapprochement, but this was going too far.

Through his conversations with Felgenhauer, Serrarius, and other conversionist and non-conversionist Millenarians, Menasseh's own messianic ideas were invigorated.[77] Where earlier he had been content to offer general ruminations about what the era of the Messiah promised and to whom, as well as a vague insinuation that the time was "near," by the mid-1650s he was looking more closely at the what, the why, and the how, if not precisely the when. Menasseh's most uninhibited say on these matters appears in what would be his penultimate treatise, the *Piedra Gloriosa* (The Glorious Stone).

The Book of Daniel, like the story of Esther, was of great importance in the early modern period to both Jews in the Sephardic diaspora and Judaizing conversos still living in Spain and Portugal. The message of redemption they saw in the divinations and visions of this Jewish exile in the ancient Babylonian court comforted them in difficult times. It sustained their messianic hopes for a future of the Jewish people freed from their captivities and reunited in the Holy Land under a new Davidic king. (Christian Millenarians saw reflected in that same biblical text their own dreams of the Fifth Monarchy under the reign of Christ.)

The subtitle of Menasseh's treatise, much of which is a commentary on Daniel, is "On the Statue of Nebuchadnezzar." He declared that this subject "touches on the totality of the history of the Hebrew people, until the end of time, and the time of the Messiah."[78] Menasseh offered an interpretation of the episode from Daniel in which Nebuchadnezzar, the King of Babylon, dreamed of a "huge and dazzling" statue—with a head of gold, breast and arms of silver, torso of bronze, legs of iron, and feet of clay and iron—that was then toppled and shattered by a

boulder (Daniel 2:31–36). In the biblical story, Daniel, habitu-
ally a bearer of bad tidings to Babylonian monarchs, explains
the king's dream as forecasting the doom facing his and subsequent kingdoms. Daniel then foretells of "a kingdom established by the God of heaven that will never be destroyed . . . it
shall shatter and make an end to all those kingdoms, it shall
itself endure forever."

It was not very difficult for Menasseh to find the messianic
import of Daniel's dream interpretation. The stone that crushes
the king's statue, "hewn from a mountain without the intervention of human hands," represents the Messiah sent by God.
Having swept away all other empires of the world—the Baby-
lonians, the Persians, the Greeks, and the Romans, represented
by the materially composite statue—he will replace them with
the Kingdom of Israel. "This stone is the Messiah, a stone that,
striking the feet of the statue, will put an end to all the kingdoms of the Fourth Monarchy, will become an immense mountain and will fill the world."[79]

Not content to provide a reading of these passages from
Daniel, Menasseh argued that the same messianic message is
present throughout the Hebrew Bible. It is there in the narratives of the patriarchs as well as in the writings of the prophets.
It is certain, he said, that "God revealed to [Moses] the entire
history of the Jews up to the end of time," and so the Torah is
full of indications about the fate of the Four Monarchies and
the establishment of the Fifth.[80] One needs only to know how
to read between the lines. "There is no prophet to whom God
has not revealed this mystery."[81] It even informs the love poetry
of the Song of Songs.

Remarkably, Menasseh argued that the stone that topples
the statue in Nebuchadnezzar's dream is in fact identical with
the stones that appear in two other well-known biblical stories.
It is the same exact rock as that on which Jacob's head rested

while he dreamed about angels going up and down a ladder and which he then set up as a sacred pillar onto which he pours oil (Genesis 28:10–19). "We have here the same stone," Menasseh insisted, "the stone of the Messiah."[82] Then there is the stone used by David, representing the Messiah, to slay the Philistine giant Goliath, who stood for both the statue of Nebuchadnezzar and the four captivities of Israel (I Samuel 17). David, Menasseh noted, had five stones in his bag. Four of them were "useless," and represent the Four Monarchies. "The fifth one stands for the one that shattered the Statue. It is the same stone on which Jacob poured oil, and the same one of which Daniel spoke."[83]

The finale of the treatise is Menasseh's extended discussion of Daniel's vision of the beasts (7:1–27). Daniel relates that during the reign of Belshazzar, Nebuchadnezzar's son, "I saw a great sea churned up by the four winds of heaven, and four huge beasts coming up out of the sea." One was a lion with eagle's wings; a second was a bear; and a third was a four-headed leopard with four bird wings on its back. Most terrifying of all was a fourth beast, "dreadful and grisly, exceedingly strong, with great iron teeth and bronze claws. It crunched and devoured, and then trampled underfoot all that was left. It differed from all the beasts that preceded it in having ten horns." One of the horns had "eyes like the eyes of a man and a mouth that spoke proud words." This last beast was killed and its carcass thrown into flames. Then, Daniel, continues,

> I saw one like a man coming with the clouds of heaven; he approached the Ancient in Years and was presented to him. Sovereignty and glory and kingly power were given to him so that all people and nations of every language should serve him; his sovereignty was to be an everlasting sovereignty which should not pass away, and his kingly power such as should never be impaired.

The four beasts were, once again, the four doomed kingdoms, while the man coming down from heaven was the Messiah. His fifth kingdom will, on Menasseh's account, be an everlasting worldly dominion.[84] "The monarchy of Israel," he insisted, "will be temporal and terrestrial," with the Davidic king sent by God ruling all nations under one law.[85] Menasseh reminded his reader, however, that the world-to-come is also a spiritual condition. "We do not so ardently aspire to it simply in order to profit from the fruits of the land of our fathers, to enjoy the leisure and pleasures of a sweet and tranquil life; we are not as carnal as certain people think." The denizens of this future monarchy will engage in "true contemplation," devoting themselves to virtue, study, and worship and thereby enjoying "a perpetual happiness and joy."[86]

As in his earlier writings, Menasseh in *Piedra Gloriosa* emphasized the universality of God's justice in the world-to-come. His mercy would be extended not only to Jews but to all righteous people—"all who adore God, each in his own way," whether by the Law of Moses or the laws of nature.[87] This afforded Menasseh the opportunity to present a code of ethics that transcended religious differences. To be righteous is

> to live with equity, to offend no one, not to take the goods of others, not to dishonor one's neighbor but to be charitable towards him, to live soberly and with temperance. How could anybody who does all this not be recompensed? . . . All adore the First Cause, each in his own way. He who lives according to the law of nature is pious and will have his reward . . . The pious of the nations of the world will have their part in the time to come.[88]

In a remark that is surely aimed both at the Dutch, in gratitude for the refuge they have provided, and at the English, in hope that they will follow suit, Menasseh added that there would be a special place in God's kingdom for those who protect rather than oppress the Jews. "The Messiah will receive those nations that do not tyrannize Israel."[89]

Menasseh, no doubt to the disappointment of Felgenhauer and others, still hesitated to speculate on when the Messiah was due. He was certain of the truth of Daniel's vision of God's providential design. "The fact that these four monarchies had a palpable existence demonstrates, unambiguously, incontestably, the infallibility of the prophecies of the dream."[90] And he remained convinced that the messianic days would arrive "soon." But he may also have had in mind Maimonides's warning that among those who will have no place in the world-to-come are those who spend too much time speculating on the world-to-come.

Menasseh was ready to publish his book in the spring of 1655. However, he thought it could use some pictures. His discussions of the toppling of Nebuchadnezzar's statue, Jacob dreaming of the ladder, David felling Goliath, and especially Daniel's graphic vision of the beasts all demanded visual aids "to better clarify what is being said."[91]

Menasseh related that he himself composed, "with great propriety," four images of just these episodes for the book. "All of this took a lot of work and industry," he wrote in his preface to the reader.[92] And a number of extant copies of the first edition of *Piedra Gloriosa* do contain such illustrations.[93] But the four etchings in these volumes, printed one to a page, are not by Menasseh. Rather, they are signed by another resident of the Vlooienburg quarter—Rembrandt Harmensz van Rijn.

From 1639 to 1659, Rembrandt owned a large house on the Sint Antoniesbreestraat, the broad boulevard across the Houtgracht from the island on which Menasseh lived. Because it was a relatively small and intimate neighborhood, and given Menasseh's prominence in the Jewish community, his reputation in the gentile world, and Rembrandt's interest in Judaica, chances are the two men met soon after Rembrandt moved to the city from Leiden in 1631.[94] They did have a number of good acquaintances in common. These included members of the Anslo clan—the Mennonite preacher Cornelis Anslo was portrayed twice by Rembrandt, and his son Gerbrand had studied Hebrew with Menasseh—and the Portuguese-Jewish physician Ephraim Bueno, Menasseh's friend and patron, who is the subject of both a painting and an etching by Rembrandt. Perhaps, then, Menasseh, dissatisfied with his own handiwork on the illustrations, simply went to an artist well known in the city for his skill with the etching needle, and who just happened to live nearby.

If this was indeed a direct collaboration between Menasseh and Rembrandt, it would not have been the first time that one of them sought the help of the other on a subject from the Book of Daniel.[95] Sometime between 1633 and 1639, Rembrandt did a painting of the "Belshazzar's Feast" episode (Daniel 5:1–30). In the biblical story, Belshazzar is giving a banquet using the vessels of gold and silver that his father had taken from the Temple sanctuary in Jerusalem when all of a sudden a very public vision emerges: a hand writing something on the palace wall. Daniel is the only member of the court who can read the message and provide an interpretation. The Aramaic text, he tells the king, says "*Mene, mene, tekel, ufarsin*," and it means, essentially, "Your days are numbered."[96]

In Rembrandt's painting, a surprised Belshazzar turns around as a hand emerges from a cloud and writes the message in Hebrew characters. The biblical text does not say *why* none of the king's guests or ministers could read the words, nor does it give any indication as to the form in which the message was written. This gave rise to some debate among the ancient rabbis as to how the writing must have looked to the confused banqueters. Were the words encrypted in some way? Were they written backward, from left to right? Were letters transposed? Or were the words to be read right to left but vertically downward rather than horizontally across?[97]

This last, vertical format of the mysterious apparition is exactly how it is depicted in Rembrandt's painting. It is also the *only* one of the rabbinic explanations presented by Menasseh in his discussion of Belshazzar in *De Termino Vitae*, where he includes a diagram of the words that resembles perfectly the image in Rembrandt's painting.[98] It is thus likely that Rembrandt, stuck on just how he should depict the divine message in his painting of a scene from Hebrew Scripture, walked down the street and over the "wood canal" to consult with a rabbi.[99]

Menasseh published *Piedra Gloriosa* in April, with a dedication to Isaac Vossius. Unlike many of his other writings, it appeared only in Spanish. This time there would be no Latin or English translations. Oddly, the most explicit of Menasseh's messianic, Fifth Monarchy writings would remain the least accessible to his Millenarian, Fifth Monarchist friends in London.

In May 1655, after nine months in England, Samuel returned to Amsterdam. He found his father in poor health but still deeply engaged in the readmission project. Samuel briefed him on the political situation, and told him about the small but organized colony of Sephardim in London among whom he and Dormido had settled.

Samuel came back bearing a title, or so it seemed. He was now presenting himself around Amsterdam—and probably to Menasseh as well—as "Dr. Samuel ben Israel Soeiro." He had always been eager to practice medicine, but as a Jew he was not allowed to matriculate in any university faculty. While in England he tried to persuade the University of Oxford to award him a doctorate, perhaps relying on his father's famous name, but the university's regents were not moved. Somehow, though, Samuel was able to come up with a "degree." He got his hands on an old University of Padua document and altered it to show that he was an Oxford-certified physician.[100] He was set on impressing his family and their community, letting everyone know that he had made good, even if it required some forgery.

High on Samuel's agenda as he brought Menasseh up to speed on the English negotiations was Cromwell's positive attitude toward Jewish settlement. Samuel told Menasseh that he had been encouraged by the Lord Protector himself to persuade his father, whom Cromwell believed would be the most effective advocate for the cause, to come to London and use his influence on behalf of the Jews. Menasseh, writing in April the following year while in London, recalls his pleasure in "finding that my coming over would not be altogether unwelcome to [his Highnesse the Lord Protector]."[101] That Menasseh's visit was indeed Cromwell's idea is confirmed by a letter to Richard Cromwell, his son and successor as England's head of state, from John Sadler, a strong proponent of readmission. "Thanks to certain letters from your royal father and other personalities of our nation, certain members of their synagogues were encouraged to send to us one of the great rabbis, Menasseh ben Israel, in order to discuss their admission and a certain liberty of commerce in some of our isles."[102]

Thus, in early September 1655, at the age of fifty, "although not yet fully recovered from a long illness, moved only by zeal and love of my people, and . . . neglecting all of my private interests," Menasseh, accompanied by Samuel, departed for London.[103] "I joyfully took my leave of my house, my friends, my kindred, all my advantages there, and the country wherein I have lived all my life time, under the benign protection, and favour of the Lords, the States Generall, and Magistrates of Amsterdam; in fine (I say) I parted with them all, and took my voyage to England."[104] He embarked upon this journey, he says in his open letter to "the Hebrew nation" composed on the eve of his departure, with both a strong sense of duty (especially to New Christians still being oppressed by the Spanish Inquisition) and great expectations.

Considering the common applause, the general good, the affliction of those of our people who are today so oppressed, who could find refuge and remedy in that most mighty commonwealth, without prejudice to any other; having regard, too, for the many souls who, dissimulating their religion, dwell scattered in so many parts of Spain and France, it was impossible for me to neglect an affair of such merit, even though it be at the cost of my faculties. I have been informed by letters and by faithful correspondents that today this English nation is no longer our ancient enemy, but has changed the Papist religion and become excellently affected to our nation, as an oppressed people whereof it has good hope.[105]

After crossing the North Sea, Menasseh and Samuel settled into rooms in a house "in the Strand, over against the New Exchange," a fashionable neighborhood near the River Thames. This was a peculiar choice of lodging, since it was both expensive and some distance from the East End—Bishopsgate Street, Bevis Marks, and Duke's Place—where most of London's small Sephardic community resided and where their clandestine meetinghouses were. The only way Menasseh could have afforded such an upscale address was if someone was subsidizing it. A very likely candidate is Cromwell himself.[106]

Not coincidentally, Menasseh and Samuel landed just before the Jewish New Year. The London Sephardim were no doubt happy to have a rabbi from the celebrated Talmud Torah congregation in Amsterdam lead them in Rosh Hashanah and Yom Kippur services. Menasseh reported that upon his arrival in London he was "very courteously received, and treated with much respect"—presumably by both his English hosts and the London Jews, including Carvajal and Dormido, who was now a permanent resident.

According to the Julian calendar, which was still in use in Protestant countries like England and the Netherlands in the mid-seventeenth century, the High Holy Days that year began in mid-September.[107] Menasseh waited until these were over before getting down to business. He had brought over with him copies of a pamphlet that he had composed and printed in Amsterdam, and in early October, with these in hand, he went to Whitehall, the seat of the Council of State. Unfortunately, Cromwell was not in attendance that day, and Menasseh was told that he could not be admitted to the chambers. The State Record for October 31 reports that "on hearing that Menasseh ben Israel, a Jew, is attending at the door with some books which he wishes to present to the Council . . . Mr. Jessop [is ordered] to go out and to receive them, and bring them in."[108]

Titled "To His Highnesse the Lord Protector of the Com-mon-wealth of England, Scotland and Ireland, The Humble Addresses of Menasseh ben Israel," the booklet, written in En-glish, lays out Menasseh's case for the readmission of the Jews and asks that England "grant us place in your Country, that we might have our synagogues, and free exercise of our religion."

No doubt aware of Cromwell's lack of interest in messianic speculation, Menasseh only briefly alluded to eschatological matters. Since "the restoring time of our Nation into their Na-tive Countrey, is very neer at hand; I believing more particu-larly that this restauration cannot be, before . . . *the dispersion of the Holy people shall be compleated in all places,* the People of God must be first dispersed into all places & Countreyes of the World." He went on to claim, rather incredibly, that England was the last place on earth where there were no Jews.

> We know, how our Nation at the present is spread all about, and hath its feat and dwelling in the most flourishing parts of al the Kingdomes, and Countreys of the World, as well as in American, as in the other three parts thereof; except onely in this considerable and mighty Island. And therefore this remains onely in my judgement, before the Messia come and restore our Nation, that first we must have our feat here likewise.[109]

Though not likely to move Cromwell, it was a clever strategy playing to the Millenarian inclinations of the pamphlet's broader audience. Did the English really want to be the ones holding up the coming of the Messiah?

For the most part, though, Menasseh limited his argument to utilitarian considerations. Of the Jews, he noted that "no [monarch] hath ever afflicted them, who hath not been by some ominious Exit, most heavily punished of God almighty. . . . And on the contrary, none ever was a Benefactor to that people, and cherished them in their Countries, who thereupon hath not presently begun very much to flourish."[110] Menasseh was only reminding Cromwell and his peers of some salient facts of English history—including the fate of Charles I—and was hopeful that now that England was a commonwealth, "the antient hatred towards [us] would also be changed into good-will."

Menasseh put a lot of store on the fact that "profit is a most powerfull motive," and so reminded the Lord Protector that throughout history those nations that have hosted Jewish populations have prospered. "It is a thing confirmed, that merchandizing is, as it were, the proper profession of the Nation of the Iews," since they have no country of their own, and thus "there riseth an infallible Profit, commodity and gain to all those Princes in whose Lands they dwell."[111]

In the "Humble Addresses" Menasseh also undertook to put to rest any concerns about the dangers of having Jews residing in England. Again, history had shown that they are good subjects, "by reason of the faithfulnesse and loyalty they show to all Potentates that receive and protect them in their countries." As for worries about Jewish usury, Menasseh noted that, first, this was neither universal among nor unique to Jews, and even among Jews it was found mainly among the Ashkenazim; and second, it was only natural that one should be allowed to "gain and get some advantage with his money," as long as it is done with moderation.[112]

Finally, there were the long-standing accusations against the Jewish people: that they kill Christian children to celebrate Passover, and that they are out to convert Christians. These are mere "slander and calumny," Menasseh insisted. Not only were they contrary to fact, but they are, just on the face of it, highly implausible, especially the blood libel. "No sacrifice nor blood is in any use by [Jews], even that blood which is found in an egg is forbidden to them, how much more mans blood?"[113]

Nothing came of this first appeal by way of the "Humble Addresses." The Council of State made no formal reply to Menasseh's pamphlet and took no action. A few weeks later, Menasseh had a second chance when he was granted an audience with Cromwell himself. He then presented the Lord Protector with a more direct and succinct request that somewhat presumptuously laid out seven conditions that would allow Jews comfortably to reside in the commonwealth. He supplemented this with letters of support he had received for the project from various Jewish communities. "I presented to his most Serene Highnesse, a petition, and some desires, which for the most part, were written to me by my brethren the Iewes, from severall parts of Europe."[114] Among the terms listed by Menasseh were that the Jews were to enjoy the same protections as other citizens, including economic freedom and judicial standing; that they be permitted public worship in synagogues; that they be allowed to purchase land for a cemetery; and that any laws "contrary to our Jewish nation be revoked so that we might live with greater security under the safeguard and protection of your most serene Highness."[115]

Cromwell, who was much in favor of readmission, brought this petition to the Council of State, which referred the matter to a special subcommittee. This subcommittee, in turn, recommended that the issue be turned over to an ad hoc body that could provide expert and informed advice. Thus began the famous Whitehall Conference. Its twenty-eight members included clergy, diplomats, lawyers, politicians, philosophers, and businessmen—including Henry Jessey, Walter Strickland (who had been part of the St. Oliver mission in The Hague), Benjamin Whichcote (the provost of Kings College, Cambridge), and Ralph Cudworth (the Regius Professor of Hebrew at Cambridge).

The conference held its first meeting on December 4, "to the intent [that] some proposalls made to his Highness in reference to the nation of the Jewes may bee considered."[116] Cromwell read Menasseh's petition to the assembly, and then charged its members to come up with recommendations on two distinct questions. First, was it lawful to admit Jews to England? And second, if it was lawful, under what conditions should they be allowed to settle?

The Whitehall Conference met over five sessions, from December 4 to 18.[117] The jurists in attendance suggested that the first issue could be easily resolved on a mere technicality. Since the original act of expulsion was issued by Edward I and not Parliament, it was valid only under that king's dominion and thus no longer binding. They concluded, "there is no Law against their coming." While this opinion may have removed any legal obstacle, it was far from settling the issue.

Throughout the two weeks that the conference was in session, England witnessed a great debate on the Jewish question. In public and private venues—newspapers, pamphlets, placards, personal letters, diplomatic reports, and ordinary conversations in the street—opinions for and against readmission were, as one observer noted, shared "with much candore and ingenuitye."[118] The economic advantages alleged by some ("they will bring much wealth into this commonwealth") were countered by fears of the increased competition that the Jewish merchants would pose to English businesses. The opportunity for advancing the conversion of the Jews was outweighed, some argued, by the danger of allowing them to mingle with Christians and convert *them* to Judaism. Feelings of sympathy for this long-suffering people and considerations of fairness—after all, Turks were allowed to reside and carry on trade in London—were met with old anti-Semitic slurs and fantastic accusations. One popular allegation had the Jews raising money to purchase St. Paul's Cathedral and convert it into a synagogue. "Very few of this nation," one foreign observer wrote, "are agreed to let them make their nest in these lands."[119] Salvetti, the Tuscan ambassador, wrote that month to his employer back home to explain that "it is a matter which generally encounters great opposition, especially from the preachers, merchants, and populace."[120] Even Menasseh's old friend, John Dury, was ambivalent. While conceding that allowing Jews into England was "expedient," he insisted that it should be done only in a way that would facilitate their conversion. This would have to include mandatory attendance at Christian sermons.[121]

The deliberations within Whitehall mirrored what was going on outside. No real consensus or even strong majority ever emerged—this despite the fact that halfway through its meetings Cromwell tried to stack the conference in his favor. If anything, the assembly was leaning against readmission. Ecclesiastic delegates to the conference, naturally unmoved by Millenarian arguments, were strongly opposed for theological reasons—after all, these were "blasphemers against Christ"—while representatives from the world of trade objected on protectionist grounds. The judicial and political members, on the other hand, tended to lean toward Jewish resettlement as a matter of pragmatism or morality, although most insisted that it would still be good to impose restrictive conditions.

In the end, it appears to have been a deadlock. Much to the annoyance of Cromwell—who, at the conference's final session, gave an impassioned speech for readmission—the Whitehall Conference concluded on December 18 without making a recommendation one way or the other. There was too much opposition among the conferees and in public opinion. Cromwell, with his power as Lord Protector, could have moved forward on his own, but it would have been politically risky. As a disappointed Menasseh recounted after the conference adjourned, because its members were made up of "Divines, Lawyers and Merchants, of different perswasions, and opinions" and whose "judgements and sentences were different . . . as yet we have had no finall determination from his most Serene Highnesse."[122]

On the bright side, neither was the idea of Jewish settlement squelched. In fact, the subcommittee of the Council of State that had convened the Whitehall Conference for advice issued its own report to the council while the meetings were still in progress. Its recommendation steered a middle course between Cromwell's willingness to allow for uninhibited settlement and the onerous restrictions that many at the conference wanted placed on Jews. This committee, considering the proposition "that the Jewes deservinge it may be admitted into this nation to trade and trafficke and dwel amongst us as providence shall give occasion," agreed that there was no legal impediment to readmission, even that "it is lawful in point of conscience." There should be some restrictions, however. The committee explicitly rejected the terms that Menasseh had proposed in his petition. It claimed that such liberties—such as public synagogues—would be "very sinfull for this or any Christian state to receive them upon." There should be no "publicke Judicatoryes, whether civill or ecclesiasticall," and the Jews would be forbidden "eyther to speake or doe anythinge to the defamation of the name of our Lord Jesus Christ or of the Christian religion." Jewish households would not be allowed to have Christian servants, nor would Jews be allowed to hold public office or do any work on the Christian sabbath. Above all, there would be serious penalties for any Jew caught proselytizing among Christians.[123]

There was still hope in some quarters that Cromwell would act. On December 21, Ambassador Salvetti wrote to the duke that "it is generally believed that His Highness is about to terminate everything by his own authority. This the Jews hope will be in their favor, although with some limitation."[124] If this was indeed Cromwell's plan, he was keeping it a secret. For the time being, it seemed that, at least officially, the campaign for the readmission of the Jews to England was stalled.

8

Denouement

All Menasseh and the London Sephardim could do now was wait. With the Council of State unwilling to decide the issue, the ball was in Cromwell's court. The Lord Protector was sympathetic to the Jewish cause, mainly because it served the English cause, but he was hesitant to act, given the tenor of public opinion. By late January 1656, the Tuscan ambassador's earlier sense that readmission was on the horizon had given way to a more pessimistic view. "In the matter of the Jews," Salvetti reported, "people do not speak as much as they used to do at the outset. Everyone now believes that the Lord Protector will not make any declaration in their favor." The more likely scenario, at least in the short run, he told his duke, was a continuation of a policy of tacit toleration. Cromwell, he suggested, would "postpone action while conniving in the meantime at religious exercise in their private houses, as they do at present."[1]

Besides, Cromwell had other, rather more pressing matters at hand. No sooner had the country signed a peace treaty with the United Provinces than it was at war on another front. In the late summer of 1655, the council had authorized a treaty with France. This essentially set England on a collision course with the third superpower, Spain. The two kingdoms had been engaged in a long-standing commercial rivalry—similar to that which occasioned the Anglo-Dutch conflict—with tit-for-tat skirmishes in the Caribbean and mutual privateering. War finally broke out in October, and the hostilities would last for another five years.

The decision that Cromwell faced regarding readmission was not unrelated to this new military venture. A resident community of Sephardic Jews could help the war effort. England was eager to improve its hand in the trans-Atlantic sugar trade, in which Portuguese-Jewish merchants still had a significant if reduced part.[2] Opening up the country to Jewish settlement, along with the capture of Spanish cane-producing colonies in the West Indies, would give England greater control over these lucrative networks. In the midst of a war initiated mainly by economic motives, Cromwell would not have needed reminding of the benefits of readmission.

A misstep by the English early in the war ended up putting the tacit accommodation of London's Jewish community to the test. Antonio Rodrigues Robles, one of the wealthy Sephardic merchants living in the city and a leader of the barely clandestine congregation, though not active in the readmission campaign, ended up playing an important role in it nonetheless.[3] In March 1656, just after the council declared that the property of Spanish citizens in the country was subject to seizure, Robles was denounced as a Spaniard by an unscrupulous Englishman. His goods—including two ships moored in the Thames—were impounded. The rest of the "New Christian" community, with their Spanish roots, now felt threatened. Would the English next come after them all as enemy aliens, perhaps as an efficient measure for dealing with merchants whom pretty much everyone knew to be Jewish?[4]

London's Jews faced a dilemma. They could either pick up their lives and move elsewhere—perhaps to Amsterdam—or finally declare themselves. The first option was unthinkable, so it was time for them to end a poorly kept secret. On March 24, a petition signed by Menasseh and six leading members of the London community—with Menasseh's signature notably on top—was presented to Cromwell. Dormido, Carvajal, and their colleagues openly announced themselves as "Hebrews at Present Residing in this citty of London," and asked that "such Protection may be graunted us in Writing as that wee may therewith meete at owr said private devotions in owr Particular houses without feere of Molestation either to owr persons famillys or estates, owr desires Being to Live Peaceably under your Highnes Governement." They also asked permission to purchase land for a cemetery, so that "those which may dey [die] of owr nation may be buryed in such a place out of the cittye as wee shall thineke convenient."[5]

At the same time, Robles appealed his case to the Admiralty Commission and the Council of State, arguing that far from being a Spaniard, he was Portuguese. More importantly, he said, he was a member of the "Hebrew Nation" whose family had been a victim of Spanish intolerance.

The community's petition and Robles's appeal together amounted to a very clever (if uncoordinated) strategy. It would force the hand of the English to finally accept that there were indeed Jews living among them and that they were deserving of some rights and prerogatives. In May, the authorities declared themselves unable to determine what exactly Robles's religion and nationality were—the fact that he was seen attending Catholic mass at the Spanish ambassador's house did not clarify matters—but they eventually ordered his ships and other property to be released. Robles was indeed to be recognized as a Jewish refugee. Moreover, in light of the letters of support he presented from other Sephardic residents, it was now unambiguously clear that his was but one of several dozen Jewish families. By not taking any action against the members of the community that stood behind Robles, the council, while not formally responding to the petition signed by Menasseh and others, essentially acknowledged the facts on the ground. As one historian notes, "an open Anglo-Jewish community was thus a new reality after the end of the Robles case."[6]

Of course, this did not put an end to disputes over the Jewish question, especially since it did not amount to a formal proclamation of readmission. As long as Cromwell refused to settle the matter once and for all, arguments for and against Jewish residence would continue as before, with unabated passion and, at least on one side, a great deal of venom.

These were the circumstances under which Menasseh—six months after issuing his "Humble Addresses" and just before the resolution of the Robles case—decided to reenter the public debate with an extraordinarily important document in the history of Jewish apologetics. It would be his final work.

The *Vindiciae Judaeorum* (A Vindication of the Jews), an essay in English that Menasseh published in April, was both his reply to contemporary opponents of settlement and a refutation of centuries of anti-Jewish prejudice and calumny.[7] Some truly scandalous pamphlets were circulating during the winter of the Whitehall Conference and into the spring. The English lawyer William Prynne, for one, published a series of tracts in which he defended the expulsion of 1290 and reviewed the standard litany of malicious vilifications. He called Jews "great Clippers and Forgers of mony," brought up the blood libel, and even accused them of crucifying English children.[8]

The Jews' gentile advocates were all too willing to respond to Prynne and his like, but Menasseh, worried about Cromwell's indecision and fearing for the cause of readmission, thought it best himself to undertake an extended defense of his people—in English, for all to read. He laid out six of the most prominent indictments against Jews and addressed each one at length, employing classical texts, historical evidence, and simple logic.

Menasseh devoted the most space in the *Vindiciae* to rebutting "the strange and horrid accusation" with perhaps the oldest pedigree, namely, "the Jews are wont to celebrate the feast of unleavened bread, fermenting it with the bloud of some Christians, whom they have for this purpose killed." Menasseh explored the origin of this slander in the "covetous ambition" of their enemies, who were eager "to gain their [the Jews'] wealth, and possesse themselves of their estates." However, he argued, not only does the Torah forbid one to kill, but Jews have as a matter of fact universally demonstrated their benevolence to all peoples. Besides, the accusation is highly implausible. Jews are forbidden to consume the blood of any animal; how would they then permit themselves to consume human blood? And why would they profane their solemn Passover holiday with such a gruesome ritual?

Menasseh then turned to the charge, long made by Christians, that Jews are idolators. It is true, he noted, that in the synagogue service they may stand up in the presence of, and even bow before and kiss, the Torah scrolls; but these are acts of piety, not adoration. Nor is it part of synagogue worship to curse Christians, asking that God "confound and root them out," or to blaspheme by uttering Christ's name "with scornfull spitting." "It is a mere calumnie to imagine, that we Iewes should pray to God, so as to give an offence to the Christians, or cause scandall, by anything in our prayers."[9] As to the claim that Jews are a threat to any Christian commonwealth because of their proselytizing, Menasseh reminded his English readers that Jews are not out to convert others. "We do not seduce anyone," he says. On the contrary, they discourage conversion and make it as difficult a process as possible. Above all, they want to make sure that the motives of the potential convert are pure, not done out of "love with some of our nation, or for any other worldly respect."[10]

Menasseh wanted to end his short treatise on a positive note, so he reviewed, once again, the economic benefits of allowing Jews to flourish in one's country. They are honest and productive businessmen, both as a matter of law—since the Torah forbids theft and the violation of oaths—and as a matter of fact. They will "always bring profit to the people of the land" that hosts them and allows them the liberty to pursue their professions. As for the rumor that the Jews are out to use their business acumen and wealth to purchase St. Paul's Cathedral and turn it into a synagogue, he dismissed it as something that "never entred into the thoughts of our nation," and was therefore not even worthy of discussion.[11]

While waiting for Cromwell and some sign that the readmission process was moving along, Menasseh took good advantage of his time in England. He brushed up on his English, made the rounds of London society, and even dined with Cromwell at his home.[12] He also dropped in to see the ambassador from the United Provinces. It is not clear whether this was just a casual visit or if the rabbi had been summoned by the diplomat. The war between England and the Republic may have been over, but their commercial rivalry continued, especially with the Navigation Act still in effect. The Dutch were likely concerned that the effort on behalf of readmission to England would, if successful, draw Sephardim away from Holland, along with their businesses and their investments in the Dutch East and West Indies Companies. Ambassador Willem Nieupoort therefore may have been looking for some reassurance from Menasseh that England's gain would not be the Dutch Republic's loss. In a letter from early December 1655 in which he reported on "the conference about the Jews," Nieupoort noted that "Menasseh ben Israel hath been to see me; and he did assure me, that he doth not desire anything for the Jews in Holland, but only for such as sit in the inquisition in Spain and Portugal."[13]

Menasseh also made the acquaintance of various luminaries of the English intellectual world. He met several times with the Cambridge philosopher Ralph Cudworth—a delegate to the Whitehall conference—in both London and Cambridge, although the two men did not hit it off. Cudworth reportedly asked Menasseh why he did not accept the truth of Christianity, while Menasseh angered Cudworth by giving him some Jewish anti-Christian literature (possibly written by Menasseh himself).[14]

Things went a little better in his meetings in London with another member of the school of philosophers known as the Cambridge Platonists, Henry More. Like Cudworth, More was a theologian. He was also a proponent of the new mechanistic philosophy of nature. However, he thought that Descartes's "machine" model of the world, which dominated natural philosophy at the time, made too much of a division between mind and body, and thus emptied the physical world of any spiritual element. At the time of his conversations with Menasseh, More was just beginning work on his treatise on the immortality of the soul. He reported that he and the rabbi discussed Jewish views on this topic "with great freedom and assurance."[15]

London was also the home of several regular gatherings of natural philosophers that would, within a few years, join to become the Royal Society. Menasseh, always interested in what was happening in the world of modern learning, may have attended some meetings of Samuel Hartlib's "circle" and of the experimental scientists at Gresham College. He paid visits to Henry Oldenburg, who would later serve as the Royal Society's corresponding secretary, and to the corpuscularian chemist Robert Boyle. Boyle had once dropped by Menasseh's house in Amsterdam when he was passing through the city. On that occasion, he and Menasseh—whom he regarded as "the famousest of the modern Rabbies"—talked about the interpretation of Scripture, so Menasseh's presence in London offered a good opportunity to renew their acquaintance and continue the conversation.[16]

A potentially more fraught occasion during Menasseh's English residency was a debate with a French Protestant theologian. Engaging in such a disputation was not only contrary to the regulations of Menasseh's home congregation in Amsterdam regarding theological discussions with gentiles, but a rather risky undertaking given English sensibilities about Jews trying to convert Christians. The "friendly and extemporaneous conversation between the most famous Jew Rabbi Menasseh ben Israel and Jean d'Espagne, Minister of New Testament," that took place on May 2, 1656, was technically not a public affair. Yet it was held not in a private home but in the French embassy in London, "with the Lord of Bordeaux, among others" present.[17]

D'Espagne, who was the pastor for a Huguenot congregation in the city, claimed to have read Menasseh's *Conciliador* and *De Creatione*, "in which," he said, "there are many excellent and rare things." He began the dialogue—which most likely took place either in French or in English—with a question about something he took Menasseh to have said in his works, namely, that a change in a person's name (such as when Abram became Abraham) can actually change that person's fortune. "Is there so much power in a new name that it can make a sick person healthy, a poor person rich, and a king from a commoner?" Menasseh replied that a change from bad fortune to good can come about only through a change in the soul, through repentance. "The change of name is only the sign of reprentence."

It is clear from this opening exchange and the subsequent

progress of the conversation that D'Espagne was out to trip Menasseh up. Puzzled by Menasseh's exegetical project in the *Conciliador*, he wanted to know how it was possible that, as he understood Menasseh, two rabbis can have diametrically opposed opinions on "matters of great import," with each "appealing to faith." If each is expressing the word of God, how could they not agree with each other? "If one rabbi should contradict another, which one should I believe?" Menasseh tried to explain away the apparent inconsistencies in Hebrew Scripture and rabbinic writings, but D'Espagne would have none of it. He persisted, and suggested that in such cases at least one of those rabbis must be speaking contrary to the faith and thus a blasphemer. Things only got worse as the dialogue continued:

MENASSEH: Do you think our rabbis are fools?

D'ESPAGNE: Well, at least crazy. For what do you think about those who think and speak about God in such a blasphemous way? Indeed, why do you not anathematize them?

MENASSEH: We are not accustomed to cursing people.[18]

D'ESPAGNE: Are you accustomed to cursing us Edomaians, as you call Christians?

MENASSEH: Not at all.

D'ESPAGNE: Let us return to the topic. You do not deny that there are Jews, indeed rabbis, who clearly defend that blasphemy. Nevertheless, you consider them as true brothers, sons of the covenant, wise men. With what right? Do you have brothers and wise men who so atrociously blaspheme against God?

MENASSEH: If there are those who blaspheme against God, it is not to be imputed to us; we do not approve their opinion.

D'Espagne accused latter-day Jews of making offerings to Satan on Yom Kippur, and claimed to have eyewitnesses to this fact; of getting so drunk on Purim that they "can no longer distinguish Haman, who is to be cursed, from Mordecai, who is to be blessed"; and of departing from the original words of Hebrew Scripture concerning the Messiah, "which your ancestors interpreted as being about Christ."

By this point, Menasseh had clearly had enough. When D'Espagne suggested that they continue their exchange in writings—"we can henceforth compete with a pen," he said—Menasseh demurred. "I have business that prevents me."

This kind of agonistic engagement with a gentile theologian may have put the London Jewish community on edge. Menasseh's relationship with the local Sephardim was not always easy, especially as things dragged on with readmission. Their justified insecurities about their situation made them especially sensitive to what was being said in the public sphere. Some of them began to feel that pushing aggressively for a formal declaration of readmission only made their situation more precarious. They had generally been allowed to go quietly about their business—albeit within the confines of the restrictions imposed upon them—and they enjoyed an informal, uncertain but (so far) functional toleration. The English civil authorities were perfectly amenable to the current arrangement, and over time official acceptance would likely and naturally come. Why not just leave well enough alone? Why force the issue and call attention to themselves?

In the absence of any resolution of the question, some of the Jews who had come over around the same time as Menasseh, anticipating great results from his mission—men like Raphael Hayim Supino, from Livorno, Italy, a scholar and merchant known in the London community as a "minister of circumcision"—began to head home.[19] Even Sephardim who had already been residing in London decided to pick up and move elsewhere. Describing this stage in his negotiations, Menasseh noted that with "no finall determination from his most Serene Highnesse [Cromwell] . . . those few Iewes that were here, despairing of our expected successe, departed hence. And others who desired to come hither, have quitted their hopes, and betaken themselves some to Italy, some to Geneva, where that Commonwealth hath at this time, most freely granted them many, and great priviledges."[20]

It is a telling indication of Menasseh's standing with the London Jews that when, in the summer of 1656, they were looking to have someone lead them regularly in worship, they bypassed him and opted for a rabbi from Hamburg, Moses Athias. Menasseh still joined services in Carvajal's home and the other residences where they were held behind closed doors, but it seems possible that he may have been outstaying his welcome.

As Cromwell continued to waver, reluctant to go against what seemed to be majority opinion—what Ambassador Salvetti called *un general disgusto* in the nation—but fearful of losing out on the economic and international political advantages of readmission, it eventually became clear to the London Jewish community, to Menasseh, and to observers that it was not going to happen anytime soon.[21] The best that could be hoped for in the near term was a continuation of the status quo. The Tuscan diplomat's earlier prediction—that the policy of "connivance [at] private prayer in their houses" would continue—was prescient.

It is noteworthy, though, that in December 1656, a house in Cree-Church Lane was rented to use as a synagogue. Just a few months later, the London Sephardim purchased land for a cemetery. It appears that the petition that Menasseh, Carvajal, Dormido, and others had submitted in March, laying out their conditions for settlement, was not entirely without effect. Somebody had to sign off for these things to happen. It was almost certainly Cromwell.

Menasseh was, of course, deeply disappointed that things had reached such an impasse. He was also embarrassed by what he must have regarded as the failure of his mission to England. As John Sadler remarked some years later to Richard Cromwell, "he [Menasseh] had stayed heere so long, that he was allmost ashamed to returne to thos that sent him; to exact theyr maintenance Heere where they found so little success, after so many Hopes."[22]

To this disappointment and shame, however, was added inconsolable sadness. On September 9, 1657, Samuel ben Israel died in London.

Menasseh was devastated. First Joseph, many years earlier in a foreign land; then his younger son, again far away from their Amsterdam home. This was more than Menasseh could take. It was time to pack things up and head back to Holland, to bury his son and grieve with his wife over their loss.

Menasseh's pain was compounded by the humiliation of having to ask Cromwell for money to travel home. It was not the first time that he sought personal financial assistance from the Lord Protector. Toward the end of 1656, when he was still not recovered from the illness he had complained about at the time of his departure from Amsterdam, he wrote to Cromwell for support.

> May it please your Highnesse, what modestie forbidds necessitie . . . compells; that having bene long time very sickly (an expensive condition) I make my moan to your Highnesse, as the alone succourer of my life, in this land of strangers, to help in this present exigence. I shall not presume to prescribe to your Highnesse but havinge had great experience of your greatnesse in compassions as well as in majestie, I lay myselfe at your feet, that am your infinit obliged supplicant & servant.[23]

Cromwell, conscious of Menasseh's efforts on behalf of a cause he supported—and perhaps feeling responsible for bringing the rabbi to England—responded by promising an annual pension of one hundred pounds, to be paid quarterly. In the end, with the State Treasury controlling the disbursement of funds and carefully guarding its expenses, only a few irregular payments were ever made.[24]

Therefore, on September 17, 1657, two years after his arrival in England, Menasseh—in profound mourning, encumbered by debts, and unable to afford the journey home with his son's body—swallowed his pride and made another plea.

> May it please your Highnesse, my only sonne, being now dead in my house, who before his departure, engaged me to accompany his corps to Holland, & I indebted here, I know not which way to turn mee but (under God) to your Highnesse for help in this condition, emploring your bowells of compassion (which I know are great and tender) to supply me with three hundred pounds, & I shall surrender my pension seal & never trouble or charge your Highnesse any more, I am very sensible considering your great kindnesse . . . how highly-bold this my petition is, but the necessitie of my present exigence & my experience of your admirable graciousness to mee have layd me prostrat at your feet, crying, Help, Most noble prince, for God's sake, your most humble supplicant.

It is a touching and sad letter, and the last thing we have from Menasseh's hand.

Cromwell wanted to satisfy Menasseh's request, but the Treasury was once again reluctant to comply. Eventually it was agreed that Menasseh would receive a one-time payment of two hundred pounds, on the condition that he renounce any further claims on the earlier pension. However, even this grant was never paid. According to Sadler, "he never gott one penny of the said 200£."[25] Menasseh's return voyage must have been funded by charity from among the London Sephardim.

Menasseh was a broken man. Bearing Samuel's body, he departed England probably in early October. He landed in the coastal town of Middelburg, in the Dutch province of Zeeland, where he buried his son.[26] Likely still suffering the ailment that had plagued him for more than two years, Menasseh himself died, in Middelburg, on November 20, 1657. His body was brought to Amsterdam and buried in the community's cemetery in Ouderkerk. The Spanish epitaph on his gravestone reads:

> He is not dead for in heaven
> he lives in supreme glory
> and his pen has earned him a memory
> that is immortal on earth.

Aristotle said that one should never pass judgment on how well a person lived and how blessed he is until the day of his death. Even then, he suggested, you cannot make a fully informed assessment until you see how his survivors and progeny fare, since their good or bad fortune can reflect on the life of the deceased. "It would be odd," he said, "if the fortunes of the descendants did not for some time have some effect on the happiness of their ancestors."[27]

By this criterion, Menasseh died not only an unhappy man, but an unfortunate one. His widow, Rachel, about whom we have so little information—aside from the proud remarks that Menasseh made early in his career about marrying into the illustrious Abrabanel family—reappears at this point, only in rather sad circumstances. After the death of her two sons, followed by the death of her husband, she was alone.[28] We can only imagine her emotional state, without much difficulty, but we do know something about her financial situation. She was destitute. Only through charitable contributions from members of the Amsterdam Portuguese community was she able to afford to bury Menasseh.[29]

Rachel wrote several letters to Cromwell asking for assistance. The English leader was sympathetic, but once again the

Exchequer declined (or was unable) to comply. She then turned to Menasseh's old colleague Sadler, who made a special plea on her behalf to Richard Cromwell, who became Lord Protector after Oliver Cromwell's death in September 1658. After reminding the younger Cromwell that it was his father who had encouraged Menasseh to come to England in the first place, and telling him that the rabbi, "with his heart ever broken with griefe on losing heer his only sonne and his presious time with all his hopes in this iland," died on his way home, "leaving a poore desolate widow," Sadler asked him, "in compassion to the said poore widow," to find for her the two hundred pounds that had been promised to Menasseh. There is no evidence, however, that this, or any, sum was ever disbursed. Rachel died in poverty.

In 1660, Charles Stuart returned from exile and assumed the throne of England as Charles II. There was no longer any secret—open or otherwise—that there was a Jewish community in London, with its own synagogue and cemetery. Despite some attempts to have the new king "enact new [laws] for the expulsion of all professed Jews out of your Majesty's dominions," their status was fairly, if still informally, secure. The congregation even brought over a rabbi from Amsterdam, *Hakham* Jacob Sasportas, one of Menasseh's former colleagues, to lead them.

In August 1664, Dormido once again took up his pen in quest of formal recognition. This time, his petition was successful. The Jews, by writ of the king, were at last officially granted the right to dwell "with favour" and "peaceably" in England.[30]

Menasseh ben Israel and Rembrandt

FEW ARTISTS in Western European history have undergone as much mythologizing as Rembrandt. His personal life, his paintings and prints, even his religious views have all been subject to much wild and romantic speculation over the centuries. He was, we have been told, a lonely and irascible genius who refused to conform to the aesthetic standards of his day; he had no interest in the demands of the market or the wishes of patrons, and painted only what he wanted to; he had an uncanny ability to capture on canvas the emotional lives of his sitters; and so on. Thus, it is no surprise that a good deal of Rembrandt scholarship in recent decades has been devoted to debunking those myths and bringing Rembrandt the man and the artist down to Dutch soil.[1]

Among the more recalcitrant myths about Rembrandt, however, are those concerning his relationship to Jews and Judaism. Rembrandt is often said to have had a profound "affinity" and "tenderness" for the Jewish people, that he, more than any other artist, had a genuine feeling for the people of the "Old Testament." He was so enamored of his Jewish neighbors in the Vlooienburg quarter of Amsterdam, the story goes, that it forever changed his art. Indeed, he is supposed to have moved to that neighborhood "to steep himself in local [Jewish] color."[2] "Rembrandt," one author says, "had a special sympathy for the Jews, as the heirs of the biblical past and as the patient victims of persecution."[3]

An important part of the mythology surrounding Rembrandt and the Jews concerns his relationship with one particular Jew: Menasseh ben Israel. It has long been claimed that the Dutch painter and the Sephardic rabbi had a very special relationship. Rembrandt and Menasseh are frequently described as neighbors, collaborators, friends, even theological soulmates. Thus, the art historian Frits Lugt, expressing a view shared by many, reports that Menasseh was "Rembrandt's intimate and highly regarded friend."[4] (The mythologizing, it should be noted, is not limited to the Rembrandt literature. The 1990 bibliography of works on Menasseh since the seventeenth century, which is not especially voluminous, contains 81 entries under the topic "Rembrandt," many of which repeat the same story; in the twenty-eight years since this bibliography was published, the quantity has probably doubled.)[5]

Recent Rembrandt scholars have brought some realism and sobriety both to the story of Rembrandt and the Jews in general, and to the case of Rembrandt and Menasseh in particular.[6] At the same time, the exhibition held at the Jewish Historical Museum in Amsterdam in 2006–2007, with the accompanying catalogue, goes a little too far in the other direction, almost eliminating any trace of Menasseh in Rembrandt's life and work.[7] Some myths are based on a kernel of truth, and there is no need to dismiss everything that has been claimed for the Rembrandt-

Menasseh connection. We should not throw out the tulips with the vase water.

What, then, do we really do know about Rembrandt's connections with Menasseh?

The story of Rembrandt and Menasseh has its ancestral roots in the eighteenth century, with the 1751 *catalogue raisonné* of Rembrandt's works by Edmé-François Gersaint, who identifies one of Rembrandt's etchings as a portrait of Menasseh and four other etchings as connected with "un livre espagnol," a book in Spanish, namely Menasseh's *Piedra Gloriosa*. However, the mythology really picks up steam in the nineteenth century, with an 1836 catalogue of Rembrandt's paintings by John Smith (who blamed Rembrandt's bankruptcy on Menasseh's nefarious influence); and a strange 1898 German young-adult novel by one J. Manefeld whose title translates as *Chiaroscuro: A Jewish Story of the Life of Rembrandt and Menasseh ben Israel*. In the book, a boy named Saul, a young refugee from eastern Europe now living in Amsterdam, is a guest at Menasseh's home on Shabbat. He also happens to sit as a model for Rembrandt, and ends up introducing the two men. A contemporary reviewer of the book for the *Wegweiser für die Jugendliteratur* (Guide to Young People's Literature) says that "we recommend this book for mature youth."[8] Books and articles in the twentieth century served only to promulgate the bromance and, in the light of new research, add new—and highly imaginative—dimensions to it.[9]

Some of the myths are dispelled easily enough by the facts.

First, there is the claim that Menasseh and Rembrandt were not just acquaintances, but friends; as one historian puts it, "the relationship with Menasseh was real and it was serious."[10] Moreover, it seems to be a commonplace that Menasseh was one of Rembrandt's neighbors on the Sint Antoniesbreestraat.

Now, as we have seen, it is highly likely that Menasseh and

Rembrandt knew (or at least knew of) each other from early on in Rembrandt's residence in Amsterdam. Their social, intellectual, and business circles overlapped to some degree, with mutual friends in the Anslo clan and Ephraim Bueno, among others.[11] The fact that they both lived in the intimate confines of the Vlooienburg/Breestraat district and that Menasseh was not only prominent in the Jewish community but enjoyed renown in the gentile realm only reinforces the likelihood of an acquaintance between the two.

Were Rembrandt and Menasseh also friends? Well, who is to say? How can we really know who in history were and were not truly friends? Correspondence between the individuals in question or others who knew them well is of course the best testimony in such matters, but in this case there are no relevant extant letters from any party. There is, in fact, no documentary evidence whatsoever to support the claim that Rembrandt and Menasseh were friends. Of course, it is certainly possible that they were, but really we have no idea. One might object that it is unlikely that in this period a painter of Dutch Reformed background and a rabbi serving a Portuguese congregation could have developed much of a rapport. And yet, we have seen how in the tolerant and cosmopolitan atmosphere of seventeenth-century Holland, amicable and cooperative relationships between gentiles and Jews—and especially the Sephardic merchants of Amsterdam—were common, particularly in business affairs but also in intellectual matters and social situations. We have also seen how Menasseh, especially, enjoyed close, warm relationships with quite a few gentiles. Still, in none of Menasseh's extant writings, whether treatises or letters, is there any mention of dealings with Rembrandt.

However, one thing we do know pretty much for certain is this: Menasseh was never Rembrandt's "neighbor on the Breestraat," and Rembrandt never "lived in a house across the street from Menasseh ben Israel," as many have alleged.[12] Rembrandt lived on the Sint Antoniesbreestraat from 1631 to 1635, as a lodger in the home of the art dealer Hendrick van Uylenburgh (whose niece, Saskia, he married), and then again from 1639 until 1659, in a house he bought right next to Van Uylenburgh's. For a brief time, from 1637 to 1639, he also lived on the Binnen-Amstel, in a house facing the back wharfs of Vlooienburg island.

Meanwhile, for most of his life Menasseh resided in (and ran his business from) a house on the "Nieuwe Houtmarkt," a vague designation for somewhere on the Vlooienburg island. He never lived on the Breestraat.[13] This is confirmed by exhaustive research undertaken in the 1930s by A. M. Vaz Dias on Rembrandt's Jewish neighbors on the Breestraat during his residence there, and Menasseh's name is nowhere to be found on the list.[14]

We can say that for two years, from 1637 to 1639, when Rembrandt was on Binnen-Amstel, he lived somewhere near Menasseh—possibly down a block or two, along the perimeter of the small Vlooienburg island. But once Rembrandt moved to the Breestraat, he left Menasseh and this crowded residential/business district behind for more genteel environs and more prosperous neighbors. The Breestraat was both the center of the city's art world and home to upscale residences of the Portuguese-Jewish professional and merchant classes. Even if Menasseh did not spend the rest of his life on the Nieuwe Houtmarkt, we can be fairly sure that he never lived on the Breestraat for yet another reason—he would not have been able to afford it. But then again, neither could Rembrandt, as we know from his bankruptcy in 1656.

The second item often cited as evidence of a close personal relationship between Menasseh and Rembrandt is an etching that Rembrandt made in 1636, the one that Gersaint identified in his *catalogue raisonné* as being "Le portrait du Juif Manassé, Ben-Israel." The scholarly consensus now, however, is that this is not a portrait of Menasseh ben Israel at all. There is, in fact, no hard evidence for thinking that it is a portrait of a rabbi or even a Jew, much less of Menasseh. On the contrary, there are good reasons for thinking that it is *not* of Menasseh. That label comes relatively late, only in the mid-eighteenth century with Gersaint, who was followed uncritically by later cataloguers.[15] Moreover, Adri Offenberg has argued that it is "highly unlikely" that Menasseh would have commissioned a portrait etching from Rembrandt in 1636, given his "dire financial straits." Offenberg also insists that the resemblance between the sitter of this etching and the subject of a Govert Flinck painted portrait from one year later also long supposed to be of Menasseh ben Israel suggests that they are "very likely" depictions of the same person, and we now know for certain that the sitter for the Flinck portrait (who, the painting tells us, was born in 1593) is not Menasseh (born in 1604).[16]

If Rembrandt did not, after all, do a portrait of Menasseh, then we have lost at least one reason for accepting another element of the mythology, namely, that Menasseh commissioned works from Rembrandt—or, as some scholars have claimed, that Menasseh was "surely [a patron] of the artist."[17] But this brings us to the broader question of the professional relationship between the rabbi and the artist, and in particular their alleged collaboration on two projects. Here we enter the realm of known unknowns.

As we have seen, the Hebraic lettering in Rembrandt's painting of Belshazzar's feast suggests that Rembrandt consulted with Menasseh on just how he should depict the message in his painting.[18] Menasseh's book was published in 1639, and depending on the dating of the painting—which most scholars now put at around 1635—this could be several years after Rembrandt had finished the work. But of course the theory about the divine writing could already have been on Menasseh's mind for a while, and he certainly could have advised Rembrandt on this in person, before writing his book. If this is indeed the case, then we would have here a personal connection and collaboration—if not a full-blown relationship—between the two men.

On the other hand, it is also possible that the connection between Rembrandt and Menasseh in this case is only indirect. Maybe one of Menasseh's students who was also among Rembrandt's acquaintances—Gerbrand Anslo or Dionysius Vossius—explained the rabbi's opinion to Rembrandt.[19] This is implausible, however, as is the suggestion that any one of a number of theologians or scholars could be responsible for advising Rembrandt on this aspect of the painting, either on the basis of their own theories or because they were familiar with Menasseh's views and communicated these to Rembrandt.[20] It seems that, among the known unknowns, the idea that Menasseh did advise Rembrandt on "Belshazzar's Feast" is fairly compelling.[21]

The more complicated case of an alleged Rembrandt-Menasseh collaboration concerns the illustrations that appear in some seventeenth-century copies of *Piedra Gloriosa* and that bear Rembrandt's signature. That these imply a direct and personal collaboration between the rabbi and the artist on this book is now the view of many commentators.[22]

However, some scholars have questioned the assumption that Rembrandt produced these images for Menasseh's book at the author's request. They cite, in part, the unsuitability of etchings to illustrate books that have more than a limited print run. It is possible, though, that the etchings *were* meant only for a limited run, perhaps as a gift to be included only in a few presentation copies of the book "for friends and people who, like Isaac Vossius"—to whom the book was dedicated—"had been involved in the book in a special way."[23]

But then there is Menasseh's remark in the book's preface "To the Reader" where he tells us that he himself composed four illustrations for the book, and the descriptions he gives of the four illustrations he prepared do not fully match the four images by Rembrandt. For example, Menasseh says that the illustration devoted to David and Goliath shows Goliath lying prostrate at David's feet (*postrado a sus pies*), whereas in Rembrandt's etching Goliath is still standing, although about to fall.[24]

Menasseh continues to refer throughout the book to the drawings "we have made," which suggests that all along he envisioned his own illustrations as an integral part of the work.[25] Moreover, the dimensions of the etching prints made by Rembrandt are such that they do not fit neatly in the copies of the book in which they appear.[26]

Finally, if there *was* a collaboration on this project between Menasseh and Rembrandt, it was short-lived. In a number of extant copies of a second edition of *Piedra Gloriosa* there are different illustrations, clearly based on Rembrandt's images but obviously by another hand, unsigned but usually identified as being by Salom Italia, the artist from the Amsterdam Portuguese-Jewish community who, as we have seen, also gave us our only confirmed portrait of Menasseh.

If the first edition of *Piedra Gloriosa* was indeed a collaboration between Menasseh and Rembrandt, these new illustrations give rise to a pressing question: Why the switch? Was Menasseh unhappy with Rembrandt's illustrations? Did he worry about the representation of God sitting on his throne in the image of Daniel's vision?[27] (In Italia's alternative version, the bodily depiction of God is replaced by an illuminated empty space above the heavenly choir.) If so, then why would he have included this and the other etchings in those copies of the first edition? Or was it all just a practical matter, with Italia's copperplate engravings ultimately better suited for reproducible book illustration?[28]

Offenberg has suggested that instead of a collaboration we should think in terms of two projects: Menasseh's book of 1655 and Rembrandt's four etchings of the same year, and they were "somehow connected with each other." Perhaps, he surmises, "Menasseh did in fact commission the illustrations from Rembrandt but did not accept the final result"; buyers of the book could then have bought the Rembrandt etchings separately and inserted them into their copies.[29] This account, of course, would leave intact a collaboration of sorts, even if in the end it was not entirely successful.

What is interesting, however, is that Rembrandt's illustrations are in only five of the extant copies of the first edition, including the copy originally owned by Isaac Vossius, still bound in its original cover in the University of Leiden library; the other extant copies lack illustrations.[30] Moreover, the Rembrandt illustrations are bound in the book *only* in Vossius's copy; in the other volumes in which they appear they are merely loose sheets. This is consistent with the theory that the illustration pages were inserted post-publication, since Vossius's final binding of the book could have been subsequent to his acquisition of it (presumably as a gift from Menasseh) as loose sheets.[31] Perhaps Vossius bought Rembrandt's rejected prints and had them bound in his copy of the book.[32]

One might take this post-publication/post-acquisition insertion theory one step further. Menasseh dedicated *Piedra Gloriosa* to Vossius. As far as we know, Vossius was not a member of Rembrandt's circle of acquaintances. However, he was connected with some of Rembrandt's patrons and sitters, including Constantijn Huygens and Jan Six. Six was a wealthy Amsterdammer, a member of the city council, an author, and the subject of an extraordinary portrait by Rembrandt. Six and Vossius were, by Vossius's own testimony, good friends. In one of his letters, Vossius good-naturedly complained about the way that Six's bidding at book auctions drives the prices up, "so unprofitable was his friendship to me. Still," he says, "we are friends and will be forever."[33]

So perhaps Menasseh had nothing directly to do with Rembrandt on this project after all. Rather, Isaac Vossius himself could have prompted Jan Six to ask Rembrandt if he would produce some illustrations for the new book by Vossius's rabbi friend in order to give Vossius's copies of the book that extra *je ne sais quoi*.[34] Vossius may have directed Six to ask Rembrandt to base his etchings on the "four sketches on sheets of paper," no longer extant, that Menasseh says he himself had provided for the book.[35] Menasseh says in his preface that these sketches "took a lot of trouble and work," and they were probably not very good, as Vossius would have seen; thus Vossius thought to turn to a true master to provide better illustrations. However, Rembrandt would likely not have responded well to the suggestion that he copy somebody else's artwork, and so Vossius, via Six, may simply have asked that Rembrandt base his illustrations on the text itself.

Alternatively, the idea to employ Rembrandt's talents could have been Six's. Menasseh approached Vossius about the book's dedication, and Vossius could have written to Six to inform him about this interesting new work on a messianic theme, with Six in turn suggesting that Rembrandt could do the illustrating.

What happened next, on this scenario, is that Vossius had the Rembrandt etchings bound in his own copy of the book, as well as inserted into several other copies for friends. This would moot any questions about Menasseh's dumping Rembrandt's illustrations after the first edition. It would also moot the question as to why etchings were used rather than engravings, since Vossius intended only a small run of the illustrations for a couple of copies of the book. At the same time, this would still be consistent with what is, as Michael Zell shows, "Rembrandt's painstaking labor to calibrate the images with the contents of the *Piedra Gloriosa*."[36]

Of course, this is just hypothesis, and it must remain hypothetical until some documentary evidence emerges to either confirm or disconfirm it. It is a plausible hypothesis, however—

no worse and maybe even better than the account that has Menasseh directly collaborating with Rembrandt, since it eliminates those nagging questions about Menasseh's removing the Rembrandt etchings from the second edition.[37] What this means, in the end, is that the idea that Menasseh commissioned Rembrandt to do the illustrations for his book is, like the statue in Nebuchadnezzar's dream, not as rock-solid as it once was.

ACKNOWLEDGMENTS

I AM EXTREMELY GRATEFUL to a number of friends and colleagues for their assistance in this project. Special thanks to Amos Bitzan, Albert Gootjes, Andrea Guardo, Jonathan Israel, David Katz, Geert Mak, James Messina, Adri Offenberg, Sina Rauschenbach, Henriette Reerink, Emile Schrijver, Gary Schwartz, Anita Shapira, Piet Steenbakkers, Wiep van Bunge, Hans Visser, David Wertheim, and Thijs Weststijn for lending their expertise in various ways, sending me relevant material, and/or reading the manuscript (in part or in whole). David Hildner and Steve Hutchison helped me navigate sixteenth- and seventeenth-century Spanish and Portuguese orthography, and I relied greatly on David Korfhagen's paleographical skills. Rachel Boertjens, curator of the Bibliotheca Rosenthaliana at the University of Amsterdam Library, was very generous with her time in providing access—both in Amsterdam and at great distance—to essential materials. Finally, my deepest gratitude

to Steven Zipperstein, whose encouragement and enthusiasm
for this book, not to mention his intellectual inspiration, made
it all possible.

My work was supported by a summer research grant from
the Graduate School of the University of Wisconsin–Madison,
and by funds provided by two endowed professorships I have
been awarded by the University of Wisconsin: the William H.
Hay II/Wisconsin Alumni Research Foundation (WARF) Professorship of Philosophy and the Evjue-Bascom Professorship
in Humanities. I also benefited greatly from a Senior Fellow-
ship at the Institute for Research in the Humanities, in the
College of Letters and Science at the University of Wisconsin–
Madison, which came with a reduction in teaching over four
years that allowed me to devote more time to research for this
book.

I dedicate this biography of Menasseh ben Israel to the
professor from whom I first heard about this remarkable rabbi
of seventeenth-century Amsterdam; a scholar who, over many
decades of incomparable research and skulduggery, contributed so much to our knowledge of Menasseh and his early
modern milieu, and who, as he transformed the nature of research into early modern philosophy and intellectual history,
was an inspiration to so many: my undergraduate teacher and,
later, friend Richard H. Popkin.

NOTES

Chapter 1. Prologue

1. The text of Mortera's sermon has been reconstructed in Saperstein 1991b.

2. *Talmud Yerushalmi*, Shekalim, ch. 2.

Chapter 2. Manoel/Menasseh

1. The archival documents related to the Inquisition's arrest, trial, and torture of Gaspar Rodrigues Nunes and his relatives are in Salomon 1983.

2. Salomon 1983, p. 110.

3. Salomon 1983, p. 114.

4. Salomon 1983, p. 127.

5. Netanyahu (1995) argues that Judaizing was not a widespread phenomenon among the New Christians.

6. See the 1648 letter to Manuel Fernandel Villareal in Adler 1904, p. 569; and *Esperança de Israel*, p. 97 (oddly, the phrase "my

native city" is missing from the English translation by Moses Wall, *The Hope of Israel*, p. 149). There is also the testimony of Francisco de Orta before the Inquisition in 1642. Orta reported on Portuguese individuals who, though born Catholics in Portugal, were living as Jews in Amsterdam. Among the names he mentioned was that of Menasseh ben Israel, "born in this city [Lisbon]" (Salomon 1983, p. 105). Hillesum (1905a, 1905b, and 1926), among others (including Méchoulan 1977), reliably puts Menasseh's birthplace in Lisbon.

7. See the document in Levy 1924. Meinsma 2006 (p. 65); Bethencourt 1904; and Salomon 1983 (p. 136) all place Menasseh's birth city in La Rochelle; Popkin (1992, p. 155) claims that Menasseh was born in La Rochelle but then raised in Lisbon.

8. See Hillesum 1905a. But there is still the question why his sister did not also hide her place of birth. Moreover, in the marriage bann, he is identified as Menasseh ben Israel, not Manoel Dias Soeiro. Would the Inquisition have been able to make the connections they were looking for? Perhaps local spies in Amsterdam could have told them that "Menasseh ben Israel" was identical to Manoel Dias Soeiro.

Menasseh ben Israel's birthplace has long been a subject of scholarly dispute. In addition to Lisbon and La Rochelle, it has also been placed on the island of Madeira, where the family fled from Lisbon (Ifrah 2001, p. 33; Roth 1945, pp. 12–13). The evidence for this, which is rather unreliable, is a document from the Inquisition's archives recording the testimony of a recent visitor to Amsterdam who had met Menasseh, who apparently told this visitor that he was born on Madeira (the text of this document is in Hillesum 1926).

9. Salomon 1983, p. 109.

10. Salomon 1983, pp. 109–110.

11. Salomon 1983, p. 126.

12. *De Termino Vitae*, p. 236.

13. *Esperança de Israel*, p. 97.

14. If Manoel was born in La Rochelle, then the departure from Lisbon would likely have been earlier than 1604, since he

was born in that year, after a layover of unknown duration in Madeira.

15. Ifrah 2001, p. 34.

16. *De Termino Vitae*, p. 236.

17. Amsterdam Municipal Archives, no. 5059, sub. 24–40 (H. Bontemantel Collection), i.c., 34. See Huussen 1993.

18. This story first appears in the *Triumpho del govierno popular* (Amsterdam, ca. 1683–1684) by Daniel Levi de Barrios (1635–1701), the poet-historian of the Portuguese-Jewish community of Amsterdam.

19. See Franco Mendes, *Memorias*, pp. 9–10.

20. Koen 1970, p. 39.

21. In his *Narraçao da vinda dos Judeos espanhoes a Amsterdam*, available in print as early as 1674.

22. On the earliest congregations in Amsterdam, see Zwarts 1928 and Vlessing 1993; Vlessing argues that the Neve Shalom congregation was earlier than Beth Jacob.

23. Quoted in Saperstein 2005, p. 149.

24. For overviews of the settlement and history of the Amsterdam Portuguese-Jewish community, see Fuks-Mansfeld 1989, Bodian 1997, and Swetschinski 2000.

25. This third congregation's original name was Ets Haim.

26. For a discussion of the challenges they faced, see Goldish 2001.

27. See Israel 1995 (pp. 360–398) on the problems of confessional unity in the Dutch Republic in the first half of the seventeenth century.

28. *Vindiciae Judaeorum*, p. 38.

29. *Conciliador*, Part II, Dedicatory Letter. "Batavia" is the ancient Roman name for the Dutch provinces.

30. *De Termino Vitae*, p. 236.

31. "Notarial Deeds Relating to the Portuguese Jews in Amsterdam Up to 1639," p. 272.

32. *Livro de Bet Haim do Kahal Kados de Bet Yahacob*, pp. 148–149, 152. For a discussion of taxation among Amsterdam's Portuguese Jews, see Swetschinski 2000, pp. 196–200.

33. On the first rabbis in Amsterdam, see Zwarts 1928. Mortera is not actually named as a *hakham* in the community's record books until 1619; see Pieterse 1968, p. 62.

34. For biographies of Mortera, see Salomon 1988 and Saperstein 2005. For a biographical study of Modena, see Cohen 1988.

35. For a study of Mortera's sermons, see Saperstein 2005.

36. Quoted in Saperstein 2005, p. 292.

37. Sanhedrin 11.1. For a study of the dispute over eternal punishment in the Amsterdam Portuguese-Jewish community, see Altmann 1972.

38. *De Termino Vitae*, p. 236.

39. "Vida de Ishac Huziel," pp. 33–34, in De Barrios, *Triumpho del Govierno Popular* (pp. 435–454). De Barrios's account of the origins of the Beth Israel congregation departs from the narrative according to which (a) Beth Israel resulted from a theological and property dispute within Beth Jacob; and (b) Joseph Pardo was that congregation's first rabbi, not his son David.

40. Fuks and Fuks-Mansfeld 1984, p. 100.

41. Previously, the work had circulated within the community in manuscript form.

42. *Conciliador*, Part II, "Al Lector," p. 8.

43. See the list of *rubissim* (teachers) in Dos Remédios 1928, vol. 2, pp. 218–219. Menasseh is listed as having been appointed as *rubi* in the Hebrew year 5382 (which corresponds to the period between the fall of 1621 and the fall of 1622). Dos Remédios says that the list is compiled from "manuscript sources [*fontes manuscritas*]," but does not indicate what these are.

44. It seems that the text was in fact printed, by Menasseh, in 1631, because it is listed in a sales catalogue published by Menasseh's son Samuel in 1652; see Yaari 1947. However, no copies of the published work are extant. A manuscript of Menasseh's Hebrew grammar is in the Bibliotheca Rosenthaliana in the University of Amsterdam Special Collections. My thanks to Rachel Boertjens, curator of the Bibliotheca Rosenthaliana, for providing me with access to the work. For discussions of the manuscript, see Offenberg 2004 and Schrijver 2011.

45. *De Termino Vitae*, p. 236.

46. Roth 1945, p. 33. Most biographical accounts, including Roth 1945 (pp. 32–33) and Ifrah 2001 (p. 47), stick with this traditional chronology. However, it is possible that Menasseh's elevation to congregational leader did not take place as soon after Uziel's death as he intimates. One scholar claims that, for a couple of years, Neve Shalom went without a rabbi altogether, with the *hazzan* Samuel Cohen carrying out the relevant duties. And when Cohen died in 1625, Isaac Aboab took over as *hazzan* and assumed the rabbinic functions. It was only in 1628, according to this account, that Menasseh began preaching to the Neve Shalom congregation, and not until 1631 that he was formally named a *hakham*; see Pieterse 1968, p. 63.

47. There is actually some dispute as to whether Aboab became the rabbi of Beth Israel or of Neve Shalom; the archival evidence suggests the latter—see Hagoort and Noach 2009, especially note 5.

Chapter 3. On the Nieuwe Houtmarkt

1. *Oeuvres de Descartes*, vol. 2, pp. 110–111.

2. He called it "a land where, if there is less honey than in the one promised by God to the Israelites, there is more milk" (Letter to Brasset, April 23, 1649, *Oeuvres de Descartes*, vol. 5, p. 349).

3. Israel 1995, p. 478.

4. Kolakowski 1969, chapter 2.

5. See Koen 1970, p. 37.

6. The burial notice in *Livro de Bet Haim do Kahal Kados de Bet Yahacob* reads: "Em 31 de Outubro se enterrou Josef ben Israel aos pees do hahão Isak Uziel" (p. 103).

7. *Sefer Nishmat Hayyim*, pp. 194–195. My thanks to Amos Bizan for his help in translating this passage.

8. *De Termino Vitae*, p. 236.

9. Her father might, in fact, have been named Samuel; a Dr. Samuel Abrabanel was buried in Ouderkerk around this time; see Roth 1945, p. 313 n. 7.

10. Roth (1945, pp. 35–36), for one, is skeptical that Rachel is descended from *those* Abrabanels.

11. Levy 1924, p. 257.

12. It is unclear which was the elder son. The fact that Joseph bore the name of his grandfather would suggest he was older; but in his book *Nishmat Hayyim*, Menasseh called him "younger" (103 recto). On this basis, Fuks and Fuks-Mansfeld (1984, p. 110) have Samuel as the elder. Roth (1945, p. 67) and Ifrah (2001, p. 49) have Joseph as the older son, as does Offenberg (2011a, p. 26). This latter view seems to me to be correct.

13. Pierre Daniel Huet, in *Huetiana*, p. 133.

14. This, at least, is what his friend Joseph Bueno said in his dedicatory letter to the *Conciliador* (unpaginated but p. xi), where he noted that at the age of twenty Menasseh was giving lessons in *gemara*.

15. *Livro de Bet Haim do Kahal Kados de Bet Yahacob*, p. 51.

16. For the text of the contract, see Fuks and Fuks 1979. On Menasseh and Briot, see Lane 1994.

17. In one of the Portuguese-Jewish community's documents of 1629, we are told that Menasseh was printing books "*en sua Caza*"; see D'Ancona 1940, p. 149. Another Sephardic printer in Amsterdam, Daniel da Fonseca, claimed to have been the first in the city to print a Hebrew book; but, as Fuks and Fuks (1979, p. 5) show, the date of the contract between Menasseh and Briot refutes that claim.

18. On Theunisz, see Dubiez 1957, p. 61.

19. See Fuks and Fuks-Mansfeld 1984, vol. 1, p. 96.

20. This may be the same Moses Halevi who would help the founders of the Amsterdam Portuguese-Jewish community.

21. The two functions were usually carried out by the same person or firm.

22. Den Boer 2008, p. 91.

23. For a study of book censorship in the seventeenth century Dutch Republic, see Groenveld 1987.

24. For a thorough study of Hebrew publishing in the Netherlands, see Fuks and Fuks-Mansfeld 1984 (especially vol. 1). See also Van Eeghen 1960–1978 and Kleerkooper 1914–1916.

25. Prins 1933, p. 149; see also Meijer 1950, 100. The full text of the Haarlem declaration for Jewish residence is in Grotius 1949, pp. 40–43 (on printing, see p. 41).

26. Grotius's recommendation on publishing is in Grotius, *Remonstrantie*, p. 124; an English translation is excerpted in Meijer 1955 (100): "The Jews may possess, use and have printed here any books, with the exception of those containing words of blasphemy or defamation. Those who have such books printed are liable to expulsion from the country and to confiscation of property, whereas those who possess and use such books are liable to confiscation of the books and a fine of fifty guilders for the first offense."

27. The full Dutch text is in Grotius, *Remonstrantie*, pp. 107–132. English excerpts, along with excerpts from the recommendations from Pauw, are in Prins 1933, pp. 150–151. For a fuller study, see Grotius, *Remonstrantie*, and Meijer 1955.

28. See Prins 1933, p. 167.

29. On Benveniste, see Fuks and Fuks-Mansfeld 1984, vol. 1, pp. 146–153.

30. Benveniste, however, was already publishing daily and Sabbath prayer books according to Ashkenaic rites by the early 1640s; see, for example, item 208 in Prins 1933, p. 157.

31. On Judah ben Mordecai and Samuel bar Moses Halevi, see Fuks and Fuks-Mansfeld 1984, vol. 1, pp. 184–199.

32. For a study of the financing of Menasseh's press, see Fuks and Fuks 1983 and the list of titles in Fuks and Fuks-Mansfeld 1984, pp. 114–135.

33. Fuks-Mansfeld 1992, p. 160.

34. For the contract between Menasseh and Laurensz, see Vieijra 1922. In fact, the contract requires Menasseh "not to leave Laurensz unoccupied except for Saturdays," but also appears to say (in wording that is rather difficult to interpret) that Laurensz may work on Saturdays "if it should be necessary to sew the bales" and that "Manace will pay him twelve stuivers for these Saturdays whether he does it or not." My thanks to Piet Steenbakkers and Wiep van Bunge for their help with this confusing text.

35. *Thesouro dos dinim*, p. iii.

36. In at least one case, involving the first volume of Menasseh's *Conciliador*, it seems that he could not publish the work in Amsterdam without the approval of the *parnassim*. This episode is discussed in the next chapter.

37. The *Sefer Elim* is in fact a three-part treatise in two volumes, with the first volume containing parts one and two, titled *Sefer Elim* and *Sefer Ma'yan Hatum*, and the second volume containing the third part, titled *Sefer Ma'yan Ganim*.

38. This may or may not be accurate; it is, in my view, more likely that Delmedigo persuaded Menasseh to publish his treatises.

39. Delmedigo's letter is excerpted in Fuks and Fuks-Mansfeld 1984, vol. i, p. 104 n. 33. For a study of Delmedigo's relationship with Menasseh, see D'Ancona 1940.

40. Delmedigo, *Sefer Elim*, p. 301.

41. *Sefer Elim*, p. 304.

42. The text of the board's minutes is in D'Ancona 1940, pp. 149–151.

43. D'Ancona 1940, pp. 125–126.

44. The text of the governors' resolution is in D'Ancona 1940, pp. 150–151.

Chapter 4. The Conciliator

1. The entry in the *Livro de Bet Haim do Kahal Kados de Bet Yahacob* reads: "En 26 de dito [Novembro] hūa menima de Menase ben Israel na careira setena entre no. 28 e 29" (p. 120 in the published version by Pieterse).

2. The full title of the work is *Conciliador o de la conveniencia de los lugares de la Sagrada. Escriptura que repugnantes entre si parecen* (Concilator, or the Agreement of the Places of Holy Scripture That Appear to Contradict Each Other).

3. As Fisher (2017, pp. 158–159) notes, what was unique about Menasseh's work was not the nature of the reconciliatory project per se—whether among Jews or Christians—but its "comprehensiveness," the attempt to address *all* of the apparently contradictory passages.

4. Question 8.

5. *Conciliador*, Part I, pp. 22–23.

6. Question 11.

7. *Conciliador*, Part I, pp. 27–28.

8. Question 121.

9. Question 128.

10. The title page says "Francofurti," but this may be a stand-in for Amsterdam. However, Katchen (1984, pp. 128–144) suggests that it actually was printed in Frankfurt.

11. For an excellent study of Menasseh's preparation of his treatises for Christian readers, and especially a comparative analysis of the Spanish originals with their Latin versions, see Rauschenbach 2012.

12. On this issue, see Méchoulan 1980, especially pp. 2–3.

13. The comment is by Samuel Sorbière; see *Sorberiana*, p. 125.

14. There is debate among scholars as to whether Vossius was or was not himself a Remonstrant. He certainly did defend the Remonstrant cause, but it is unclear whether this was out of ideological sympathy with its tenets or simply as a matter of the principle of toleration. He does express, in a letter, a "distaste for all partisanship" (quoted in Rademaker 2010, p. 480). Rademaker (especially p. 487) offers a brief discussion of this topic and provides references.

15. It is unclear how Gerardus first made the rabbi's acquaintance, but it was apparently well before the Vossius family moved to Amsterdam. In his letter to Simon Beaumont of November 1632, Vossius mentioned that Dionysius had been studying with Menasseh already for six years (*jam ab sexennio*); Vossius, *Gerardi Joan. Vossii et Clarorum Virorum ad eum Epistolae* (henceforth abbreviated as: *G. J. Vossii Epistolae*), vol. 1, n. 185, p. 208.

16. G. J. Vossius to Chris. Stupesky, 13 January 1637, Vossius, *G. J. Vossii Epistolae*, vol. 1, n. 295, p. 293.

17. Vossius, *Theses Theologicae et Historicae*, p. 253.

18. November 1632, Vossius, *G. J. Vossii Epistolae*, vol. 1, n. 185, p. 208.

19. G. J. Vossius to Antonio van der Linden, 4 April 1647, Vossius, *G. J. Vossii Epistolae*, vol. 1, n. 536, p. 452.

20. See G. J. Vossius's letter to Isaac Vossius, 1 July 1642, Amsterdam University Library, J 86 h (cited by Blok 2000, p. 57).

21. See Katchen 1984.

22. The label is from Roth 1945, p. 106.

23. On the growing interest and expertise in Hebraic studies among Dutch scholars in the seventeenth century, see Katchen 1984.

24. On this see Rauschenbach 2018.

25. *Vindiciae Judaeorum*, in Wolf 1901, p. 124.

26. *Conciliador*, Part II, Dedicatory Letter, unpaginated but on p. v.

27. See the "Greeting to the Reader" of the Latin *De Fragilitate Humana*.

28. The more well read among them may have been struck (unfavorably) by the similarity between Menasseh's account of the creation of human beings (as single creatures with two heads and two sets of limbs) and the fanciful tale told by Aristophanes in Plato's dialogue *Symposium*.

29. Cited in Katchen 1984, p. 142. For an account of his affair, see also Blok 1977.

30. Barlaeus to Van der Myle, 10 May 1634, in Barlaeus, *Casparis Barlaei Epistolarum Liber*, Letter 241, p. 510.

31. For a biographical sketch of Barlaeus, see Blok 1977.

32. Diary of Episcopius, Chapter 3, fol. 24. The diary is in the University of Amsterdam library; my thanks to Rachel Boertjens, curator of the Bibliotheca Rosenthaliana, for providing access to it. Episcopius refers to "D. Vossius" not because it is Dionysius, but because the "D" stands for "Doctus," meaning "learned" or "scholar."

33. 7 November 1633, *Epistolae Celeberrimorum Virorum*, Letter 37, pp. 125–126.

34. Barlaeus to Van der Myle, 10 May 1634, in Barlaeus, *Casparis Barlaei Epistolarum Liber*, Letter 241, p. 511. This is from a letter that Barlaeus gave to Menasseh to take to Van der Myle on the

chance that the States might reverse their rejection of the dedication. For an account of Barlaeus's epigram and the events that followed, see Blok 1977.

35. Samuel Sorbière, after noting that Menasseh, with whom he was well acquainted, was not especially skilled in Latin, said that he wrote the *Conciliador, De la Resurreccion,* and *De Creatione* "in Lusitanian" and had them translated into Latin by Dionysius Vossius, Vorstius, "and other friends" (see the entry "Menasses-Ben Israel" in his *Sorberiana,* p. 125).

36. Menasseh here criticized a view that was later propounded by his friend Isaac La Peyrère in his work *Prae-Adamitae,* that there were human beings before Adam. On Menasseh and La Peyrère, see Popkin 1974.

37. Roth calls it "pedantic, pretentious and trivial" (1945, p. 91); and Offenberg says it is "a rather trivial booklet" (2011a, p. 19). Although these judgments may be true, it remains the case that the work offers us insight into problems and theories that Menasseh took seriously.

38. *Epigramma in Problemata Clarissimi viri Manassis Ben-Israel, De Creatione,* in *De Creatione Problemata XXX,* p. vi:

Si sapimus diversa, Deo vivamus amici,
doctaque mens precio constet uqique suo.
Haec fidei vox summa meae est. Haec crede Menasse.
Sic ego Christiades, sic eris Abramides.

39. Certain Reformed critics of Barlaeus focused, especially, on the phrase *"Deo vivamus amici,"* which if read in a certain way— "we are friends to God"—seems to suggest an equality of standing before God.

40. July 1637, Vossius, *G. J. Vossii Epistolae,* vol. 1, n. 308, p. 301.

41. The texts of these disputations are in Voetius, *Selectarum Disputationum Theologicarum Pars Secunda* (i.e., vol. 2), pp. 77–155.

42. *Selectarum Disputationum Theologicarum Pars Secunda,* pp. 111 and 131.

43. *Selectarum Disputationum Theologicarum Pars Secunda,* p. 102.

44. He also insisted that "the Talmudic books should not be read promiscuously and without precautions," although he allowed that "they should not be destroyed" (*Selectarum Disputationum Theologicarum Pars Secunda*, p. 111).

45. *Selectarum Disputationum Theologicarum Pars Secunda*, p. 110. There was, in fact, a great deal of diversity even within the more orthodox Reformed camp regarding the Jews from both a theological and political perspective; Voetius's extremism was not universally shared by all conservatives.

46. For a discussion of Voetius's role, see Prins 1933, pp. 159–162, and Blok 1977.

47. See, for example, Albiac 1994, pp. 300–325, and Katchen 1984, p. 149. In Maimonides, *Commentary on the Mishnah*, Sanhedrin 10, the thirteenth "fundamental principle" is "the belief in the resurrection of the dead."

48. See Da Costa's memoir, *Exemplar Humanae Vitae*, in Gebhardt 1922, pp. 105–123 (pp. 108–109).

49. Da Costa 1993, p. 343.

50. This is according to Da Costa's own report (Gebhardt 1922, p. 112).

51. For a discussion of the role this issue might have played in the community's excommunication of the philosopher Spinoza, see Nadler 2001.

52. On the dating and a reconstruction of Mortera's lost (unpublished) treatise, see Saperstein 1991.

53. Biblical texts on resurrection and immortality are hard to find, although passages such as Isaiah 26:19 ("Oh, let your dead revive! Let corpses arise! Awake and shout for joy, You who dwell in the dust!—For your dew is like the dew on fresh growth; You make the land of the shades come to life") and Daniel 12:2 ("Many of those that sleep in the dust of the earth will awake, some to eternal life, others to reproaches, to everlasting abhorrence") were clearly suggestive enough to inspire a long tradition of rabbinic commentary on resurrection.

54. For a thorough presentation of this debate over eternal punishment, as well as the relevant texts, see Altmann 1972.

55. Oddly, Rosenbloom (1994) refers to Menasseh's "silence" on this topic, and speculates that "he preferred noninvolvement rather than express an opinion" (p. 245) and that he declined to take a side one way or the other.

56. Menasseh seems, in fact, to have tailored the Latin versions of his works to his gentile audience, introducing changes in both form and content from the Spanish versions; on this, see Rauschenbach 2012 and 2016.

57. *De Resurrectione Mortuorum*, unpaginated but on p. xiv.

58. Quoted in Roth 1945, pp. 46–47. See also Ifrah 2001, p. 51.

59. Prins 1933, p. 157. On L'Empéreur, see also Van Rooden 1989.

60. Amsterdam Municipal Archives, *Resolutieboek van Burgermeesteren en Oud-Burgemeesteren, 1603–1649*, fol. 109 recto.

61. The text of the letter is in Méchoulan 1980. The work in question is *De Termino Vitae*, and it was in fact published by Menasseh, with his name on the cover, in 1639; I return to this in the next chapter.

62. See Van der Wall 1985, p. 59.

63. November 1632, Vossius, *G. J. Vossii Epistolae*, vol. 1, n. 185, p. 208.

64. The texts of these letters are in Méchoulan 1979.

65. *Conciliador*, Part II, final page of unpaginated "Letter to Reader."

66. The text of this letter from 1647 is in Blok 2000, p. 59 n. 49.

67. Menasseh's name, at least, was familiar to Grotius as early as July 1637, when he was mentioned in a letter from Gerardus Vossius relating the affair over the Barlaeus epigram; see Vossius, *G. J. Vossii Epistolae*, vol. 1, n. 308, p. 301.

68. Autograph manuscript copies of Menasseh's letters to Grotius are in the Bibliotheca Rosenthaliana, and can be found online at http://cf.uba.uva.nl/en/collections/rosenthaliana/menasseh/brieven.html. My thanks to Steven Hutchison for his help in transcribing the texts of these letters.

69. Grotius to Gerardus Vossius, 30 October 1638, *The Cor-*

respondence of Hugo Grotius, Part 9, n. 3823; *Briefwisseling van Hugo Grotius,* vol. 9, p. 664.

70. Grotius to Menasseh ben Israel, 8 October 1639, *The Correspondence of Hugo Grotius,* Part 10, n. 4326; *Briefwisseling van Hugo Grotius,* vol. 10, pp. 649–650.

71. Barlaeus, *Vindiciae Epigrammatis,* p. 7.

72. 1 July 1642, in the collection of the Amsterdam University Library, J 86 h, quoted in Blok 2000, p. 57 n. 46.

73. *Vindiciae Judaeorum,* in Wolf 1901, p. 137.

74. "Echo Hebreae," in *De Resurrectione Mortuorum,* unpaginated.

75. *Dissertatio de fragilitate humana,* pp. 3–4.

76. As Rauschenbach (2016) puts it, "everybody knew that exchanging knowledge with Christians was playing with fire, because it not only threatened the status of Jewish communities, but also provided Christians with new weapons against Judaism and the Jews" (pp. 64–65).

77. Fuks and Fuks-Mansfeld 1984, p. 106; Kleerkoper 1914–1916, p. 1467.

78. According to Fuks and Fuks-Mansfeld 1984, "this contract . . . came to nothing" (p. 112).

79. Fuks-Mansfeld 1992, p. 158.

80. See Fuks and Fuks-Mansfeld 1984, p. 107.

81. Gnirrep and Offenberg 2012.

82. The text of the letter is in Méchoulan 1979, p. 15.

Chapter 5. "I am not my own master"

1. On the merger agreement, see Wiznitzer 1958–1959.

2. M. Fokkens, *Beschrijvinghe der Wijdtvermaarde koopstadt Amsterdam* (1622), quoted in Gans 1971, p. 46. This synagogue should not be confused with the large synagogue complex that now stands on the Mr. Visserplein, which was not built until 1675.

3. See Fuks-Mansfeld 1989, p. 64. De Hooghe made a series of prints of people, sites, and activities among Amsterdam's Jews.

4. That Menasseh did end up with teaching is evident from

a letter he wrote in 1648 complaining about the hours he had to spend in the school; the text of the letter is in Adler 1904, p. 572.

5. For the document laying out the terms of the merger, including the ranking of the rabbis, see *Livro dos Acordos da Naçao e Ascamot*, fols. 77–88; Menasseh's and the other rabbis' assignments are specified in section 22 on fol. 81. Accessible online as #41 at https://archief.amsterdam/inventarissen/inventaris/334.nl.html#A01504000003. A transcription can be found in Barrios's *Triumpho del Govierno Popular*, the text of which is in Pieterse 1968, pp. 155–167; on Menasseh's assignment, see item 22 on p. 160.

6. *De Termino Vitae*, II.2, p. 49.

7. *De Termino Vitae*, II.8, p. 114.

8. *De Termino Vitae*, III.10, p. 222. See also *De la Fragilidad Humana*, II.14.i, p. 69.

9. *De Termino Vitae*, II.6, p. 194.

10. *De Termino Vitae*, III.1, pp. 118–119. For a study of Menasseh's views on free will and their historical context, see Méchoulan 1996, pp. 7–77.

11. *De Termino Vitae*, Dedicatory Letter.

12. The text of the letter is in Méchoulan 1980.

13. On Sephardic Jews and the trans-Atlantic slave trade, see Zemon Davis 2016.

14. On the role that Dutch Jews played in the sugar trade, see Blom 1937. For a general overview of the early history of the Jews in Brazil, see Wiznitzer 1960, as well as Swetschinski 2000, pp. 114–116.

15. Vossius, *G. J. Vossii Epistolae*, vol. 1, n. 372, p. 345.

16. 2 February 1640, *The Correspondence of Hugo Grotius*, Part 11, n. 4499; *Briefwisseling van Hugo Grotius*, vol. 11, p. 60.

17. *De Termino Vitae*, pp. 236–237.

18. *De Termino Vitae*, pp. 235–236. Croesus was the wealthy king of Lydia. The reference to Thersites is odd, since in Homer's *Iliad* (Book II) he is portrayed as a lowly and detestable character. Perhaps the meaning is that Thersites is beneath dignity, and so should not expect any honor or respect.

19. The *ma'amad*'s records of the event, from which the quo-

tations that follow are taken, are in the *Livro dos Acordos da Naçao e Ascamot*, fols. 55–56 and 69–70. They are accessible online as #71, 78, and 79 at https://archief.amsterdam/inventarissen/inventaris /334.nl.html#A01504000004. They are transcribed in Gebhardt 1922, pp. 212–219.

20. The most important study of the function of the *herem* among Amsterdam's Sephardim in the seventeenth century is Kaplan 1984. For an overview of offenses for which one would earn a *herem* in the Talmud Torah congregation, see Wiznitzer 1958–1959.

21. For a study of Spinoza's case, see Nadler 2001.

22. *Livro dos Acordos da Naçao e Ascamot*, fol. 70, accessible online as #79 at https://archief.amsterdam/inventarissen/inventaris /334.nl.html#A01504000004. On 8 September 1647, the page on which the *herem* against Menasseh was recorded was pasted over with a piece of paper by the *ma'amad*, "out of respect."

23. *Conciliador*, Part II, p. 87.

24. As a preface to the section of the work dealing with the Book of Kings; see Part II, pp. 87–88.

25. Ephraim's burial record is at *Livro de Bet-Haim do Kahal Kados de Talmud-Torah*, p. 37.

26. The date of Aboab's departure and Menasseh's appointment to take over his teaching duties is confirmed in the *Livro dos Acordos da Naçao e Ascamot*, fol. 96. Accessible online as #92 at https://archief.amsterdam/inventarissen/inventaris/334.nl.html #A01504000062; also cited in Pieterse 1968, document 17, p. 168. Contrary to Roth (1945, p. 61) and Ifrah (2001, p. 54), Aboab was not Mortera's "senior colleague" but in fact fourth in rank, so his departure did not mean that Menasseh was promoted to second in rank in the rabbinate, which was still held by David Pardo; see the merger document in Barrios, *Triumpho del Govierno Popular*, in Pieterse 1968, p. 159.

27. See the agreement signed by Menasseh and the *parnassim* transferring Aboab's teaching duties to Menasseh in the *Livro dos Acordos da Naçao e Ascamot*, fol. 96; also in Pieterse 1968, document 17, p. 168. See also the letter transcribed in Adler 1904, p. 568. What Menasseh said to his correspondent was that his "income"

was "500 cruzados," using the name of the Portuguese currency. Presumably "income" referred only to his rabbinic salary, and he must have been using the word *cruzado* as shorthand for money, i.e., Dutch guilders. Otherwise, 500 cruzados converted into guilders would, in the early seventeenth century, mean over 1,500 guilders (see Souza 2004, p. xvi), which would be an extraordinary salary.

28. The *parnassim* appointed Leão to take over Menasseh's class on 24 October 1648 (8 Heshvan 5409); see the document in the *Livro dos Acordos da Naçao e Ascamot*, fol. 256. Accessible online as #172 at https://archief.amsterdam/inventarissen/inventaris/334 .nl.html#A01504000064.

29. The letter, from 1648, is in Adler 1904.

30. Adler (1904) had suggested that the recipient of the letter was Gerardus Vossius, but Roth's claim (1945) that it was Villareal is now generally accepted.

31. See Roth 1945, pp. 135–139, who says that among the papers in the Inquisition's dossier on Villareal was the letter from Menasseh.

32. Things would get even worse for Jews operating in Brazil when the Portuguese finally retook Pernambuco from the Dutch in 1654. We can assume that by that point Menasseh was no longer involved there as a merchant.

33. Adler 1904, p. 571.

34. I have translated from the Dutch text in *Menasse ben Israel's VVelkomst*. The Portuguese text is in Menasseh, *Gratulaçao de Menasseh ben Israel*.

35. For the text of this letter, see Méchoulan 1978.

36. See the entry for 2 June 1642 (4 Sivan 5402/48th Day of the Omer), *Livro dos Acordos da Naçao e Ascamot*, fol. 128. Accessible online as #108 at https://archief.amsterdam/inventarissen/inven taris/334.nl.html#A01504000005.

37. On Beelthouwer and his writings, see Zilverberg 1969.

38. Beelthouwer, *Schildt der Christenen*, pp. 56–57.

39. For the few known details of Italia's life and a catalogue of his known works, see Narkiss 1956 and 1957.

40. See Assaf and Bilski 2011 for a discussion and catalogue of Italia's Esther scrolls.

41. "I would be glad to know if your Lordship's brother-in-law was present in the synagogue. I think I saw him, but because of my poor eyesight, I cannot be sure" (Méchoulan 1978, p. 81).

42. In his "Life of Menasseh ben Israel," in *The Term of Life*, p. viii. Pocock was relying on someone else's description, since he was not yet born when Menasseh died.

43. Offenberg (2011b) has shown that the author of the poem is David Jesurun, a member of a Portuguese-Jewish family in Amsterdam with which Menasseh enjoyed good relations.

44. Franckenberg, *Briefwechsel*, pp. 161, 180. For an insightful discussion of Italia's portrait of Menasseh, see Perlove 2006.

45. In the end, it was used as the frontispiece for the Latin edition of *The Hope of Israel, Spes Israelis*.

46. *De la Fragilidad Humana*, "To the Reader," unpaginated, but p. v.

47. *De la Fragilidad Humana*, "To the Reader," unpaginated, but p. vi.

48. See, for example, Maimonides, *Sefer ha-Mitzvot*, Mitzvot lo-ta'aseh, 32–33.

49. *De la Fragilidad Humana*, pp. 2–3.

50. Menasseh did overlook some rabbinic literature that cites the earliest patriarchs as examples of individuals who led a life without sin; see, for example, *Mekhilta de Rabbi Yishmael* 48a (on Exodus 16.10). For a discussion of the background to Menasseh's *De la Fragilidad Humana*, see Méchoulan 1996.

51. *De la Fragilidad Humana*, II.16.ii, pp. 78–79. The words in brackets appear in the Latin but not the Spanish edition.

52. *De la Fragilidad Humana*, II.10.v, p. 49.

53. *Sefer Nishmat Hayyim*, p. 340. He is here following Maimonides in his *Commentary on the Mishnah*, Tractate Makhot.

54. *De la Fragilidad Humana*, II.14.i, p. 69.

55. *De la Fragilidad Humana*, II.14.i, p. 69.

56. Their responses ranged from refutation to cooptation; see Rauschenbach 2016.

57. For example, the theologian Johannes Hoornbeck in his *Teshuvat Yehuda sive Pro convincendis et convertendis Judaeis libri octo* of 1655. On this, see Rauschenbach 2016, p. 75.

58. Beelthouwer, *Schildt der Christenen*, pp. 17–20.

59. Item 38 of the community's *Ascamot*, or regulations, says: "No one should dispute nor argue matters of religion with the *goyim* in order to convince them to follow our Holy Law, nor say any scandalous words to them regarding their beliefs. To do otherwise would be to disturb the liberty that we enjoy and make us hateful for the sake of something that is neither commanded by law or an obligation" (*Livro dos Acordos da Nação e Ascamot*, fol. 25, accessible online as #56 at https://archief.amsterdam/inventarissen /inventaris/334.nl.html#A01504000004).

60. There is no record of any such order in the *Livro dos Acordos da Nação e Ascamot*.

61. This suggests that Menasseh did not actually sell the firm to Aboab but merely handed it over to him for some time.

62. The catalogue is reproduced in Fuks and Fuks-Mansfeld 1981, pp. 40–45.

63. Archief van de Burgemeesteren, *Resolutieboek van de Heeren Burgermeesteren* 1603–1794 (A. 1603 Maart 29–1649 Januari 28), 29 April 1648, fol. 208v. Accessible online as #172 at https://archief .amsterdam/inventarissen/inventaris/5024.nl.html.

64. This is the explanation preferred by Hillesum (1917, p. 28).

65. Coymans signed his letter *mercator sapiens*, or "wise merchant." This was a familiar economic/social class in the Dutch Golden Age comprising gentlemen engaged in business who also maintained strong scholarly interests and used their wealth to support intellectual projects. They constituted a significant part of the attendees at the Amsterdam Athenaeum Illustre. For a study of this phenomenon, see Rauschenbach 2013.

66. The text of the letter is in Méchoulan 1982. The exchange of books went in both directions. In early 1652, Menasseh wrote to Colvius, a Millenarian, to see if he might obtain from him a copy of the treatise *De Tribus Imposteribus* (*On the Three Impostors*), a notorious anonymous work attacking the prophetic foundations of

Judaism, Christianity, and Islam (the three "impostors" being Moses, Jesus, and Muhammed). Menasseh was seeking to learn what objections the "profane" had against "Moses and his writings" in connection with his study of a work titled *De Divinatione Pentateuchi*. The text of Colvius's letter to Claude Saumaise (6 June 1652) with this information is in a note by Susanna Åkerman, in the Richard Popkin Papers in the William Andrews Clark Library, UCLA, Box 17, folder 37.

67. For Sorbière's comments on Menasseh and details of their meetings, see Sorbière, *Sorberiana*, pp. 124–125.

68. *Sorberiana*, p. 125.

69. Fuks and Fuks-Mansfeld 1981, p. 38. They, among others (including Roth 1945), claim that Menasseh sent Joseph to Poland in 1650; but it makes more sense to date this in 1649, when Menasseh's other son, Samuel, took over the printing business.

70. Roth 1945, pp. 67–68. There is no record of Joseph's burial in Amsterdam (Ouderkerk), so presumably he was interred in Poland.

71. 10 March 1651. The autograph of the letter in Spanish is in the Bibliotheca Rosenthaliana. A Dutch translation is in Hillesum 1899, pp. 48–52.

Chapter 6. The Hope of Israel

1. Levi/Montezinos gave his report on 19 September 1644, to be exact. The report appeared as a preface to Menasseh's *Esperança de Israel/The Hope of Israel*.

2. I will use the term "Indians" to refer to the indigenous people of the Americas only because that is how they are referred to in the sources I am discussing, to avoid confusion.

3. *Esperança de Israel*, p. 4; *The Hope of Israel*, p. 106.

4. *Esperança de Israel*, p. 10; *The Hope of Israel*, p. 109.

5. Thorowgood, *Jewes in America*, unpaginated, final page.

6. *Esperança de Israel*, pp. 41–42; *The Hope of Israel*, pp. 124–125.

7. On these and other views, see Popkin 1989.

8. "An Epistolicall Discourse of Mr. John Dury, to Mr.

Thorowgood. Concerning his conjecture that the Americans are descended from Israelites," in Thorowgood, *Jewes in America,* unpaginated preface.

9. II Esdras 13:39–41.

10. In 1649, Dury wrote to Menasseh to get a copy of Montezinos's deposition and gave it to Thorowgood to put in his book, which was finally published in 1650—the first printed, and thus widely available, version of Montezinos's adventure.

11. Thorowgood, *Jewes in America,* p. 37.

12. "An Epistolicall Discourse of Mr. John Dury, to Mr. Thorowgood. Concerning his conjecture that the Americans are descended from Israelites," in Thorowgood, *Jewes in America,* unpaginated preface.

13. Essentially, Dury put together three things: 1, the theory that the native peoples of America were the Lost Tribes of Israel (which he read in Thorowgood); 2, the report about Montezinos discovering a Jewish people in America; and 3, biblical prophecies about what the discovery and return of the Lost Tribes would mean in terms of the coming of the Messiah.

14. "An Epistolicall Discourse of Mr. John Dury, to Mr. Thorowgood. Concerning his conjecture that the Americans are descended from Israelites," in Thorowgood, *Jewes in America,* unpaginated preface. On Dury's correspondence with Menasseh and transcriptions of Menasseh's three letters to Dury, see Van der Wall 1985.

15. The text of one of Homes's letters to Menasseh (24 December 1649), with a postscript by Jessey, is extant in Felgenhauer, *Bonum Nuncium,* pp. 103–106.

16. John, Revelation, chapter 20. Most Christians of the time did not share this Millenarian vision; see Van der Wall 1989, pp. 177–178.

17. Cited in Popkin 1984a, p. 353.

18. Rabbi Leão, of course, certainly did not share his collaborators' conversionist aims.

19. Cited in Popkin 1988, p. 8.

20. Popkin 1988, p. 9.

21. In his preface, Menasseh claimed, as justification for this vocalized edition of the Mishnah: "I saw many of the most wise and learned of my people stuttering over the pronunciation of many words instead of being precise. Few comprehend the conjugation of the verbs and the laws of accentuation, nor the pronouns, and so do not know their right from their left. I said to myself in my heart, the time has come to serve God and to open an entry to students who have been reading for days and years, to make it easier for them with pointing and signs to lighten their burdens, for the meanings are hidden and sealed"; for the text of the prefaces by Menasseh and Leão, see Popkin and Katz 1988.

22. Popkin 1984a, p. 353.

23. For a discussion of Dury's *A Seasonable Discourse Written by Mr. John Dury upon the earnest requests of many*, in which he laid out the plan for the college, see Popkin 1984a, pp. 354–356.

24. See his letters included in Felgenhauer's *Bonum Nuncium*, pp. 92–96 (p. 96): "Menasseh quoque confert nonnihil ad Exitum Israelis & Introitum Gentilium."

25. *Assertion du règne de mille ans*, p. 35 (quoted in Méchoulan and Nahon 1987, p. 50).

26. Méchoulan (1982, p. 24) notes that "the prophesies on which Millenarianism was grounded were, most often, common to both Christians and Jews, but their interpretations diverged radically."

27. On this, see Saraiva 1972.

28. Felgenhauer, *Bonum Nuncium*, p. 104.

29. See, for example, *De Resurrectione Mortuorum*, p. 314.

30. For a study of this episode and its sources, see Saraiva 1972.

31. Quoted in Saraiva 1972, p. 47.

32. 25 November 1649. The Latin text of the letter is in Van der Wall 1985, pp. 60–61.

33. In the *Dedicatoria al Lector* of the Spanish edition, Menasseh said that "as a new person of great quality and letters from England has asked me to write more about this topic, I have written this publication in the Latin language, although with some care."

I am skeptical that he wrote it in Latin, however, and believe that the original was composed in Spanish and translated into Latin by one of his friends, as was the case with other works; Méchoulan and Nahon (1987) concur, and provide arguments to this effect (pp. 62–63).

34. *Esperança de Israel*, p. 42; *The Hope of Israel*, pp. 124–125.

35. *Esperança de Israel*, p. 23; *The Hope of Israel*, p. 115 n. 43.

36. *Esperança de Israel*, p. 120; *The Hope of Israel*, p. 161.

37. This remark appears in the 1650 English translation by Moses Wall but not the Spanish original; see *The Hope of Israel*, p. 115.

38. *Esperança de Israel*, pp. 93–94; *The Hope of Israel*, pp. 146–147.

39. *Esperança de Israel*, p. 97; *The Hope of Israel*, p. 148.

40. *Esperança de Israel*, p. 95; *The Hope of Israel*, p. 148.

41. 23 December 1649, in Van der Wall 1985, p. 61.

42. 14 July 1650, in Van der Wall 1985, p. 62.

43. *Conciliador*, Part III, p. 180.

44. *Conciliador*, Part III, pp. 184–185.

45. The other is his concordance to biblical passages in the Midrash Rabbah, the *Sefer Pene Rabbah*.

46. On Menasseh's account, the reunion with the resurrected body does not take place until the Messianic era/world-to-come.

47. In *De la Resurreccion*, Menasseh limited himself to explaining how, on the Day of Judgment, "some are destined for eternal life, others for an ignominious and eternal punishment" (III.7, pp. 306–307).

48. *Sefer Nishmat Hayyim*, Part I, ch. 12, p. 31.

49. *Sefer Nishmat Hayyim*, Part I, ch. 13.

50. For a study of this, and a perhaps overly sober assessment of Menasseh's "importance" among rabbinic authorities, see Kasher 1989.

51. The standard biography of Queen Christina is Åkerman 1991.

52. For a magisterial study of Isaac Vossius and his intellectual circle, see Blok 2000.

53. See Le Blon's letter to Christina, 25 October 1650, in Kernkamp 1903, pp. 54–55.

54. Autographs of the four letters from Menasseh to Isaac Vossius are in the Bibliotheca Rosenthaliana at the University of Amsterdam Special Collections, accessible online at http://cf.uba .uva.nl/en/collections/rosenthaliana/menasseh/brieven.html. Transcriptions and translations into Dutch of the first two letters, from 1651, are in Hillesum 1899, pp. 47–52. All of the letters are discussed in Bethencourt 1904a, which also includes transcriptions and translations into French of the third (1652) and fourth (1655) letters. The Spanish original of the third letter is transcribed in Offenberg 1985, and an English translation is in Offenberg 2011a, p. 31. The Spanish original of the fourth letter, and an English translation, are in Offenberg 1989a.

55. Vossius to Saumaise, 4 July 1638; the text of this excerpt from the letter is in Blok 2000, p. 59 n. 54.

56. Blok 2000, pp. 60–61.

57. Quoted in Blok 2000, p. 61 n. 58.

58. Quoted in Blok 2000, p. 60.

59. Unfortunately, Vossius's end of the correspondence is not extant.

60. A translation of this letter of 2 February 1652 is in Offenberg 2011a, p. 31.

61. For an account of this extended dispute, see Blok 2000, pp. 383–392.

62. Blok 2000, p. 398.

63. Letter from Cornelius Tollius to Johann Friedrich Gronovius, quoted in Blok 2000, p. 392.

64. Preface to Huet, *Demonstratio Evangelica*, p. 3.

65. Preface to Huet, *Demonstratio Evangelica*, p. 3.

66. *Huetiana*, pp. 225–226.

67. *Huetiana*, pp. 226–227.

68. As of November 1652, it seems the books had not arrived in Stockholm—or at least, not at the queen's court. In a pair of letters that month to Vossius, Borchart told him that "the way things are, Master Menasseh should not count on his money very soon,"

and "the Hebrew library of Master Menasseh has not arrived. I have often spoken about him with the Queen, who certainly means him well. But there is no money here" (quoted in Blok 2000, p. 414).

69. *Conciliador*, Part II, "Al Lector," final page. This was written in 1641, around the midpoint of his rabbinic career.

Chapter 7. The English Mission

1. For a study of this episode in Dutch Jewry, see Israel 1989.
2. Israel 1989, p. 144.
3. Salomon 1988, p. xlviii.
4. Israel 1989, pp. 146–147.
5. Salomon 1988, p. xlviii.
6. Pieterse 1968, p. 170.
7. Salomon 1988, p. xlviii. Aboab was then earning more than Mortera.
8. *Livro dos Acordos da Naçao e Ascamot*, fol. 358. Accessible online as #223 at https://archief.amsterdam/inventarissen/inventaris /334.nl.html#A01504000005.
9. Salomon 1988, p. xlviii.
10. *Livro dos Acordos da Naçao e Ascamot*, fol. 341. Accessible online as #215 at https://archief.amsterdam/inventarissen/inventaris /334.nl.html#A01504000005.
11. *Livro dos Acordos da Naçao e Ascamot*, fol. 344. Accessible online as #216 at https://archief.amsterdam/inventarissen/inventaris /334.nl.html#A01504000005.
12. This was on 12 April 1654; *Livro dos Acordos da Naçao e Ascamot*, fol. 363. Accessible online as #226 at https://archief.amster dam/inventarissen/inventaris/334.nl.html#A01504000005.
13. The Spanish original was dedicated to the *parnassim* of Talmud Torah.
14. *The Hope of Israel*, pp. 99–100.
15. Schorsch (1978) argues that readmission to England was in fact not among the initial motivating factors for the composition of *The Hope of Israel*; rather, Menasseh wanted to dissociate himself from a Christian missionary effort in the Americas that was grounded in the idea that the American Indians were Israelites

that needed to be converted. It was, he claims, only shortly after first writing the work that he came to see its potential for the re-admission project.

16. *Vindiciae Judaeorum*, p. 143.

17. Letter to an unknown correspondent, September 1647, in Wolf 1901, pp. lxxvii–lxxviii.

18. Quoted in Katz 1982, p. 177.

19. My discussion of the settlement of the Jews in England is indebted to the fuller accounts by Katz 1982; Wolf 1901; and Roth 1945, chapter 10.

20. Katz 1982, p. 23.

21. Salvetti to Senator Bali Gondi, 7/17 December 1655; the text of this letter is in Roth 1928, pp. 137–138.

22. The Spanish text and a translation of this letter are in Roth 1928, pp. 116–117.

23. And yet, in London Menasseh reportedly told the Dutch ambassador to England that he "doth not desire any thing for the Jews in Holland, but only for such as sit in the Inquisition in Spain and Portugal"; see the ambassador's letter in Adler 1893–1894, p. 48.

24. *Vindiciae Judaeorum*, Section 7, in Wolf 1901, p. 143.

25. *Esperança de Israel*, p. 79; *The Hope of Israel*, p. 140.

26. *Vindiciae Judaeorum*, Section 7, in Wolf 1901, p. 143.

27. See Roth 1928, p. 114, and Roth 1945, p. 207.

28. Mary Cary, *The Little Horns Doom & Downfall* (1651), cited in Katz 1982, p. 42.

29. On English support for resettlement, see Katz 1982, ch. 3.

30. Cited in Katz 1982, p. 187.

31. Cited in Roth 1945, p. 198.

32. The text of Wall's preface is in Wolf 1901, p. 9.

33. Wolf 1901, p. 58.

34. Katz 1982, p. 162.

35. Cited in Katz 1982, p. 178.

36. "A Breife Epistle to the Learned Manasseh Ben Israel," unpaginated dedicatory letter.

37. "A Breife Epistle," p. 14.

38. "A Breife Epistle," p. 16.

39. *Vindiciae Judaeorum*, p. 5 (in Wolf 1901, p. 111). Elsewhere he noted: "the Ambassadors of England . . . were received in our Synagogue with as great pomp and applause, Hymns and cheerfulnesse of minde, as ever any Soveraigne Prince was" ("To His Highnesse the Lord Protector . . . The Humble Addresses of Menasseh Ben Israel," in Wolf 1901, p. 77).

40. The relevant record from the State Papers is in Adler 1893–1894, p. 44.

41. *Vindiciae Judaeorum*, p. 38 (in Wolf 1901, p. 144).

42. Katz 1982, pp. 190–191; Roth 1945, p. 211.

43. Quoted in Katz 1982, p. 190.

44. The text is in Roth 1928, p. 116.

45. Menasseh may, in fact, have been waiting for Christina in Antwerp, perhaps having heard about her abdication from Vossius; see Offenberg 1989a, pp. 269–270. Popkin (1974), on the other hand, argues that Menasseh was not in Antwerp until that December.

46. Pieterse 1968, pp. 19–20.

47. This was the theory proposed by Bethencourt (1904a), but Offenberg (1989a) offers a refutation of that interpretation. See also Roth 1945, pp. 173–174, and Katz 1983–1984.

48. Isaac Vossius to Nicholas Heinsius, 20 August 1654, in *Sylloges Epistolarum*, vol. 3, pp. 676–677 (Ep. XCIII). Offenberg (1989a) corrects Bethencourt's reading of this letter.

49. See Bethencourt 1904a, p. 103.

50. On Menasseh and La Peyrère, see Popkin 1974 and 1984b. Popkin argues that La Peyrère was an influence on Antonio Vieira, and that by 1655 a highly ecumenical Menasseh "was moving toward a Judeo-Christian position similar to those of Vieira" and La Peyrère, and "presenting a view of Jewish Messianism almost compatible with Vieira's Judeo-Christian Millenarianism" (1984b, p. 19).

51. The text of the letter, in the original Spanish and translated into English, is in Offenberg 1989a, pp. 271–272.

52. 10 March 1651. A complete Dutch translation of this letter,

originally written in Spanish, is in Hillesum 1899, pp. 48–52; an English translation of the relevant passage is in Offenberg 1989a, p. 267. The Spanish autograph is accessible at http://cf.uba.uva.nl /en/collections/rosenthaliana/menasseh/brieven/ivossius1.jpg.

53. It does not even appear among the books listed as "ready for the Presse" in a personal bibliography that Menasseh appended to the *Vindiciae Judaeorum;* see the catalogue reprinted in Wolf 1901, p. 147. Offenberg (1989a), however, suggests that "probably the response [by Vossius and Christina] to this proposal was a positive one, since exactly four years later Menasseh was engaged in printing the work, although apparently without the promised support of the Queen" (p. 268). He proposes that the *Humas o cinco Libros de la Ley Divina* published in 1654–1655 was in fact "the first part of the first volume" of a (Jewish) *Biblia Española*, and that the "Maecenas" was, instead of Christina, the Amsterdam pensionary and ambassador to Sweden Conrad van Beuningen.

54. Turnbull 1947, p. 273.

55. See his letter to "All Persons of the Hebrew Nation . . . ," in Roth 1928, p. 116.

56. Letter from David Nassi to Manoel Martinez Dormido, 20 November 1654, quoted in Israel 1989, p. 157. The letter is extant only in a contemporary English translation.

57. Jacob del Monte to Manoel Martinez Dormido, 26 November 1654, quoted in Israel 1989, p. 158. The letter is extant only in a contemporary English translation.

58. Israel 1989, p. 160.

59. Wolf (1901, pp. xxxii–xxxiii) suggests that Menasseh was reluctant to go because of his own precarious standing among the Jews in Amsterdam.

60. Roth 1945, pp. 212–213. On Dormido, see also Wolf 1901, pp. xxxii–xxxiv, and Israel 1989, pp. 154–160. Despite having the same name, Abrabanel, Dormido was apparently not related to Menasseh's wife; see Roth 1945, p. 337 n. 39.

61. Israel (1989, p. 155) says that "during the first Anglo-Dutch War [Dormido] seems to have passed intelligence from Amsterdam to London."

62. Quoted in Katz 1982, p. 194; see also Israel 1989, p. 156.

63. Quoted in Katz 1982, p. 194.

64. Recorded in the State Papers, in Adler 1893–1894, p. 44.

65. Roth 1945, p. 220; Israel 1989, p. 156.

66. We do not know whether this was when Menasseh and Felgenhauer first got acquainted; more likely, they had known each other for some time through mutual friends.

67. "Dedicatio," in Felgenhauer, *Bonum Nuncium:* "Non plures elapsi sunt dies, quando Reverentiam tuam prima facie viderim, in hospitio dilecti nostri Petri Serarii, Amici, ubi primus noster sermo erat de Messiah, quanquam brevissimus."

68. "Dedicatio," in Felgenhauer, *Bonum Nuncium Israeli,* unpaginated; see also p. 32.

69. Felgenhauer, *Bonum Nuncium Israeli,* pp. 32–33.

70. Felgenhauer, *Bonum Nuncium Israeli,* p. 10.

71. Psalm 94:8, in Felgenhauer, *Bonum Nuncium Israeli,* p. 15.

72. Menasseh's letter is in Felgenhauer, *Bonum Nuncium Israeli,* pp. 87–91.

73. Felgenhauer, *Bonum Nuncium,* pp. 87–88.

74. This is in fact a reprint of the "panegyric in praise of the eminent, most outstandingly wise and noble man, Menasseh ben Isreal" by Rosales that first appeared in 1639 at the end of Menasseh's *De Termino Vitae.*

75. Van der Wall (1989, p. 168) notes that "this volume was made in close cooperation between Menasseh and the Bohemian chiliast."

76. Roth 1945, p. 156.

77. Popkin (1984b) argues that it is important to distinguish between the influence on Menasseh by conversionist and non-conversionist Millenarian friends, thereby contrasting men like La Peyrère and Vieira with English Millenarians such as Dury, Homes, and Jessey and the Germans Felgenhauer, Mochinger, and Von Franckenberg.

78. *Even yeqarah. Piedra Gloriosa o de la Estatua de Nebuchadnesar,* v.

79. *Piedra Gloriosa,* p. 25.

80. *Piedra Gloriosa*, p. 139.

81. *Piedra Gloriosa*, p. 176.

82. *Piedra Gloriosa*, p. 102.

83. *Piedra Gloriosa*, pp. 164–165.

84. Menasseh's interpretation of these verses from Daniel take up the final ten sections of *Piedra Gloriosa*, pp. 186–259.

85. Menasseh alerted his reader to the fact that he, unlike other commentators, did not take Daniel here to be referring to some Last Judgment. In his view, the messianic era, or the world-to-come, though involving the resurrection of the dead, is not the same as the time of final reckoning before God. He thereby followed Maimonides, who insisted that "the 'days of the Messiah' refers to a time in which sovereignty will revert to Israel and the Jewish people will return to the land of Israel" (*Commentary on the Mishnah*, Sanhedrin 11). On the other hand, Maimonides, unlike Menasseh, distinguished between the world-to-come and the Messianic era.

86. *Piedra Gloriosa*, p. 59.

87. Rauschenbach (2018), however, has questioned this "universalist" reading of Menasseh. In the *Piedra Gloriosa* in particular, she is doubtful that "Menasseh's vision of the fifth monarchy was a vision of universalism and religious unity." Rather, she claims, "it was a vision of Jewish triumph, rule and revenge, a world turned upside down," with Jews ruling over Christians.

88. *Piedra Gloriosa*, p. 242.

89. *Piedra Gloriosa*, p. 245.

90. *Piedra Gloriosa*, "Dedicatory Letter," pp. iii–iv.

91. *Piedra Gloriosa*, "To the Reader," p. v.

92. *Piedra Gloriosa*, "To the Reader," pp. v–vi.

93. The etchings are bound with the text in only one of these volumes—the one belonging to Vossius himself, now in the Leiden University library; in the other copies they are inserted as loose sheets.

94. For recent studies of Judaic themes (in some cases from a Millenarian and conversionist perspective) in Rembrandt's art, see Zell 2002. See also Perlove and Silver 2009.

95. A collaboration on *Piedra Gloriosa* is not certain, and the relationship between Menasseh and Rembrandt has been subject to much romantic mythologizing over the centuries; see my Appendix.

96. The Aramaic words are units of measurement in order of declining value.

97. See *Talmud Bavli*, Sanhedrin 22a.

98. *De Termino Vitae*, p. 160. Menasseh was writing this book around the time that Rembrandt was working on the Belshazzar painting.

99. The suggestion of a Rembrandt-Menasseh collaboration here was first made by Dyserinck (1904, pp. 160–161). The argument was expanded by Hausherr (1963), and the thesis has since become a commonplace in the literature. Menasseh's book was published in 1639, and depending on the dating of the painting—which most scholars now put at around 1635—this could be several years after Rembrandt had finished the work. But the theory about the writing would certainly have been on Menasseh's mind for a while, and he could have advised Rembrandt on this in person, before writing his book.

100. Roth 1945, pp. 221–222; Katz 1982, pp. 197–198. That the doctorate was a forgery was not discovered until the late nineteenth century by John Griffith, Keeper of the Archives, Wadham College, Oxford. For the Latin text of the diploma and Griffith's report proving it a forgery, see Adler 1893–1894, pp. 48–54. No one suspected the ruse in Samuel's lifetime; his gravestone identifies him as "Do Doctor Samuel, F[ilho] Do Haham Menasseh Ben Israel."

101. *Vindiciae Judaeorum*, in Wolf 1901, p. 144.

102. Sadler to Cromwell, in 1658, quoted in Ifrah 2001, pp. 159–160.

103. Letter to "All Persons of the Hebrew Nation . . . ," 2 September 1655, in Roth 1928, p. 116. Wolf (1901, p. xxxvii n. 4) says that Menasseh and Samuel were accompanied by a "retinue of three rabbis," including another member of the Amsterdam rabbinate, Jacob Sasportas; however, I have not found any evidence to support this claim.

104. *Vindiciae Judaeorum*, in Wolf 1901, p. 144.

105. Letter to "All Persons of the Hebrew Nation . . . ," 2 September 1655, in Roth 1928, p. 116.

106. Wolf (1899, p. 147) believes that this confirms that Menasseh "was the guest of the Protector."

107. September 22. According to the Gregorian calendar, Erev Rosh Hashanah was on October 1.

108. Adler 1893–1894, p. 44.

109. "Humble Addresses," in Wolf 1901, p. 79.

110. "Humble Addresses," in Wolf 1901, p. 76.

111. "Humble Addresses," in Wolf 1901, pp. 81–82.

112. "Humble Addresses," in Wolf 1901, p. 100.

113. "Humble Addresses," in Wolf 1901, p. 102.

114. *Vindiciae Judaeorum*, in Wolf 1901, p. 144.

115. The petition is in Wolf 1901, pp. lxxxiii–lxxxiv.

116. From the letter of charge sent to the members of the conference; see Katz 1982, p. 205.

117. See the account of the conference's meetings in Katz 1982, pp. 208–228.

118. John Thurloe to Henry Cromwell, 17 December 1656, in Adler 1893–1894, p. 48.

119. Salvetti to Senator Bali Gondi, 14/24 December 1655; the text of this letter is in Roth 1928, p. 138.

120. Salvetti to the Grand Duke, 21/31 December 1655; the text of this letter is in Roth 1928, pp. 138–139.

121. Katz 1982, p. 217.

122. *Vindiciae Judaeorum*, in Wolf 1901, p. 144.

123. The text of the report is in Wolf 1901, pp. lxxxiv–lxxxv, and in Adler 1893–1894, p. 45.

124. Salvetti to the Grand Duke, 21/31 December 1655; the text of this letter is in Roth 1928, p. 138.

Chapter 8. Denouement

1. Salvetti to the Grand Duke, 18/28 January 1656; the text of this letter is in Roth 1928, p. 141.

2. The Portuguese recapture of Brazil naturally had an ad-

verse effect on the role played by Amsterdam's Jews in the growing, transport, and commerce of sugar.

3. See Wolf 1901, p. lxii.

4. On the Robles affair, see Roth 1945, pp. 257–261; and Katz
1982, pp. 235–238.

5. The text of the petition is in Wolf 1901, pp. lxxxv–lxxxvi.

6. Katz 1982, p. 238.

7. Its subtitle is "A Letter in Answer to certain Questions
propounded by a Noble and Learned Gentleman, touching the
reproaches cast on the Nation of the Jewes; wherein all objections
are candidly, and yet fully cleared." The "gentleman" in question
is William Prynne.

8. See especially his *A Short Demurrer to the Jews long-discontinued Remitter into England* (London, 1656).

9. *Vindiciae Judaeorum*, in Wolf 1901, pp. 133–134.

10. *Vindiciae Judaeorum*, in Wolf 1901, p. 137.

11. *Vindiciae Judaeorum*, in Wolf 1901, p. 118.

12. Pococke, in his introduction to his translation of *De Termino Vitae*, notes that Menasseh was "once civilly entertain'd by
the Protector at his Table" (*The Term of Life*, p. iv).

13. An extract from this letter is printed in Adler 1893–1894,
p. 48. It is also possible that what the Dutch ambassador needed
reassurance about was not that Menasseh was scheming to move
the Jews from Holland to England, but rather that he was not trying to leverage additional rights and privileges for the Jews in
Holland.

14. Popkin 1992, p. 346; Popkin, however, provides no evidence for these reports, and it would seem to have been both an
imprudent thing to do and contrary to Menasseh's character. But
see Katz 1982, p. 234 n. 2.

15. More makes this comment in his "Annotations" to a work
by Joseph Glanvill and George Rust, *Two choice and useful Treaties:
the one Lux Orientalis or an Enquiry into the Opinion of the Eastern
Sages concerning the Praeesitence of Souls . . . The other, a Discourse of
Truth* (London, 1682), p. 27. See Van den Berg 1989, pp. 98–99.

16. See "Some considerations touching the style of the Holy

Scriptures," in *The Works of the Honourable Robert Boyle* (vol. 2), where Boyle recalls "the famousest of the modern Rabbies, Menasse ben-Israel (one time I made him a visit at his own house in Amsterdam)" (p. 280). He also calls Menasseh "the greatest rabbis of this age" (p. 301).

17. A Latin transcript of their dialogue was published in 1671, after both men had died, in Jean D'Espagne, *Quatre Petits Traittez de Jean Despagne*, pp. 111–123.

18. Interestingly, this debate took place just two months before the Amsterdam Portuguese-Jewish community decided to "excommunicate, expel, curse and damn" the young Baruch Spinoza for his "abominable heresies and monstrous deeds." For the full text of this *herem*, see Nadler 2001, p. 2.

19. On Supino, see Roth 1928, pp. 118–126.

20. *Vindiciae Judaeorum*, in Wolf 1901, pp. 144–145.

21. Salvetti to the Grand Duke, 18/28 January 1656; the text of this letter is in Roth 1928, p. 140.

22. State Papers, John Sadler to Richard Cromwell, 4 January 1658; the text of this letter is in Wolf 1901, pp. lxxxvii–lxxxviii.

23. The text of this letter is in Wolf 1901, pp. lxxxvi–lxxxvii.

24. The payments were to begin in February 16, 1657; at least two payments, of twenty-five pounds each, were made that year (Katz 1982, p. 241).

25. Letter to Richard Cromwell, in Wolf 1901, p. lxxxviii.

26. It is unclear why Menasseh buried Samuel in Middelburg rather than bringing the body to Amsterdam, to be buried in the Ouderkerk cemetery. One plausible explanation is that Menasseh himself was too ill to continue the journey, since he died so soon after Samuel's interment. This would mean that Menasseh had every intention of returning to Amsterdam, contrary to Roth (1945, pp. 272–273), who says that Menasseh "had some idea of remaining there [in Middelburg] as *Haham* of the community." Katz says that Menasseh died in Middelburg "en route" to Amsterdam (1982, p. 241). Moreover, Roth claims that in Middelburg "a number of refugees from Brazil had established themselves, not without some difficulty, upon the fall of Pernambuco—among them, Menasseh's

own brother, Ephraim Soeiro. It was in the latter's house that he took up his residence" (1945, p. 272); Roth seems unaware that Ephraim had, in fact, died in 1640. Ifre, on the other hand, suggests that it was Menasseh's "brother in-law, Ephraïm Abravanel," who lived in Middelburg (2001, p. 260); however, we do not know of any brother of Rachel named Ephraim—perhaps he means Jonah?

27. *Nicomachean Ethics*, 1100a30.

28. We do not know anything more about Menasseh and Rachel's daughter, Hannah/Gracia, other than her marriage to Samuel Abrabanel in 1646. If she was still alive, she would have been forty-two years old and living with her own family. In his letter to Richard Cromwell in 1658, John Sadler mentions Menasseh's "widow & relations," but we do not know to whom he is referring.

29. See John Sadler to Richard Cromwell, in Wolf 1901, p. lxxxviii.

30. On these final stages in the process of readmission, see Roth 1945, pp. 276–284; Katz 1982, pp. 242–243.

Appendix: Menasseh ben Israel and Rembrandt

1. Two prominent examples are Schwartz 1985 and Alpers 1988.

2. Roth 1945, p. 168.

3. Janson 1974, p. 426.

4. Lugt 1915, p. 87. Perlove calls Menasseh "Rembrandt's friend and patron" (1993, p. 47).

5. Coppenhagen 1990. See, for example, the introductory essay by Mireille Hadas-Lebel and Henri Méchoulan to *La Pierre Glorieuse de Nabuchodonosor, ou La Fin de l'Histoire au XVIIe siècle*, pp. 24–25.

6. See especially Zell 2002, chapter 3; Schwartz 2006, pp. 299–305; and Perlove and Silver 2009.

7. Alexander-Knotter et al. 2007.

8. Manefeld 1898. The review is in *Wegweiser für die Jugendliteratur* 13 (September, 1906), pp. 51–52.

9. Perhaps the most fanciful contribution is that of Valen-

tiner, who has Menasseh—"who lived opposite to Rembrandt's house" and, "it must surely be assumed, was a friend of Rembrandt's for twenty years"—introducing the painter and the young philosopher Spinoza in his home (1957, p. 20). Interestingly, Landsberger takes a rather conservative position. With regard to whether Rembrandt "was a close friend of Rabbi Manasseh ben Israel," he says that "while this is not unlikely, there is no evidence to this effect" (1946, p. 34).

10. Schama 1999, p. 607.

11. See Perlove 1993, especially pp. 56–57.

12. See, for example, Roth 1945, p. 169; Schwartz 1985, p. 175; Haussherr 1963; and Schama 1999, p. 418.

13. See also Offenberg 2011a, p. 7; and Dudok van Heel 1994, p. 26.

14. Vaz Dias 1930. The idea that Menasseh did live on the Breestraat near Rembrandt is apparently due to a case of mistaken identity: Rembrandt did have a neighbor named Emanuel Dias, while Menasseh used as a business alias his original Portuguese name, Manoel Dias Soeiro; see Alexander-Knotter et al. 2007, p. 20, and Offenberg 2011a, pp. 7–8.

15. For an assessment of Gersaint's reasoning, see Dudok van Heel 1994.

16. Offenberg 2011a, pp. 6–8, and Offenberg 1992. See also Dudok van Heel 1994; Dubiez 1992a; Salomon 1992; and Alexander-Knotter et al. 2007. Schwartz initially identifies the sitter of the Rembrandt etching as Menasseh (1985, p. 176), but later retracts this claim (2006, p. 191). Dubiez believes that the Rembrandt etching is a portrait of Rabbi Saul Levi Mortera, and that the Flinck painting is a portrait of David Pardo, one of the early rabbis of the Amsterdam Sephardim (1992a). Dudok van Heel argues against Dubiez's identifications.

17. Perlove and Silver 2009, p. 372.

18. The suggestion of a Rembrandt-Menasseh collaboration here was first made by Dyserinck 1904. The argument was expanded by Hausherr 1963, and the thesis has since become a commonplace in the literature.

19. This is the suggestion of Offenberg 2011a, p. 22.

20. Thus Alexander-Knotter et al. say that "We do not know whether Menasseh must have been Rembrandt's only source for this knowledge. There were many theologians and scholars who also dealt with Jewish topics and Hebrew texts" (2007, p. 46). The publication of the book in 1639 and the range of dates for the painting (1635–1639) make it even more unlikely that one of these theologians or scholars read Menasseh's book and then, on that basis, advised Rembrandt.

21. Zell notes that Protestant and Catholic exegetes generally avoided the issue of the unreadability of the message "by assuming that God had blinded them to the prophecy," and concludes that "Rembrandt therefore most likely learned the sequence from Menasseh" (2002, p. 62). On the dating issue, he suggests that "Menasseh might well have written out the inscription in this [vertical] arrangement for Rembrandt before the book appeared" (p. 62). Perlove and Silver regard a collaboration here as "most likely" (2009, p. 134), while Schama says that Menasseh "almost certainly supplied the painter with the additionally esoteric effect of having the Hebrew/Aramaic letters read in vertical columns rather than horizontally from right to left" (1999, p. 418). Schwartz initially says that, with respect to this painting, "we must assume that Rembrandt derived his information directly from Menasseh" (1985, p. 175). In subsequent work, however, he is more skeptical that Rembrandt received any Jewish help here (Schwartz 2006, pp. 301–302), and eventually outright rejects the idea that Menasseh had any involvement in Rembrandt's painting (Schwartz 2009). Alexander-Knotter et al., in keeping with the general tenor of their study, are equally suspicious, saying that "it is also uncertain whether Rembrandt had personal contact with Menasseh regarding the Hebrew inscription on *Belshazzar's Feast*" (2007, p. 20).

22. See, for example, Van de Waal 1954–1955; Perlove and Silver 2009, p. 134; the catalogue *Rembrandt et la Nouvelle Jérusalem: Juifs et Chrétiens à Amsterdam au Siècle d'Or*, no. 177 (Sigal-Klagsbald 2007); and many others, including Nadler 2003, p. 137. Méchoulan says that "the rabbi went, quite naturally, to Rembrandt, not only

because he is the greatest artist of his time, but also because he knows that the painter reads the Bible without outside commentary" (1996, p. 24). He suggests, moreover, that Menasseh commissioned the illustrations from Rembrandt for his book "to give it more weight, to show the world the catholicity of his message" (2007, p. 79). Even those who tend to be skeptical or highly conservative about a Rembrandt-Menasseh relationship tend to make an exception for this project; see, for example, Schwartz 2006, p. 301. A prominent dissenter, however, is Dubiez, who says "the idea that Menasseh would have had a share in this can best quickly be forgotten" (1992b, p. 28). See also Offenberg 2011a, p. 23, and Alexander-Knotter et al. 2007, pp. 24–26.

23. This, at least, is the explanation provided by Blok 2000, p. 419.

24. *Piedra Gloriosa*, "Al Lector," p. v.

25. For example, in Part VII, with reference to Jacob's dream of the angels on a ladder: "En esta conformidad avemos hecho la pintura baxando los tres Angeles" (*Piedra Gloriosa*, p. 87).

26. This has been established by Offenberg 2011a, p. 23.

27. This was first suggested by Solomons 1906; see also Landsberger 1946.

28. Munz 1952, vol. 2, p. 89.

29. Offenberg 2011a, pp. 23–24. This suggestion was first made by Solomons 1906.

30. Besides the copy that is in the University of Leiden library, there are copies in the Museum het Rembrandthuis, Amsterdam; the library of the Jewish Theological Seminary, New York; the Institut Néerlandais de Paris; and the Petit Palais, Paris.

31. Dubiez 1992b, p. 27. Zell, however, who claims that "Rembrandt's illustrations of Menasseh's text reflect an exceptional degree of cooperation," argues against this post-acquisition insertion theory (2002, pp. 81–84).

32. Dubiez 1992b, pp. 27–28.

33. Isaac Vossius to Nicolas Heinsius, 8 July 1651, in *Sylloge Epistolarum a viris illlustribus scriptarum*, vol. 3, no. 52, pp. 617–618. My thanks to Geert Mak for bringing this letter to my attention.

34. My thanks to Gary Schwartz for suggesting the Jan Six connection.

35. *Piedra Gloriosa*, pp. v–vi.

36. Zell 2002, p. 83.

37. As for Italia's engravings, which also appear only in some copies of the treatise, they too can be explained by an owner of the book commissioning illustrations for his and other copies. This would likely be someone from the Amsterdam Portuguese-Jewish community, who naturally would turn to a Jewish artist from within the community for such work.

BIBLIOGRAPHY

Primary Sources

Works by Menasseh

Most of these texts are accessible online at the University of Amsterdam's Bibliotheca Rosenthaliana (Special Collections) digital research collection devoted to Menasseh ben Israel: cf.uba.uva.nl/en/collections/rosenthaliana/menasseh/collectie.html.

Safah Berurah (manuscript, Montezinos Library, Ets Hayim, #EH 47 D7).

Sefer Peneh Rabbah (Amsterdam: Menasseh ben Israel, 1628).

Conciliador, Part I (Amsterdam: Menasseh ben Israel, 1632); Part II (Amsterdam: Nicolas Ravesteyn, 1641); Part III (Amsterdam: Samuel ben Israel Soeiro, 1650); Part IV (Amsterdam: Samuel ben Israel Soeiro, 1651).

De Creatione Problemata XXX (Amsterdam: Menasseh ben Israel, 1635).

De Resurrectione mortuorum Libri III (Amsterdam: Joannes Janssonium, 1636).

De la Resurreccion de los Muertos, libros III (Amsterdam: Menasseh ben Israel, 1636).

De Termino Vitae (Amsterdam: Menasseh ben Israel, 1639).

The Term of Life, translated by Thomas Pocock (London: Thomas Baker, 1709).

De la Fragilidad Humana, y Inclinacion del Hombre al Peccado (Amsterdam: Menasseh ben Israel, 1642).

[Modern edition: *De la fragilité humaine et de l'inclination de l'homme au péché* (Paris: Cerf, 1996).]

Menasse Ben Israels VVelkomst, uyt sijns Volcks naem, aen de Hooghgebooren, Prince van Oranjen Frederic Henric, als hy met de Doorluchtigste Koningin Henriette Maria, Gemalin des Hoogh-gebiedende Karolvs, Koninghs van Engelandt, Vrankrijck ende Yrlandt, onse Synagoge besocht (Amsterdam: Menasseh ben Israel, 1642).

Gratulaçao de Menasseh ben Israel, Em nome de sua Naçao, Ao Celsissimo Principe de Orange Frederique Henrique Na sua vinda a nossa Synagoga de T. T. Em companhia da Serenissima Raynha Henrica Maria (Amsterdam: Menasseh ben Israel, 1642).

Thesouro dos Dinim (Amsterdam: Menasseh ben Israel, 1645–1647).

Miqveh Yisrael, Esto es, Esperança de Israel (Amsterdam: Samuel ben Israel Soeiro, 1650).

[Modern edition: *The Hope of Israel*, trans. Moses Wall, eds. Henri Méchoulan and Gérard Nahon (Oxford: Oxford University Press for the Littman Library, 1987).]

Sefer Nishmat Hayyim (Amsterdam: Samuel Abarbanel Soeiro, 1651).

'Even yeqara. Piedra Gloriosa o de la Estatua de Nebuchadnesar (Amsterdam: Menasseh ben Israel, 1655).

[Modern edition: *La Pierre Glorieuse de Nabuchodonosor, ou La Fin de l'Histoire au XVIIe siècle*, trans. Mireille Hadas-Lebel and Henri Méchoulan (Paris: J. Vrin, 2007).]

"To his Highnesse The Lord Protector of the Commonwealth of England, Scotland and Ireland, The Humble Addresses of Menasseh ben Israel" (Amsterdam: Menasseh ben Israel, 1651?).

Vindiciae Judaeorum (London: R. D., 1656). [The text is reproduced in Wolf 1901.]

Other Primary Sources

Arckenholtz, Johan, *Mémoires pour servir à l'histoire de Christine reine de Suède*, vol. 1 (Amsterdam: Pierre Mortier, 1751).

Barlaeus, Caspar, *Vindiciae Epigrammatis . . . Adversus improbas Theologi cujusdam Anonymi criminationes* (Amsterdam: Johannes Blaeu, 1636).

Barlaeus, Caspar, *Casparis Barlaei Epistolarum Liber* (Amsterdam: Joannis Blaeu, 1667).

Barrios, Daniel Levi de, *Triumpho del Govierno Popular y de la Antiguedad Hollandesa* (Amsterdam, 1683–1684).

Beelthouwer, Jan Pietersz, *Schildt der Christenen Tegen alle On-Christenen* (Amsterdam: Nicolas van Ravesteyn, 1649).

Boyle, Robert, *The Works of the Honourable Robert Boyle*, ed. Thomas Birch, 6 vols. (London: J. and F. Rivington, 1722).

Da Costa, Uriel, *Examination of the Pharisaic Traditions*, trans. H. P. Salomon and I. S. D. Sassoon (Leiden: Brill, 1993).

Delmedigo, Joseph Solomon, *Sefer Elim* (Odessa: M. A. Belinson, 1864).

Descartes, René, *Oeuvres de Descartes*, eds. Charles Adam and Paul Tannery, 11 vols. (Paris: J. Vrin, 1964–1971).

D'Espagne, Jean, *Quatre Petits Traittez de Jean Despagne* (Geneva: Samuel De Tourness, 1671).

Epistolae Celeberrimorum Virorum (Amsterdam: Janssonius-Waesbergius, 1715).

Felgenhauer, Paul, *Bonum Nuncium Israeli. Quod offertur Populo Israel & Iudae in hisce temporibus novissimis de Messiah* (Amsterdam: George Trigg, 1655).

Franckenberg, Abraham von, *Briefwechsel: Abraham von Franckenberg*, ed. Joachim Telle (Stuttgart: Frommann-Holzboog, 1995).

Franco Mendes, David, *Memorias do estabelecimento e progresso dos Judeos portuguezes e espanhoes nesta famosa citade de Amsterdam*, eds. L. Fuks and R. G. Fuks-Mansfeld, *Studia Rosenthaliana* 9 (1975).

Grotius, Hugo, *Briefwisseling van Hugo Grotius*, eds. P. C. Molhuysen, B. L. Meulenbroek, P. P. Witkam, H. J. M. Nellen, and C. M. Ridderikhoff (The Hague: Martinus Nijhoff, 1928–2001).

Grotius, Hugo, *The Correspondence of Hugo Grotius*, digital edition, 1st edition. October 2009. Online at http://grotius.huygens.knaw.nl.

Grotius, Hugo, *Remonstrantie nopende de ordre dije in de landen van Hollandt ende Westvrieslandt dijent gestelt op de Joden*, ed. Jakob Meijer (Amsterdam: Joachimsthal, 1949).

Huet, Pierre Daniel, *Demonstratio Evangelica* (Amsterdam: Jansson-Waesberg, 1680).

Huet, Pierre Daniel, *Commentaria de rebus ad eum pertinibus* (Amsterdam, 1718).

Huet, Pierre Daniel, *Huetiana, ou Pensées Diverses de M. Huet Evesque d'Avranches* (Paris: Jacques Etienne, 1832).

Livro de Beth Haim do Kahal Kados de Bet Yahacob, ed. Wilhelmina C. Pieterse (Assen: Van Gorcum, 1970).

Livro de Bet-Haim do Kahal Kados de Talmud-Torah, Comessado em Pesah do Anno de 5399 em Amsterdam, eds. Lydia Hagoort and Wilhelmina C. Pieterse (Amsterdam: Gemeente Amsterdam Stadsarchief, 2008). Available online: https://www.amsterdam.nl/stadsarchief/archief/downloads/beth-haim.

Livro dos Acordos da Naçao e Ascamot, in the Municipal Archives of the City of Amsterdam, Archive 334: Archives of the Portuguese Jewish Community in Amsterdam, Inventory 19 (Ascamot A, 5398–5440 [1638–1680]). Available online: https://archief.amsterdam/inventarissen/inventaris/334.nl.html#.

"Notarial Deeds Relating to the Portuguese Jews in Amsterdam Up to 1639," *Studia Rosenthaliana* 7 (1973).

Prynne, William, *A Short Demurrer to the Jews long-discontinued Remitter into England* (London, 1656).

Sorbière, Samuel, *Sorberiana, ou bons mots, rencontres agréables, pensées judicieuses, et observations curieuses de M. Sorbière* (Paris: Veuve Mabre-Cramoisy, 1732).

Spencer, Edward, "A Breife Epistle to the Learned Manasseh Ben

Israel. In Answer to His, Dedicated to the Parliament" (London, 1650).

Sylloges Epistolarum a Viris Illustribus Scriptarum, ed. Pieter Burman, 5 vols. (n.p.: Samuel Luchtmans, 1727).

Thorowgood, Thomas, *Jewes in America, Or, Probabilities that the Americans are of that Race* (London: Tho. Slater, 1650).

Voetius, Gisbertus, *Selectarum Disputationum Theologicarum*, 5 vols. (Utrecht: Johannes à Waesberge, 1648–1669).

Vossius, Gerardus Joannis, *Theses Theologicae et Historicae*, 3rd edition (The Hague, 1658).

Vossius, Gerardus Joannis, *Gerardi Joanii Vossii et Clarorum Virorum ad eum Epistolae*, 2 vols., coll. Paulo Colomesio (London: Laurentius Kroniger, 1690).

Secondary Sources

Adler, E. N. (1893–1894). "A Homage to Menasseh ben Israel," *Transactions of the Jewish Historical Society of England* 1: 25–54.

Adler, E. N. (1904). "A Letter of Menasseh ben Israel," *Jewish Quarterly Review* 16: 562–572.

Åkerman, Susanna (1991). *Queen Christina and Her Circle* (Leiden: Brill).

Albiac, Gabriel (1994). *La Synagogue Vide* (Paris: Presses Universitaires de France).

Alexander-Knotter, Mirjam, Jasper Hillegars, and Edward van Voolen (2007). *De 'joodse' Rembrandt: De mythe ontrafeld* (Zwolle: Uitgeverij Waanders/Joods Historisch Museum Amsterdam).

Alpers, Svetlana (1988). *Rembrandt's Enterprise: The Studio and the Market* (Chicago: University of Chicago Press).

Altmann, Alexander (1972). "Eternality of Punishment: A Theological Controversy Within the Amsterdam Rabbinate in the Thirties of the Seventeenth Century," *Proceedings of the American Academy for Jewish Research* 40: 1–88.

Assaf, Sharon, and Emily D. Bilski (2011). *Salom Italia's Esther Scrolls and the Dutch Golden Age* (Amsterdam: Menasseh ben Israel Institute and Jewish Historical Museum).

Bethencourt, Joao Leao Cardoso de (1904a). "Lettres de Menasseh ben Israel à Isaac Vossius, 1651–1655," *Revue des Etudes Juives* 49: 98–109.

Bethencourt, Joao Leao Cardoso de (1904b). "Menasseh ben Israel," *Jewish Chronicle*, May 20, 1904, p. 17.

Blok, F. F. (1973). "Quelques humanistes de la Jerusalem de l'Occident," *Humanists and Humanism in Amsterdam: Catalogue of an Exhibition in the Trippenhuis, Amsterdam* (Amsterdam: University of Amsterdam), pp. 9–32.

Blok, F. F. (1977). "Caspar Barlaeus en de Joden. De Geschiedenis van een Epigram," *Nederlands Archief voor Kerkgeschiedenis* 57: 179–209.

Blok, F. F. (2000). *Isaac Vossius and His Circle* (Leiden: Brill).

Blom, H. I. (1937). *The Economic Activities of the Jews of Amsterdam in the Seventeenth and Eighteenth Centuries* (Williamsport, Pa.: Kennikat Press).

Bodian, Miriam (1997). *Hebrews of the Portuguese Nation: Conversos and Community in Early Modern Amsterdam* (Bloomington: Indiana University Press).

Chajes, J. H. (2003). *Between Worlds: Dybbuks, Exorcists, and Early Modern Judaism* (Philadelphia: University of Pennsylvania Press).

Cohen, Mark R. (1988). *The Autobiography of a Seventeenth-Century Rabbi: Leon Modena's Life of Judah* (Princeton: Princeton University Press).

Coppenhagen, J. H. (1990). *Menasseh ben Israel: A Bibliography* (Jerusalem: Misgav Yerushalayim, Institute for Research on the Sephardi and Oriental Jewish Heritage).

Dan, Joseph (1989). "Menasseh ben Israel: Attitude Towards the Zohar and Lurianic Kabbalah," in Yosef Kaplan, Henri Méchoulan, and Richard H. Popkin, eds., *Menasseh ben Israel and His World* (Leiden: Brill), pp. 199–206.

D'Ancona, J. (1940). "Delmedigo, Menasseh ben Israel en Spinoza," *Bijdragen en Mededelingen van het Genootschap voor de Joodse Wetenschap in Nederland* 7: 105–152.

Den Boer, Harm (2008). "Amsterdam as 'Locus' of Iberian Printing in the Seventeenth and Eighteenth Centuries," in Yosef

Kaplan, ed., *The Dutch Intersection: The Jews and the Netherlands in Modern History* (Leiden: Brill), pp. 87–110.

Dohrman, Menahem (1989). *Menasseh ben Israel* [Hebrew] (Kibbutz ha-Meuhad).

Dos Remédios, Mendes (1928). *Os Judeus em Portugal*, 2 vols. (Coimbra: Universidade de Coimbra).

Dubiez, F. J. (1957). "De Hebreeuwse Boekdrukkerij van Menasseh ben Israel in Amsterdam," *Ons Amsterdam* 9: 60–64.

Dubiez, F. J. (1992a). "Rembrandt en de rabbijn—maar welk?," *Vrij Nederland*, April 15, 1992, p. 6.

Dubiez, F. J. (1992b). "Drie beeldende kunstenaars en drie rabbijnen te Amsterdam in de zeventiende eeuw," *Kroniek van het Rembrandthuis* 91: 23–29.

Dudok van Heel, S. A. C. (1994). "Rembrandt en Menasseh ben Israel," *Kroniek van het Rembrandthuis* 93: 22–29.

Dyserinck, Johannes (1904). "Eene Hebreeuwsche inscriptie op eene schilderij van Rembrandt," *De Nederlandsche Spectator* 49: 160–161.

Fisher, Benjamin (2017). "God's Word Defended: Menasseh ben Israel, Biblical Chronology, and the Erosion of Biblical Authority," in Dirk van Miert, Henk Nellen, Piet Steenbakkers, and Jetze Touber, eds., *Scriptural Authority and Biblical Criticism in the Dutch Golden Age* (Oxford: Oxford University Press), pp. 155–174.

Fuks, Leo (1955–1957). "Wat heeft Menasseh Ben Israel geschreven en wat is er van gedrukt? In memoriam Menasseh Ben Israel's 300ste sterfjaar (20 november 1657)," in *Het Boek* (Second Series) 32: 330–335.

Fuks, Leo, and R. Fuks (1979). "The First Hebrew Types of Menasseh ben Israel," *Studies in Bibliography and Booklore* 12: 3–8.

Fuks, Leo, and R. Fuks (1983). "The Financiers of Menasseh Ben Israel's Printing House in Amsterdam, 1627–1655," in *Yad le-Heman. The A.M. Haberman Memorial Volume* (Lod: Mekhon Haberman), pp. 313–320.

Fuks, Leo, and R. G. Fuks-Mansfeld (1981). "Menasseh ben Israel as a Bookseller in the Light of New Data," *Quarendo* 11: 34–45.

Fuks, Leo, and R. G. Fuks-Mansfeld (1984). *Hebrew Typography in the Northern Netherlands, 1585–1815. Historical evaluation and descriptive bibliography.* 2 vols. (Leiden: E. J. Brill).

Fuks, Leo, and M. H. Gans (1957). *Menasseh Ben Israel 1604–1657. Catalogus van de tentoonstelling, georganiseerd door het Genootschap voor de Joodse Wetenschap en het Joods Historisch Museum* (Amsterdam: Joods Historisch Museum).

Fuks-Mansfeld, R. G. (1989). *De Sefardim in Amsterdam tot 1795: Aspecten van een joodse minderheid in een Hollandse stad* (Hilversum: Uitgeverij Verloren).

Fuks-Mansfeld, R. G. (1992). "The Hebrew Book Trade in Amsterdam in the Seventeenth Century," in C. Berkvens-Stevelinck, H. Bots, P. G. Hoftijzer, and O. S. Lankhorst, eds., *Le Magasin de l'Univers: The Dutch Republic as the Centre of the European Book Trade* (Leiden: E. J. Brill), pp. 155–168.

Gans, Mozes H. (1971). *Memorboek: History of Dutch Jewry from the Renaissance to 1940,* trans. Arnauld J. Pomerans (Baarn: Bosch & Keuning).

Gebhardt, Carl (1922). *Die Schriften des Uriel da Costa* (Amsterdam: Menno Hertzberger).

Gnirrep, Kees, and Adri Offenberg (2012). "Menasseh ben Israel as a Supplier of Books to the Municipal Library in Amsterdam in 1635 and 1639," *Quaerendo* 42: 293–307.

Goldish, Matt (2001). "The Amsterdam Portuguese Rabbinate in the Seventeenth Century: A Unique Institution Viewed from Within and Without," in Chaya Brasz and Yosef Kaplan, eds., *Dutch Jews As Perceived By Themselves and By Others. Proceedings of the Eighth International Symposium on the History of the Jews in the Netherlands* (Leiden: Brill), pp. 9–19.

Groenveld, S. (1987). "The Mecca of Authors? States Assemblies and Censorship in the Seventeenth-Century Dutch Republic," in A. C. Duke and C. A. Tamse, eds., *Too Mighty to Be Free: Censorship and the Press in Britain and the Netherlands* (Zutphen: De Walburg), pp. 63–86.

Hagoort, Lydia, and Ben Noach (2009). "'Een lauwer op zijn graf gelegd!' Een korte beschrijving van leven en werken van chacham Isack Aboab da Fonseca," *De Misjpoge* 22: n.p.

Haussherr, Reiner (1963). "Zur Menetekel-Inschrift auf Rembrandt's Belsazarbild," *Oud Holland* 78: 142–149.

Henriques de Castro, David (1950). *De Synagoge der Portugees-Israëlietische Gemeente te Amsterdam* (Amsterdam: n. p.).

Hillesum, Jeremias Meijer (1898a). "Bijdragen tot de geschiedenis van Menasseh Ben Israel, I," *Achawah. Maandblad van den bond voor Israëlietische godsdienstonderwijzers* vol. 5, no. 43: 4.

Hillesum, Jeremias Meijer (1898b). "Bijdragen tot de geschiedenis van Menasseh Ben Israel, II," *Achawah. Maandblad van den bond voor Israëlietische godsdienstonderwijzers* vol. 5, no. 44: 1.

Hillesum, Jeremias Meijer (1899). "Menasseh ben Israel," *Amsterdamsch Jaarboekje voor 1899* 2: 28–56.

Hillesum, Jeremias Meijer (1905a). "Waar werd Menasseh Ben Israel geboren?," *Centraal Blad voor Israëlieten in Nederland* 21: 23.

Hillesum, Jeremias Meijer (1905b). "Een belangrijk historisch feit herdacht," *Centraal Blad voor Israëlieten in Nederland* 21: 36.

Hillesum, Jeremias Meijer (1906). "Menasseh Ben Israel's Epitaph," *Jewish Chronicle*, no. 1925 (23 February 1906): 17.

Hillesum, Jeremias Meijer (1916). "Menasseh Ben Israel (1604–1657)," *Het Boek* (Second Series) 5: 145–152.

Hillesum, Jeremias Meijer (1917). "Uit de geschiedenis der Joden te Amsterdam," *Elsevirs Maandblad* 54: 25–33, 112–125.

Hillesum, Jeremias Meijer (1926). "Een kleine bijdrage tot de geschiedenis van Menasseh Ben Israel alias Manuel Dias Soeiro," *Nieuw Israëlietisch Weekblad*, 31 December 1926: 10.

Hillesum, Jeremias Meijer (1927). "Bijdrage tot de bibliographie van Menasseh Ben Israel's geschriften," *Het Boek* (Second Series) 16: 353–363.

Huussen, Arend H., Jr. (1993). "The Legal Position of Sephardi Jews in Holland, circa 1600," in Jozeph Michman, ed., *Dutch Jewish History* 3 (Assen: Van Gorcum), pp. 19–41.

Ifrah, Lionel (2001). *L'Aigle d'Amsterdam: Menasseh ben Israel (1604–1657)* (Paris: Honoré Champion, 2001).

Israel, Jonathan (1989). "The Dutch Sephardic Colonization Movement of the Mid-Seventeenth Century (1645–1657)," in Yosef Kaplan, Henri Méchoulan, and Richard H. Popkin, eds., *Menasseh ben Israel and His World* (Leiden: Brill), pp. 139–163.

Israel, Jonathan (1995). *The Dutch Republic: Its Rise, Greatness, and Fall, 1477–1806* (Oxford: Oxford University Press).

Janson, H. W. (1974). *History of Art* (Englewood Cliffs, N.J.: Prentice-Hall).

Kaplan, Yosef (1984). "The Social Functions of the *Herem* in the Portuguese Jewish Community of Amsterdam in the Seventeenth Century," in Jozeph Michman, ed. *Dutch Jewish History* I (Tel Aviv: Tel Aviv University), pp. 111–155.

Kaplan, Yosef, Henri Méchoulan, and Richard H. Popkin, eds. (1989). *Menasseh ben Israel and His World* (Leiden: Brill).

Kasher, Asa (1989). "How Important Was Menasseh ben Israel?," in Yosef Kaplan, Henri Méchoulan, and Richard H. Popkin, eds., *Menasseh ben Israel and His World* (Leiden: Brill), pp. 220–227.

Katchen, Aaron (1984). *Christian Hebraists and Dutch Rabbis* (Cambridge, Mass.: Harvard University Press).

Katchen, Aaron (1987). "Menasseh ben Israel the Apologist and the Christian Study of Maimonides' *Mishneh Torah*," in Isadore Twersky and Bernard Septimus, eds., *Jewish Thought in the Seventeenth Century* (Cambridge, Mass.: Harvard University Press), pp. 201–220.

Katz, David S. (1981). "Edmund Gayton's Anti-Jewish Poem Addressed to Menasseh ben Israel, 1656," *Jewish Quarterly Review* 71: 239–250.

Katz, David S. (1982). *Philo-Semitism and the Readmission of the Jews to England, 1603–1655* (Oxford: Clarendon Press).

Katz, David S. (1983–1984). "Menasseh ben Israel's Mission to Queen Christina of Sweden," *Jewish Social Studies* 45: 57–72.

Katz, David S. (1989). "Henry Jessey and Conservative Millenarianism in Seventeenth-Century England and Holland," in Jozeph Michman, ed., *Dutch Jewish History* 2 (Assen: Van Gorcum), pp. 75–93.

Katz, David S. (1993). "Isaac Vossius Among the English Biblical

Critics, 1670–1689," in Richard H. Popkin and A. J. Vanderjagt, eds., *Scepticism and Irreligion in the Seventeenth and Eighteenth Centuries* (Leiden: Brill), pp. 142–184.

Katz, David S. (1994). *The Jews in the History of England, 1485–1850* (Oxford: Oxford University Press).

Kayserling, M. (1877). *The Life and Labours of Menasseh ben Israel,* trans. F. de Sola Mendes (London: Wertheimer, Lea and Company).

Kernkamp, G. W. (1903). *Verslag van een onderzoek in Zweden, Noorwegen en Denemarken naar archivalia belangrijk voor de geschiedenis van Nederland* (The Hague: W. P. van Stockum).

Kleerkooper, M. M. (1914–1916). *De Boekhandel te Amsterdam voornamelijk in de 17e eeuw. Biografische en geschiedkundige aanteekeningen,* 5 vols. (Amsterdam: W. P. Van Stockum).

Klijnsmit, Anthony J. (1988). "Amsterdam Sephardim and Hebrew Grammar in the Seventeenth Century," *Studia Rosenthaliana* 22: 144–164.

Koen, E. M. (1970). "The Earliest Sources Relating to the Portuguese Jews in the Municipal Archives of Amsterdam up to 1620," *Studia Rosenthaliana* 4: 25–42.

Kolakowski, Leszek (1969). *Chrétiens sans église* (Paris: NRF/Editions Gallimard).

Kromhout, David, and Irene Zwiep (2017). "God's Word Confirmed: Authority, Truth, and the Text of the Early Modern Jewish Bible," in Dirk van Miert, Henk Nellen, Piet Steenbakkers, and Jetze Touber, eds., *Scriptural Authority and Biblical Criticism in the Dutch Golden Age* (Oxford: Oxford University Press), pp. 133–154.

Landsberger, Fritz (1946). *Rembrandt, the Jews and the Bible* (Philadelphia: Jewish Publication Society).

Lane, John A. (1994). "Nicolaes Briot and Menasseh ben Israel's First Hebrew Types," in Adri Offenberg, Emile Schrijver, and F. J. Hoogewoud, eds., *Bibliotheca Rosenthaliana: Treasures of Jewish Booklore: Marking the 200th Anniversary of the Birth of Leeser Rosenthal, 1794–1994* (Amsterdam: Amsterdam University Press), pp. 25–29.

Levy, Solomon (1924). "Menasseh ben Israel's Marriage Banns," *Jewish Historical Society of England Transactions* 10: 254–257.

Lugt, Fritz (1915). *Wanderlingen met Rembrandt in en om Amsterdam* (Amsterdam: P. N. van Kampen).

Manefeld, J. (1898). *Helldunkel: Eine jüdische Erzahlung aus dem Leben Rembrants und Mannasse ben Israels* (Mainz: n.p.).

Méchoulan, Henri (1977). "Menasseh ben Israel et l'expérience de l'exil," in *Philosophes ibéro-américains en exil* (Toulouse: Université de Toulouse-Le Mirail), pp. 71–78.

Méchoulan, Henri (1978). "A propos de la visite de Frédéric-Henri, Prince d'Orange, à la synagogue d'Amsterdam," *LIAS* 5: 81–86.

Méchoulan, Henri (1979). "Lorsque Saumaise consultait Menasseh Ben Israel: deux lettres inédites du rabbin d'Amsterdam à l'humaniste de Leyde," *Studia Rosenthaliana* 13: 1–17.

Méchoulan, Henri (1980). "Le problème du Latin chez Menasseh ben Israel et quelques implications religieuses et politiques à propos d'une lettre inédite à Beverovicius," *Studia Rosenthaliana* 14: 1–6.

Méchoulan, Henri (1982). "Menasseh ben Israël au centre des rapports judéo-chrétiens en Holland au XVIIe siècle dans une lettre inédite d'Isaac Coymans à André Colvius," *Studia Rosenthaliana* 16: 21–24.

Méchoulan, Henri (1996). "Introduction," in Menasseh ben Israel, *De la fragilité humaine et de l'inclination de l'homme au péché* (Paris: Les Éditions du Cerf), pp. 7–71.

Méchoulan, Henri (2007). "Esquisse d'un portrait présumé de Menasseh Ben Israël à travers quelques dédicaces," in *Rembrandt et la Nouvelle Jérusalem: Juifs et Chrétiens à Amsterdam au Siècle d'Or* (Paris: Musée d'art et d'histoire du Judaïsme), pp. 73–81.

Méchoulan, Henri, and Gérard Nahon (1987). "Introduction," in Menasseh ben Israel, *The Hope of Israel* (Oxford: Oxford University Press for the Littman Library), pp. 1–95.

Meijer, Jacob (1950). "Hugo Grotius' 'Remonstrantie,'" *Jewish Social Studies* 17 (1955): 91–104.

Meinsma, K. O. (2006). *Spinoza et son cercle* (Paris: J. Vrin).

Melnick, Ralph (1981). *From Polemics to Apologetics* (Assen: Van Gorcum).

Munz, Ludwig (1952). *Rembrandt's Etchings*, 2 vols., translated by N. Maclaren (London: Phaidon).

Nadler, Steven (2003). *Rembrandt's Jews* (Chicago: University of Chicago Press).

Nadler, Steven (2018). "A Source for Menasseh ben Israel's Printer's Mark," *Zutot: Perspectives on Jewish Culture* 14.

Nadler, Steven (2001). *Spinoza's Heresy: Immortality and the Jewish Mind* (Oxford: Oxford University Press).

Narkiss, Mordecai (1956). "The Oeuvre of the Jewish Engraver Salom Italia, Part I," *Tarbiz* 25: 441–451 [in Hebrew].

Narkiss, Mordecai (1957). "The Oeuvre of the Jewish Engraver Salom Italia, Part II," *Tarbiz* 26: 87–101 [in Hebrew].

Nellen, Henk (2015). *Hugo Grotius: A Lifelong Struggle for Peace in Church and State, 1583–1645* (Leiden: Brill).

Netanyahu, Benzion (1995). *The Origins of the Inquisition in Fifteenth-Century Spain* (New York: Random House).

Offenberg, Adri (1985). "Brief van Menasseh ben Israel aan Isaac Vossius, 2 februari 1652," in *Historische sprokkelingen uit de Universiteit van Amsterdam* (Amsterdam: Universiteitsbibliotheek van Amsterdam), pp. 55–64.

Offenberg, Adri (1989a). "Menasseh ben Israel's Visit to Christina of Sweden at Antwerp," *LIAS* 16: 265–274.

Offenberg, Adri (1989b). "Some Remarks Regarding Six Autograph Letters by Menasseh ben Israel in the Amsterdam University Library," in *Menasseh ben Israel and His World*, ed. Yosef Kaplan, Henri Méchoulan, and Richard H. Popkin (Leiden: Brill), pp. 191–198.

Offenberg, Adri (1992). "Nogmaals Rembrandt en de rabbijn—rabbijn?," *Vrij Nederland*, August 15, 1992, p. 6.

Offenberg, Adri (2004). "A Mid-Seventeenth-Century Manuscript of the (unpublished) Hebrew Grammars of Menasseh ben Israel and Isaac Aboab da Fonseca Recovered," *Zutot: Perpsectives on Jewish Culture* 3: 98–107.

Offenberg, Adri (2011a). "Menasseh ben Israel (1604–1657): A Biographical Sketch," *Menasseh ben Israel Instituut Studies* 6.

Offenberg, Adri (2011b). "David Jeserun and Menasseh ben Israel," *Zutot* 8: 31–40.

Perlove, Shelley (1993). "An Irenic Vision of Utopia: Rembrandt's *Triumph of Mordecai* and the New Jerusalem," *Zeitschrift für Kunstgeschichte* 56: 38–60.

Perlove, Shelley (2006). "Identity and Exile in Seventeenth-Century Amsterdam: A Portrait of Menasseh ben Israel by Salom Italia," in T. J. Broos, M. Bruyn Lacy, and T. F. Shannon, eds., *The Low Countries—Crossroads of Cultures* (Münster: Nodus Publikationen), pp. 11–32.

Perlove, Shelley, and Larry Silver (2009). *Rembrandt's Faith: Church and Temple in the Dutch Golden Age* (University Park: Pennsylvania State University Press).

Pieterse, Wilhelmina C. (1968). *Daniel Levi de Barrios als Geschiedschrijver van de Portugees-Israelietische Gemeente te Amsterdam in Zijn "Triumpho del Govierno Popular"* (Amsterdam: Scheltema & Holkema).

Popkin, Richard H. (1974). "Menasseh ben Israel and Isaac La Peyrère," *Studia Rosenthaliana* 8: 59–63.

Popkin, Richard H. (1980). "Jewish Messianism and Christian Millenarianism," in Pierre Zagorin, ed., *Culture and Politics from Puritanism to the Enlightenment* (Berkeley: University of California Press), pp. 67–90.

Popkin, Richard H. (1984a) "The First College of Jewish Studies," *Revue des études juives* 143: 351–364.

Popkin, Richard H. (1984b). "Menasseh ben Israel and Isaac La Peyrère, II," *Studia Rosenthaliana* 18: 12–20.

Popkin, Richard H. (1988). "Some Aspects of Jewish-Christian Theological Interchanges in Holland and England, 1640–1700," in J. van den Berg and E. G. E. Van der Wall, eds., *Jewish-Christian Relations in the Seventeenth Century* (Dordrecht: Kluwer), pp. 3–32.

Popkin, Richard H. (1989). "The Rise and Fall of the Jewish Indian Theory," in Yosef Kaplan, Henri Méchoulan, and Richard H.

Popkin, eds., *Menasseh ben Israel and His World* (Leiden: Brill), pp. 63–82.

Popkin, Richard H. (1992). *The Third Force in Seventeenth-Century Thought* (Leiden: Brill).

Popkin, Richard H., and David Katz (1988). "The Prefaces by Menasseh ben Israel and Jacob Judah Leon Templo to the Vocalized Mishnah (1646)," in Johannes van den Berg and Ernestine G. van der Wall, eds., *Jewish-Christian Relations in the Seventeenth Century* (Dordrecht: Kluwer), pp. 151–153.

Postma, Ferenc, and Arian Verheij (2009/2010). "In Signum Benevoli Affectus I: Seven Album Inscriptions by Menasseh ben Israel," *Zutot: Perpsectives on Jewish Culture* 6: 35–47 and 7: 75–79.

Prins, Izak (1933). "De Oud-Hollandsche drukpersvrijheid ten opzicht van het Joodsche Boek," *Bijdragen en Mededeelingen van het Genootschap voor de Joodsche Wetenschap in Nederland* 5: 147–176.

Rademaker, C. S. M. (2010). "At the Heart of the Twelve Years' Truce Controversies: Conrad Vorstius, Gerard Vossius, and Hugo Grotius," in Jeanine de Landtsheer and Henk J. M. Nellen, eds., *Between Scylla and Charybdis: Learned Letter Writers Navigating the Reefs of Religious and Political Controversy in Early Modern Europe* (Leiden: Brill), pp. 465–489.

Rauschenbach, Sina (2012). *Judentum für Christen: Vermittlung und Selbstbehauptung Menasseh ben Israels in den gelehrten Debatten des 17. Jahrhunderts* (Berlin: De Gruyter).

Rauschenbach, Sina (2013). "Elzeverian Republics, Wise Merchants, and New Perspectives on Spain and Portugal in the Seventeenth-Century Dutch Republic," *De Zeventiende Eeuw* 29: 81–100.

Rauschenbach, Sina (2016). "Christian Readings of Menasseh ben Israel: Translation and Retranslation in the Early Modern World," in David J. Wertheim, ed., *The Jew as Legitimation: Jewish-Gentile Relations Beyond Antisemitism and Philosemitism* (London: Palgrave/Macmillan), pp. 63–82.

Rauschenbach, Sina (2018). "Jewish Universalism? Menasseh's Final Remarks on History and the End of Times," in Sina Rauschenbach, ed., *Sefardische Perspektiven/Sephardic Perspectives, Jahrbuch Zentrum Jüdische Studien Berlin-Brandenburg* (Berlin: Hentrich & Hentrich).

Révah, I. S. (1958). "Menasseh ben Israel et Ropicanefma de Joao de Barros," *Revista de Filologia* 4: 25–27.

Roest, Meijer (1867). "Nog iets over het graf van Menasseh Ben Israel," *Nieuw Israëlietisch Weekblad* 13: 12.

Rosenbloom, Noah (1994). "Menasseh ben Israel and the Eternality of Punishment Issue," *Proceedings of the American Academy for Jewish Research* 60: 241–262.

Roth, Cecil (1928). "New Light on the Resettlement," *Transactions of the Jewish Historical Society of England* 11: 112–142.

Roth, Cecil (1945). *A Life of Menasseh ben Israel: Rabbi, Printer, and Diplomat*, 2nd ed. (Philadelphia: Jewish Publication Society).

Salomon, Herman Prins (1983). "The Portuguese Background of Menasseh ben Israel's Parents As Revealed Through the Inquisitorial Archives at Lisbon," *Studia Rosenthaliana* 17: 105–146.

Salomon, Herman Prins (1988). *Saul Levi Mortera en zijn "Traktaat Betreffende de Waarheid van de Wet van Mozes"* (Braga: Barbosa & Xavier).

Salomon, Herman Prins (1991). "Menasseh Ben Israel, Saul Levi Mortera et le 'Testimonium Flavianum,'" *Studia Rosenthaliana* 25: 31–40.

Salomon, Herman Prins (1992). "Nogmaals Rembrandt en de rabbijn—maar welk?," *Vrij Nederland*, July 25, 1992, p. 6.

Saperstein, Marc (1991a). "Saul Levi Morteira's *Treatise on the Immortality of the Soul*," *Studia Rosenthaliana* 25: 131–148.

Saperstein, Marc (1991b). "Saul Levi Morteira's Eulogy for Menasseh ben Israel," in Dan Cohn-Sherbok, ed., *A Traditional Quest: Essays in Honor of Louis Jacobs, Journal for the Study of the Old Testament*, Supplement Series 114: 133–153.

Saperstein, Marc (2005). *Exile in Amsterdam: Saul Levi Morteira's Sermons to a Congregation of "New Jews"* (Cincinnati: Hebrew Union College Press).

Saraiva, A. J. (1972). "Antonio Vieira, Menasseh ben Israel et le Cinquième Empire," *Studia Rosenthaliana* 6: 25–56.

Schama, Simon (1999). *Rembrandt's Eyes* (New York: Knopf).

Schorsch, Itmar (1978). "From Messianism to Realpolitik: Menasseh ben Israel and the Readmission of the Jews to England," *Proceedings of the American Academy for Jewish Research* 45: 187–208.

Schrijver, Emile (2011). "Twee Portugees-joodse grammatica's," in Jane Steenbergen and Karel van der Toorn, eds., *Papieren Pracht uit de Amsterdamse Gouden Eeuw* (Amsterdam: Vossiuspers Universiteit van Amsterdam), pp. 138–143.

Schwartz, Gary (1985). *Rembrandt: His Life, His Paintings* (New York: Viking).

Schwartz, Gary (2006). *The Rembrandt Book* (New York: Abrams).

Schwartz, Gary (2009). "Rembrandt's Hebrews," *Jahrbuch der Berliner Museen* 51: 33–38.

Shapiro, James (1997). *Shakespeare and the Jews* (New York: Columbia University Press).

Sigal-Klagsbald, Laurence (2007). *Rembrandt et la Nouvelle Jérusalem: Juifs et Chrétiens à Amsterdam au Siècle d'Or* (Paris: Musée d'art et d'histoire du Judaïsme).

Silva Rosa, J. S. da (1927). "Menasseh ben Israel als grondlegger der Hebr. Typographie in Nederland," *De Vrijdagavond*, January 7, 1927.

Slotki, Judah Jacob (1964). *Menasseh ben Israel, His Life and Times* (London: Jewish Religious Educational Publications).

Solomons, Israel (1906). "The Second Series of Illustrations for the *Piedra Gloriosa* of Menasseh ben Israel," *The Jewish Chronicle*, July 27, 1906, pp. 31–40.

Souza, G. B. (2004). *The Survival of Empire: Portuguese Trade and Society in China and the South China Sea, 1630–1754* (Cambridge: Cambridge University Press).

Swetschinski, Daniel M. (2000). *Reluctant Cosmopolitans: The Portuguese Jews of Seventeenth-Century Amsterdam* (London: The Littman Library of Jewish Civilization).

Turnbull, George Henry (1947). *Hartlib, Dury and Comenius: Gleanings from Hartlib's Papers* (Liverpool: University Press of Liverpool).

Valentiner, W. R. (1957). *Rembrandt and Spinoza: A Study of the Spiritual Conflicts in Seventeenth-Century Holland* (London: Phaidon).

Van de Waal, Henri (1954–1955). "Rembrandts Radierungen zur Piedra Gloriosa des Menasseh ben Israel," *Imprimatur: Jahrbuch für Bücherfreunde* 12: 52–60.

Van den Berg, Jan (1989). "Menasseh ben Israel, Henry More and Johannes Hoornbeeck on the Pre-existence of the Soul," in Yosef Kaplan, Henri Méchoulan, and Richard H. Popkin, eds., *Menasseh ben Israel and His World* (Leiden: Brill), pp. 98–116.

Van der Wall, Ernestine (1985). "Three Letters by Menasseh ben Israel to John Durie: English Philojudaism and the 'Spes Israelis,'" *Nederlands Archief voor Kerkgeschiedenis* 65: 46–63.

Van der Wall, Ernestine (1989). "Petrus Serrarius and Menasseh ben Israel: Christian Millenarianism and Jewish Messianism in Seventeenth-Century Amsterdam," in Yosef Kaplan, Henri Méchoulan, and Richard H. Popkin, eds., *Menasseh ben Israel and His World* (Leiden: Brill), pp. 164–190.

Van Eeghen, Isabella Henriette (1960–1978). *De Amsterdamse Boekhandel, 1680–1725*, 6 vols. (Amsterdam: Scheltema & Holkema/N. Israel).

Van Rooden, Pieter (1989). *Theology, Biblical Scholarship, and Rabbinical Studies in the Seventeenth Century: Constantijn l'Empéreur (1591–1648), Professor of Hebrew and Theology at Leiden* (Leiden: Brill).

Vaz Dias, A. M. (1930). "Wie waren Rembrandt's Joodsche Buren," *De Vrijdagavond*, October 10, 1930, pp. 22–26, and October 17, 1930, pp. 40–45.

Vieijra, D. (1922). "Dienstovereenkomst tusschen Menasseh ben Israel en zijn drukker B. Laurensz," *Nieuwe Israëlitisch Weekblad*, April 28, 1922, p. 12.

Vlessing, Odette (1993). "New Light on the Earliest History of the Amsterdam Portuguese Jews," in Jozeph Michman, ed., *Dutch Jewish History* 3 (Assen: Van Gorcum), pp. 43–75.

Wiznitzer, Arnold (1958–1959). "The Merger Agreement and the Regulations of Congregation 'Talmud Torah' of Amsterdam (1638–1639)," *Historia Judaica* 20–21: 109–132.

Wiznitzer, Arnold (1960). *The Jews of Colonial Brazil* (New York: Columbia University Press).

Wolf, Lucien (1899). "Menasseh ben Israel's Study in London," *Transactions of the Jewish Historical Society of England* 3: 144–150.

Wolf, Lucien (1901). *Menasseh ben Israel's Mission to Oliver Cromwell* (London: MacMillan/Jewish Historical Society of England).

Yaari, Avraham (1947). *Mi-bet defuso shel Menasheh Ben Israel* (Jerusalem).

Zafran, Herbert C. (1977–1978). "Amsterdam: Center of Hebrew Printing in the Seventeenth Century," *Jewish Book Annual* 35: 47–55.

Zell, Michael (2002). *Reframing Rembrandt: Jews and the Christian Image in Seventeenth-Century Amsterdam* (Berkeley: University of California Press).

Zemon Davis, Natalie (2016). "Regaining Jerusalem: Eschatology and Slavery in Jewish Colonization in Seventeenth-Century Suriname," *The Cambridge Journal of Postcolonial Literary Inquiry* 31: 11–38.

Zilverberg, S. B. J. (1969). "Jan Pieterszoon Beelthouwer (ca. 1603–ca. 1669)," *Studia Rosenthaliana* 3: 156–167.

Zwarts, Jacob (1928). "De Eerste Rabbijnen en Synagogen van Amsterdam naar archivalische bronnen," *Bijdragen en Mededeelingen van het Genootschap voor de Joodsche wetenschap in Nederland* 4: 147–242.

Jewish Lives is a prizewinning series of interpretive
biography designed to explore the many facets of Jewish identity.
Individual volumes illuminate the imprint of Jewish figures upon
literature, religion, philosophy, politics, cultural and economic
life, and the arts and sciences. Subjects are paired with authors to
elicit lively, deeply informed books that explore the range and
depth of Jewish experience from antiquity to the present.

Jewish Lives is a partnership of Yale University Press
and the Leon D. Black Foundation.

Ileene Smith is editorial director.
Anita Shapira and Steven J. Zipperstein are series editors.